T0293092

Reflective Practice for Coaches

This practical evidence-based guide to running Reflective Practice professional development programmes provides a dynamic and engaging resource for a wide range of coaches.

Reflective Practice is a proven learning and development approach that involves consciously and deliberately thinking about experiences to develop insights and apply these within coaching practice. McCormick argues that it is vital that coaches regularly reflect on their work to develop and grow professionally, and this book provides a definitive and rich source of material on how and what to reflect on. Topics include how to reflect as an individual coach; working in pairs and small groups; applying reflective practice in a training context; and how to run advanced group sessions for coaches. The book features a wide range of practical workbook exercises to challenge the reader's current practice and extend their capability, as well as an evidence-based guide to enhancing skills in recently developed areas such as Unified Protocol Cognitive Behavioural Therapy, Internet Supplemented Acceptance and Commitment Therapy, and Using Schema Therapy with Mindfulness Techniques.

Written by a highly experienced executive coach, this book is full of practical and effective ways to become more capable and proficient. It is essential reading for any career, life or executive coach who wishes to enhance their coaching capability through reflective practice, as well as for coaching training organisations, senior executive coaches offering sessions for other coaches, and academic institutions offering coaching qualifications.

Iain McCormick PhD is the founder of the Executive Coaching Centre in Auckland, New Zealand. He trained in clinical psychology, subsequently completing a PhD in work stress. Iain has been coaching and consulting for 30 years, working in Canada, Hong Kong and New Zealand.

Reflective Practice for Coaches

A Guidebook for Advanced Professional Development

Iain McCormick

Routledge
Taylor & Francis Group

LONDON AND NEW YORK

First published 2023
by Routledge
4 Park Square, Milton Park, Abingdon, Oxon OX14 4RN

and by Routledge
605 Third Avenue, New York, NY 10158

Routledge is an imprint of the Taylor & Francis Group, an informa business

British Library Cataloguing-in-Publication Data
A catalogue record for this book is available from the British Library

Library of Congress Cataloging-in-Publication Data
Names: McCormick, Iain, author.
Title: Reflective practice for coaches : a guidebook for advanced professional
    development / Iain McCormick.
Description: Abingdon, Oxon ; New York, NY : Routledge, 2023. | Includes
    bibliographical references and index.
Identifiers: LCCN 2022036775 (print) | LCCN 2022036776 (ebook) |
    ISBN 9781032258133 (hardback) | ISBN 9781032258027 (paperback) |
    ISBN 9781003285144 (ebook)
Subjects: LCSH: Personal coaching. | Counseling. | Critical thinking.
Classification: LCC BF637.P36 M363 2023 (print) | LCC BF637.P36
    (ebook) | DDC 158.3—dc23/eng/20221017
LC record available at https://lccn.loc.gov/2022036775
LC ebook record available at https://lccn.loc.gov/2022036776

ISBN: 978-1-032-25813-3 (hbk)
ISBN: 978-1-032-25802-7 (pbk)
ISBN: 978-1-003-28514-4 (ebk)

DOI: 10.4324/9781003285144

Typeset in Goudy
by Apex CoVantage, LLC

Contents

About the Author

Iain McCormick PhD is the founder of the Executive Coaching Centre in Auckland, New Zealand. He initially trained in clinical psychology, working in the forensic sector, and subsequently completed his PhD studying work stress during a long overland traverse of Antarctica. Iain then moved into organisational consulting, becoming a Partner in Deloitte for some years, working in Canada and New Zealand. He subsequently moved to Hong Kong where he helped build a consulting firm that was sold to a US multinational. He returned to New Zealand in 2000 and started the Executive Coaching Centre in Auckland. He currently coaches a wide range of boards of directors, chief executives and senior managers. He has conducted many thousands of individual and team coaching sessions over 30 years. Iain has been running intensive reflective practice sessions with coaches since 2020. He is a Fellow of the New Zealand Psychological Society and has published a wide range of articles on coaching, organisational psychology and psychometrics.

Acknowledgements

I dedicate this book to my wife, Kerry, and my two sons, Cam and Olly.

Many thanks to Barbara Kennedy whose initial question started my journey into reflective practice. To Stewart Forsyth for his challenge to write this workbook. To David Graham for his enduring interest in my work. To Jonathan Black and Bridget Jelley for their energy, enthusiasm and undying support. To Richard Siegert for those long chats over dinner.

To the wonderful group of coaches and leaders who attended my initial reflective practice sessions: Maree, Barbara, David, Dianne, Libby, Stewart, Jonathan, Mel, Trish, Bridget, Dane, Nailia, Sarah, Stephanie, Willem, John, Rebekah, Gretchen, Hannah, Tara.

Many thanks to Professor Jonathan Passmore who reignited my passion for writing.

Many thanks to Professor James Bennett-Levy for his valuable input early in the process of writing the book.

Many thanks to Zoe Thomson, Commissioning Editor, Psychology at Taylor & Francis Group.

To Emeritus Professor Tony Taylor (1926–2021), my great teacher, mentor and dear friend.

Author's Note

The examples, case studies and anecdotes provided in this book are drawn from my coaching, consulting and teaching conducted over many years. Names and a wide range of identifying details about these people have been changed to protect their privacy. Many of the case studies in this book are composites drawn from a range of different clients, students and contacts seen over the course of my work.

Part I
Introduction to Reflective Practice for Coaches

This part of the book provides an overall introduction to reflective practice for coaches and covers:

- What reflective practice is and why it is critically important.
- The practical steps to reflective practice.
- The range of models or types of reflective practice.

DOI: 10.4324/9781003285144-1

1
Reflective Practice

A Critical Focus

INTRODUCTION TO THE CHAPTER

This chapter covers:

- The purpose of this workbook.
- The structure of this workbook's parts and chapters.
- How the reader can usefully engage in reflective practice.
- What the international professional coaching bodies say about the value of reflective practice.
- What reflective practice is.
- A practical guide to start the process of awareness building, deliberation and self-regulation.
- A summary of the research on the effectiveness of reflective practice.
- The relationship between reflective practice, coaching, training and supervision.
- How reflective practice relates to the range of different coaching models.

The Purpose of This Workbook

This book aims to provide coaches with an understanding of how reflective practice can be applied as a powerful professional development method. Reflective practice is designed to be an interesting and dynamic approach to professional development that coaches will find valuable on an ongoing basis.

This workbook can be used in multiple ways:

- As a source of information for students learning coaching with practical examples including case studies and exercises.

DOI: 10.4324/9781003285144-2

- As a workbook for individual coaches wanting to improve their capability.
- As a basis for running peer-based reflective practice sessions.
- As a guide for facilitators who want to set up and run reflective practice professional development groups.
- As a source of information for participants who want to be involved in these groups and are curious about how they work.
- As a workbook for coaching training or educational organisations.

The Structure of This Workbook's Parts and Chapters

This workbook is in five parts. Part I introduces the idea of reflective practice as a method of professional development for coaches then sets out the practical steps required to undertake it. Part II provides material on how to set up group reflective practice sessions including building psychological connection and safety for participants. Also, the use of baseline measures in reflective practice are set out in this section. Part III has extensive material on what coaching is and its effectiveness, and a section on rapid, solution-focused coaching which is the predominant model of coaching used in this workbook. It also introduces the skills that are needed by coaches and provides a range of self-assessment and reflective practice exercises. Part IV sets out a range of innovative therapeutic methods and techniques that can be used in conjunction with coaching. Part V contains a range of reflective questions relevant to the book as a whole and sets out how any coach can set up their own reflective practice.

The chapters in this workbook contain evidence-based information, practical case studies, which are used to illustrate the approach, and reflective practice exercises that can be used by either individual coaches working on their own through this book or by facilitators or educators who are training others.

Engaging in Reflective Practice

Readers are encouraged to try the exercises in this book because engagement in the reflective practice process is highly correlated with the level of benefit gained by participants (Bennett-Levy & Lee, 2012). Readers may want to try the reflective practice exercises on their own, with a colleague or in small groups. If individuals want to work with others using these exercises it is very important to read Part II of this workbook and establish sound psychological connection, safety and confidentiality before proceeding into discussing any personal material.

The International Professional Coaching Bodies and Reflective Practice

Each of the major international professional coaching bodies have specified the importance of reflective practice as a key competency for coaches.

The International Coaching Federation (ICF) is a not-for-profit body that is 'dedicated to advancing the coaching profession by setting high standards, providing independent certification and building a worldwide network of trained coaching professionals' (ICF, 2021, p. 1). In July 2020 the organisation had over 41,000 members in 147 countries with over 30,000 coaches holding ICF Credentials (ICF, 2020). As part of their role ICF have developed a set of core competencies to increase understanding about the mindset and skills that are required in effective coaching. These competencies are used as part of the assessment process for ICF Credentials. The ICF Core Competencies are in four logically connected domains: The Foundation, Co-Creating the Relationship, Communicating Effectively and Cultivating Learning and Growth. Updated Core Competencies were released in October 2019 and revised in July 2021. The update included changes to the *Embodies a Coaching Mindset* competency and now includes the phrase, 'Develops an ongoing reflective practice to enhance one's coaching' (ICF, 2019, p. 2).

The ICF emphasis on the competency of reflection is also seen in the European Mentoring and Coaching Council (EMCC) Global Competence Framework V2 (EMCC, 2015). The EMCC's purpose is 'to develop, promote, and set the expectation of best practice in mentoring, coaching, and supervision globally for the benefit of society' (EMCC, 2021, p. 1). In August 2019 it had over 6,000 members located in 90 countries. Their Capability Indicator *Understanding Self* includes the phrase 'Builds further self-understanding based on a range of theoretical models and structured input from external sources with rigorous reflection on experience and practice' (EMCC, 2015, p. 6).

The Association for Coaching is an independent and not-for-profit professional body, that was established in 2002 and is committed to developing best practice and raising coaching standards worldwide. It has members in over 80 countries, drawn from academic institutions, professional coaches and trainers of coaches. Its purpose is to 'inspire and champion coaching excellence, to advance the coaching profession and make a sustainable difference to individuals, organizations and society' (AC, 2021a, p. 1). Their Coaching Competency Framework No. 9 *Undertaking Continuous Coach Development*, includes the following:

- Actively reflects on coaching practice and outcomes.
- Acts on own critical reflections and client feedback to improve coaching practice.
- Participates in regular coaching supervision to reflect on, and improve practice.

(AC, 2021b, p. 5)

The Chartered Institute of Personnel and Development (CIPD, 2021) states that 'Reflective practice is the foundation of professional development; it makes meaning from experience and transforms insights into practical strategies for personal growth and organisational impact' (p. 2).

These major international bodies clearly indicate the importance of reflective practice as a core requirement for any coach.

What Reflective Practice Is

> Schön (1987) described professional practice as being in a flat place where we can't see very far. Everyone would love to work on a high place from which all the near valleys and far hills are in view. Everyday life, work and learning rarely have signposts, definitive maps, or friendly police to help with directions.

(Bolton & Delderfield, 2018, p. 3)

Dewey (1933), an early pioneer in reflective practice in education defined reflective practice as 'the active, persistent and careful consideration of any belief or supposed form of knowledge in the light of the grounds that support it and the further conclusions to which it tends' (1933, p. 9). Dewey's work contains several key ideas about reflection:

- It involves active, conscious, deliberate thinking.
- It is a type of rational and logical problem solving.
- It produces ideas that are ordered and linked in a meaningful way.

Reflective practice has been defined as the 'deliberate, purposeful, metacognitive thinking and/or action . . . to improve . . . professional practice' (Sellars, 2017, p. 2) and there are many different models, theories, and levels of reflection that focus on the:

- *Situations* and circumstances that stimulate involvement in the reflective process.

- *Process* of reflection which includes the different types of reflection, concepts and views on how the results should be implemented.
- *Content* of the reflection, which includes how the ideas are analysed, reviewed, discussed and challenged.
- *Outcome* of the reflection and how it improves professional practice.

Grant et al. (2002) defines reflective practice as the 'inspection, evaluation and clear understanding of one's thoughts, feelings and behaviour' (p. 821). They suggested there were three elements to this reflection: the need or motivation for self-reflection, the time spent and engagement in reflective practice and the clarity and insight gained from it.

Reflective practice can be better understood by contrasting it with thoughtful action.

Table 1.1 The difference between thoughtful action and reflective practice

Thoughtful action	*Reflective practice*
Is done spontaneously – the decision to think about a subject is made in a second.	Requires time and conscious effort to plan and process, and action is the outcome.
Does not happen on a regular basis and is generally unpredictable as the frequency is determined by triggering events and situations.	Is a planned deliberate cycle.
Can occur at any time.	Occurs after action and typically involves a written record of the process and outcome.
Is not part of a continuous improvement process but typically relates to an event or action.	Is an integral part of continuous improvement and professional development.
Does not involve an intentional opportunity to learn.	Involves a deliberate attempt to learn.

Source: adapted from Phillips et al. (2000, p3.2).

Gore and Zeichner (1991) suggests that there are four types of reflective practice:

1. Academic reflection which involves considering questions such as 'Do I know the research content in this area well?', 'Am I well organised in presenting the key ideas?' and 'Am I innovative and creative in order to engage and sustain the interest of my clients?'
2. Social efficacy reflection which is the belief that collectively *we can achieve success* and involves considering questions such as 'Am I implementing what I know from the research in my area of work?', 'Have I adopted proven strategies that will maximise the chances of success?' and 'Is my evidence-based practice meeting the needs of my clients?'
3. Developmental reflection, which involves asking questions relevant to the age and stage of the client; for example, 'Am I collaborating with my clients to develop the right learning experiences that are appropriate to their age and developmental stage?' and 'Is our agreed action plan going to meet the client's current emotional needs?'
4. Critical reflection which involves asking values-based questions, such as, 'What is the purpose of my coaching?', 'Are my beliefs in accord with that of the organisation I am coaching in?'

By contrast, Van Manen (1977) outlines three areas of reflection:

1. Technical reflection, which focuses on whether the coach has the competencies that are required to achieve their professional goals. In the coaching context relevant questions are: 'Do I have the ability to clearly explain what coaching is and is not?' and 'Do I have the skills to deal with clients who are in a career crisis?'
2. Practical reflection, which focuses on whether the coach has the processes or the means to achieve the goals. In coaching relevant questions are: 'Can I establish a highly collaborative relationship with this client?' and 'Can I address this problem within the number of coaching sessions allocated by the client organisation?'
3. Ethical reflection, which focuses on moral considerations. In coaching relevant questions are: 'Can I be honest about the progress of my client, even though I know that saying he is not making progress will disadvantage me financially?' and 'Do I want to support an organisation that is making no progress towards sustainability?'

Reflective practice helps build coaching capability through a three-step process:

•   Reflection involves coaches asking questions about the impact of their sessions, which leads to,

- Awareness or building understanding about themselves, which leads to,
- Self-regulation or the maturity to know when to say or do what, despite how the coach feels (Hullinger et al., 2019).

These authors go on to present a four-element reflective practice model with the coach considering:

1.   Their own internal responses in-the-moment of coaching, reflecting, gaining awareness and self-regulation for the benefit of this client in this session.
2.   Their own internal responses generally in coaching, reflecting for the benefit of their practice as a whole.
3.   Observing others' responses in-the-moment, then reflecting for the benefit of their clients.
4.   Observing others' responses generally in coaching, then reflecting for the benefit of the profession as a whole.

The CIPD (2021) argue that reflection deepens learning. Reflecting assists the learner to better understand why something is being learned and what has been learned. It enables learning to be integrated, internalised and personalised. The CIPD suggest that reflective practice is not only intellectual but also an emotional and physical activity that is closely linked to our values and identity. Reflective practice is seen as an essential part of skill development, but it also enhances the ability of the learner to deal with stress and challenges, manage emotions, make effective decisions and develop productive relationships. The CIPD present three steps that are needed to become a reflective practitioner:

1.   Developing the skill of critically thinking through past experiences which can be done by reliving the experience, noting what was going on, analysing the situation and capturing new insights.
2.   Noticing the dynamic thoughts, feelings and sensations as they happen, and making choices based on these.
3.   Applying these insights in our professional practice.

Passmore and Sinclair (2020) suggest that reflective practice comes in a range of forms which include:

- Coaching supervision – professional guidance by an experienced practitioner using interactive reflection, evaluation, and the sharing of expertise.

- Peer group reflection – colleagues providing observation, reflection and feedback.
- Individual journaling – coaches keeping a written record of their thoughts, feelings and reflections.
- Mentor coaching – professional assistance from an experience coach that may include achieving coaching competency at a desired credential level.
- Coaching feedback – a peer or supervisor observing coaching practice or listening to recordings of client work followed by debrief and commentary.

Reflective Practice Questions

A range of questions which have been developed to assist the reflective coach in this process and these are set out below.

Gibbs (1988) developed a reflective guide to learning which consisted of five steps:

- Description – what do I think was happening at this time?
- Feelings – what was I feeling and thinking during the experience?
- Evaluation – what was good and bad from my perspective about the experience?
- Analysis – what sense can I make of the situation, what insights did I gain and what else could I have done?
- Action plan – based on my reflection, what will I do next.

Winter and Katrivesis (2016) outlines a similar reflective practice cycle that consists of the following:

- Describe the current situation – 'What is going on?' 'What assumptions have I made?'
- Reflect on what happened – 'What is my take on the situation?' 'Are my assumptions reasonable?' 'What skills are needed in this situation?' 'Do I have these skills?'
- Act to improve – 'What would I do differently next time?' 'What are the implications for my work?'
- Review my actions – 'Has there been a change?' 'What have I learned?' 'Who can I share this learning with?'

Passmore and Sinclair (2020) encourage coaches to use the eight practical questions called the Henley8, which include the following:

1. What did I observe?
2. What was my response?

3.   What does this say about me personally?
4.   What does this tell me about myself as a coach or leader?
5.   What strengths does this offer?
6.   What are the potential pitfalls?
7.   What did I learn?
8.   What might I do differently next time?

Reflective Practice Techniques

There are a wide range of reflective techniques which are summarised below (Bisson, 2017; Bolton & Delderfield, 2018; de Haan, 2019).

The Six-minute Write

This approach involves free form writing for a short set period of time. The steps are:

- Write continuously for six minutes nonstop.
- Write anything you like on any topic that comes to mind.
- Don't review or revise it.
- Let it flow and do not worry about spelling or grammar.
- Write anything that you think of – you do not have to re-read it.
- Whatever you write is important and it's yours.

The Narrative

The steps involved in this type of story writing are:

- Have a focus to your writing and make it a story about your experience.
- Pick the first story that enters your head.
- Write for between 20 and 40 minutes.
- Try just to write and not to think or plan out your story.
- Document the situation as you remember it with the details that you can remember.
- It can be fiction – you do not have to be accurate.
- Do not edit at this stage, just write.
- Form is not important – it does not need a beginning, middle and end.
- Write down as many of the details as you can – feelings, tone of voice and so on.

- Write down your reactions to your story.
- Suspend judgement about your story.

The Journal

This is an ongoing record of your thoughts, feelings and experiences in a particular part of your life. Regularly asking 'what, how or why' questions can help to stimulate continued writing. Examples are:

- What did I observe in this coaching session?
- What are the five things that strike me most about this client?
- What did I learn from this client today?
- How could I have done a better job of coaching today?
- What is another approach or technique that I could have used with this client today?

The Opposing Lists

Reflect on your experience and write a series of lists – what was good about the situation, what was bad? 'Should I do A or should I do B?' 'What are the advantages or disadvantages of doing this?' These lists which take opposing perspectives on issues are very helpful in deepening our understanding.

Unsent Letters

If the coach or client feels anger or frustration towards someone, they can try writing never-to-be-sent letters. These letters help to vent feelings if they are written in an unconstrained and uncensored way. Alternatively two letters can be written, one to the person who frustrates the writer and then a reply can be written back. This helps build a sense of perspective on the issue.

Internal Mentor

Write to your 'wise self' about a problem and ask for support and guidance. Write a response back to yourself using all your trustworthy wisdom. Questions to ask your internal mentor may include:

- How well am I applying what I have been taught at university about coaching in my practice?
- How can I be a better coach?

- How can I keep up to date with the evidence-based approach to coaching?
- How should I challenge my clients when they just want to repeatedly vent?
- Am I offering this organisation value-for-money?

Internal Saboteur

Nearly everyone has an inner critic that tells us the reasons that we will not succeed or are not good enough. The saboteur is often formed in childhood from painful experiences that have been witnessed or experienced. Having picked up these critical messages the individual then replays them repeatedly. Coaches or clients can be asked to 'Spend 5 minutes writing down exactly what the internal saboteur is saying, then spend time thinking about this and write down your challenges to these unhelpful thoughts'.

The Metaphor

A metaphor is a figure of speech where one thing becomes representative of another; for example, I could eat a horse, meaning, I am hungry. In reflective practice, metaphors can be used in the following ways:

- If my coaching work were an animal, what would it be?
- If my problem were the weather, what would it be?
- If my challenge was a colour, what would it be?
- If my attitude was a piece of furniture, what would it be?
- If my clients were a form of transport, what would they be?

The idea of using a metaphor in reflective practice is to challenge the individual to think in a fresh new way about an issue.

Critical Moments

These are a type of turning point in a conversation, coaching session or reflection in which a thought, comment or action decisively changes the direction of an idea flow. de Haan (2019) in his book *Critical Moments in Executive Coaching: Understanding the Coaching Process through Research and Evidence-Based Theory* uses this qualitative method to better understand executive coaching. Critical moments are useful in any reflective practice and can be uncovered by asking 'Describe briefly one critical moment (an exciting, tense or significant moment) with one of your clients. Think about what was critical in the coaching journey, or a moment when you did not quite know what to do.' (p. 21). Once the moment has been captured then it can be written down and the coach can ask:

- Why is this moment critical?
- What does it suggest is important to me?
- How might I use this critical moment to inform my coaching?
- What will I do better or differently next time?

Reflective Practice Exercise: My Reflective Practice

What are the important ideas that are contained in the chapter so far? Write these below.

How much do I reflect on my coaching?

Not at all 1   2   3   4   5   6   7   8   9   10 A great deal

How do I want to improve?

Academic reflection: How up to date with the coaching research and literature am I?

Not at all 1   2   3   4   5   6   7   8   9   10 Very up to date

How do I want to improve?

Social efficacy reflection: Am I implementing what I know from the research in order to maximise my effectiveness?

Not at all 1   2   3   4   5   6   7   8   9   10 A great deal

How do I want to improve?

Development reflection: Is what I am doing in coaching directly relevant to the age and stage of my clients?

Not at all 1   2   3   4   5   6   7   8   9   10 Very directly related

How do I know this?

How do I want to improve?

Critical reflection: Are my values aligned with the values of the organisations I work in?

Not at all 1   2   3   4   5   6   7   8   9   10 Very aligned

How do I want to improve?

Technical reflection: When was the last time I critically reviewed my competencies? Do I have the full range of technical skills to deliver real value to my clients?

Practical reflection: Can I consistently form a truly collaborative relationship with my clients? How do I want to improve in this area?

Ethical reflection: Would I consistently exit myself from coaching if I felt I was not adding value to the client or the organisation? How do I want to improve in this area?

Reflective Practice Exercise: Becoming a Reflective Practitioner

How can I take the following three steps to become a more reflective practitioner:

1. Developing the skill of critically thinking through past experiences which can be done by reliving the experience, noting what was going on, analysing the situation and capturing new insights.
2. Noticing the dynamic thoughts, feelings and sensations as they happen, and making choices based on these.
3. Applying these insights in my professional practice.

My action plan is:

Reflective Practice Exercise: Reflective Techniques

What reflective techniques do I want to use? The six-minute write, the narrative, the journal, the opposing lists etc.?

How often do I want to use this technique?

How will I hold myself accountable?

Research on the Effectiveness of Reflective Practice

This section presents a sample of research that can enable any coach to have confidence that their reflective practice is evidence-based. The section is not designed as a comprehensive review of the effectiveness of the literature but simply as an indication of the research.

In their review, Ruth-Sahd (2003) found that reflective practice had value, when assessed by qualitative participant feedback, in a wide range of settings including higher education, nursing, social work, science education, pastoral education, and management and leadership training. They indicated that the benefits of reflective practice have been widely recognised in the United States, Canada, United Kingdom, New Zealand, Australia, Finland and Hong Kong. The studies they reviewed identified that the positive outcomes included:

- Better integration of theoretical concepts into practice (Scanlan et al., 2002).
- Improved learning from experience (Atkins & Murphy, 1993).
- Greater self-esteem through learning (Johns, 1995).
- Better acceptance of professional responsibility (Johns, 1995).
- Greater social and political emancipation (Taylor, 2001).
- Expanded clinical knowledge and skills (Paget, 2001).

van Goethem et al. (2014) undertook a meta-analysis and assessed the effect of community service and reflective practice on adolescent development based on 49 studies (24,477 participants, 12–20 years old). They found that that community service had a positive impact on academic, personal, social and civic outcomes. Importantly, they concluded that reflection was essential to achieve these results.

Lines et al. (2021) used evidence from 24 independent randomised controlled trials or experiments on the impact and performance of teams who reflected upon their progress and used this to adapt their functioning. They found a significant positive overall effect from reflection on both outcomes and performance behaviours.

Barbagallo (2021) used a meta-synthesis to examine qualitative data of nursing students' perceptions and experiences of reflective practice and suggested that high quality reflection resulted in an improvement in professional practice.

Self-practice has also been used to enhance the skills of therapists. Bennett-Levy et al. (2001, 2015) and Haarhoff and Thwaites (2016) suggested that for Cognitive Behaviour Therapy (CBT) practitioners, a reflective programme enhanced understanding of the CBT model, built therapeutic skills, developed confidence as a therapist and improved belief in the therapeutic model. Participants typically reported having a deeper sense of what the therapy was all about and better reflective skills – a key metacognitive competency needed for continuous learning. Reflective practice has also demonstrated improvements in the therapist's attitude towards their clients including both better interpersonal skills and enhanced empathy for clients. Participants report personal insights and changes in their own lives as well as enhanced capability as a therapist. Reflective practice had the potential for improving therapists' development because it integrated knowledge development with practical and conceptual skills while impacting on both the individual's personal life and their work as a therapist (Bennett-Levy et al., 2015). Haarhoff (2006) reported that reflective practice may also increase therapists' resilience and decrease the likelihood of burnout.

Gale and Schröder (2014) undertook a meta-synthesis of studies examining therapists' experiences of using CBT to assist themselves. Their literature search identified 378 papers and ten were included in their study as they met their research quality criteria. Their analysis identified three broad constructs: the experience of self-reflection, outcomes of the reflection and implications for training. They found that reflective practice enabled therapists to experience the benefits and challenges of being in the client's shoes. This increased therapists' empathy and confidence. At a practical level they identified the following three points:

- Reflective practice using CBT can be a useful training and development strategy.
- Therapists can develop an ongoing 'self-care' case study, repeatedly recording reflections and sharing these with peers, rather than using reflective practice as a one-off experience.

- Reflective practice can increase therapists' empathy for clients and provide experience of the difficulties clients encounter (p. 373).

While the research above applies to CBT there is no reason to believe that the same positive outcomes will not apply to the development of coaches. However, research to confirm this is clearly needed.

Reflective Practice, Coaching Training Programmes and Supervision

While reflective practice is effective in developing capability it is not a substitute for academic and other professional training programmes for coaches. However, it is suitable for a wide range of coaches who have undertaken their basic training and now want to expand their capability in an engaging and experiential environment. One advantage of reflective practice sessions for coaches is that they can attend these many times and will typically find each session is different and interesting.

Reflective practice is also not a substitute for coaching supervision. However, it can be used as a supplement that provides a different focus because in reflective practice coaches can work on their own issues or personal problems. Bisson (2017) has argued for the importance of supervision in supporting reflective learning and practice for coaches. Reflective practice ensures that the coach is wholeheartedly engaged in the learning and professional development process. Bisson suggests that creating an opportunity for reflective practice immediately after the supervision elements of the session will help the coach to consolidate their learning and skill development.

Summary

This chapter covered:

- The purpose of this workbook.
- The structure of the workbook's parts and chapters.
- How the reader can usefully engage in reflection.
- What the international professional coaching bodies say about the value of reflection.
- What reflective practice is.
- A practical reflective practice guide to start the process of awareness building, deliberation and self-regulation.

- A summary of the research on the effectiveness of reflection.
- The relationship between reflective practice, coaching, training and supervision.

The aim at this point in the book is to have the reader interested in sharpening their coaching skills and capability by using more self-reflection.

2
Practical Steps to Reflective Practice

INTRODUCTION TO THE CHAPTER

This chapter presents the practical steps needed to run a wide range of reflective practice sessions. The chapter includes:

- How reflective practice fits well with the concept of adult learning.
- How to design reflective practice sessions.
- The seven types of reflective practice.
- Case studies to illustrate these different types of reflective practice.
- Reflective practice exercises that the student or coach can work on.

The aim of this chapter is to enable coaches to feel confident and comfortable in running a wide range of reflective practice sessions.

The Value of Professional Development

The world of executive coaching is becoming increasingly complex and is constantly changing, so continuing professional development is critically important to maintain competence and keep up to date with evidence-based practice. Passmore and Sinclair (2020) suggest that maturity as a coach is 'an ongoing and lifelong journey of development and growth' (p. 5).

However, having summarised the research into the value of continuing professional development, Green (2006) concludes its ability to improve the effectiveness of practitioners is 'one of the most prevalent professional myths' (p. 16). Kennedy (2021) argues that a great deal is known about how to make learning powerful, effective and transformative for adults but that this is almost never applied in the development of coaches. To enhance

DOI: 10.4324/9781003285144-3

professional development, there is a need to draw on areas such as andragogy (Knowles, 1984) action-focused reflection (Kolb, 1984), first/second-order change (Watzlawick et al., 1974) and transformational learning (Mezirow, 1991). Kennedy (2021) cites a small-group reflective practice programme for mid to late career coaches as an example of effective learning that takes professional development to the next level (McCormick, 2021b; Jelly & McCormick, 2022).

Reflective Practice as Adult Learning

Reflective practice is designed to be a practical, engaging and dynamic approach to professional development that coaches will find valuable on repeated occasions. As such it is designed around adult learning principles (Knowles, 1980).

Merriam (2001) argues that there are five characteristics of the adult learner, who is someone that:

1. Is independent and can direct his or her own learning.
2. Has gained a wealth of life experiences that is a rich resource for learning.
3. Has learning needs closely related to their work role.
4. Is problem-centred and interested in immediate application of skills and knowledge.
5. Is motivated to learn by internal rather than external factors.

There are several models of adult learning that can be used to understand and enhance reflective practice and professional development. David Kolb (1984) documented the 'experiential learning cycle' and suggested it had four phases in which the client:

1. Has a specific and concrete learning experience.
2. Observes and reflects on the learning experience and reacts to it.
3. Relates this learning to prior experience and knowledge.
4. Identifies the implications for action from the learning experience that can be tested and applied in different situations.

Kolb (1984) places considerable emphasis on how the individual reflects on the experience of learning. This reflection provides the basis for the individual to relate to and integrate past experience and knowledge. This leads to greater self-awareness, behaviour change and the active development of new capability.

Gibbs (2001) produced an adult learning model for reflecting on experience when something goes wrong, which is summarised here:

- Description – what occurred during the experience?
- Feelings – what was my range of thoughts and feelings?
- Evaluation – what did I enjoy and not enjoy about the experience?
- Analysis – how can I understand the situation and what can I do better next time?
- Action plan – based on my analysis, what steps do I now want to take?

Cercone (2008) has a range of practical suggestions about how learning programmes can be made relevant to their adult audience. A range of these suggestions are presented in Table 2.1 and the approach adopted in reflective practice for coaches is detailed.

Table 2.1 How adult learning can be applied to reflective practice

Adult learning suggestion	*Reflective practice approach for coaches*
Encourage learners to formulate their own learning objectives, giving them more control over their learning.	Ensure all reflective practice sessions start with clients describing what they want to examine and work on in the session.
Assist learners to identify resources and devise strategies to achieve their objectives.	Actively encourage participants to find and use resources such as this workbook, research papers and their own experience.
Increase interactions with regular practice and feedback sequences.	Provide many opportunities for practice and feedback in any session.
Acknowledge the accumulated experiences of the participants as valuable educational resources.	At the beginning of any session give participants an opportunity to talk about their background including their journey into coaching, so their accumulated experiences are directly tapped into.

(Continued)

Table 2.1 (Continued)

Adult learning suggestion	Reflective practice approach for coaches
Encourage and reinforce self-sufficiency through timely feedback.	Ensure each participant is given feedback and encouraged to think about the insights they gained in the session and how they can apply these in their own practice.
Develop a learner portfolio or personal scrapbook to capture the knowledge, skills and abilities they have gained.	Encourage participants to keep a journal and write down the insights gained during the session.
Encourage learners to articulate problems.	Ensure all sessions start with clients describing what the issues are that they want to work and reflect on.
Include tasks that let the participants use their knowledge and experience.	In all reflective practice exercises, let the participants use their knowledge and experience.

Transformative Learning

Transformative learning is the process of changing the frame of reference or the habitual way of thinking or point of view. It involves changing how we see ourselves, what we believe and how we live our lives (Mezirow 1991). A transformational learning experience typically has the following phases (Mezirow 1991).

- A disorienting dilemma. This is a situation where a learner's thoughts or beliefs are challenged. It is the 'light bulb' moment when the learner has a new insight into something that they haven't understood before. This challenging or uncomfortable situation starts the transformational learning.
- Self-examination. The second phase typically involves an exploration of the learner's beliefs and understandings. They think through how the disorienting dilemma connects to their experience.
- Critical evaluation of assumptions. Learners then typically move on to take a fresh look at their assumptions and review them analytically. They come to understand that some past assumptions were incorrect, so they can

then move to accept new ideas and beliefs. This enables the learner to be less biased about their past.

- Planning new actions. Following their opening to new ideas and beliefs learners can start to plan a course of action. They can develop a strategy to learn new ideas, try new behaviours, think new thoughts.
- Gaining of knowledge or skills. Carrying out the plan can enable the learner to embrace the transformational learning. They can acquire new skills, with a different and powerful new perspective. It may take extra effort, but the new learning can be real and lasting.
- Exploring new roles. Trying out new skills, actions and tactics is important in transformational learning. It is a critical part of success. It is not just acquiring new information but actively experiencing the change.
- Developing self-efficacy. This involves the individual believing that they can complete a task. As learners experience transformative learning they build confidence and a self-belief in their ability.

Designing Reflective Practice Sessions

The design of reflective practice sessions for executive coaches can usefully be informed by the work in designing these types of sessions for therapists. Several studies over the last 20 years have suggested that reflective practice is a valuable adjunct to traditional therapy training and this work can be used in professional development for coaches. Freeston et al. (2019) present a guide to designing, adapting and implementing reflective practice programmes using three key principles: process issues, content issues and the structure of the programmes.

Process Issues

- Effective reflective practice programmes need a careful match between the level of development of the practitioner and the types of learning used.
- The learning challenge needs to be neither too low (boring) nor too high (intimidating).
- The programme should add new experiences at a rate that allows them to be easily understood, processed and integrated.
- Reflection is a key to the success of the programme and includes techniques such as self-questioning, logical analysis and problem solving. Reflection turns experience into expertise by integrating existing information with powerful insights.

Content Issues

- Participants should develop their abilities in areas that are directly related to their work practice.
- The programme should aim to develop self-reflective knowledge and skills by clearly giving participants the opportunity to reflect on their experience, what it felt like to be in that role, what happened in the experience and how it can be applied to their own practice.

Structure Issues

- A well-defined structure is important to the programme. This could include a discussion on the nature of self-reflection, an agreement on psychological safety, a discussion around the relevant approach, time to experience the therapeutic intervention, an opportunity for the participant to reflect on the experience and to gain feedback if a group format is used.
- All group programmes need a leader who is highly capable, participants that have a high degree of trust in the process; the roles of leader and participants must be clearly defined, there must be sufficient time allowed for both the practice and the reflective practice phases, a commitment from the leader to resolving all issues raised in the session and a programme that is evaluated.

The Seven Types of Reflective Practice

Reflective practice is a very flexible approach to professional development and can be applied in many ways (McCormick, 2022a).

1. Individual Informal Reflection

Useful research has been undertaken on the value of informal reflective practice in organisations. Di Stefano et al. (2016) found that employees of call centres who spent 15 minutes reflecting about lessons learned at the end of the day performed 23% better than those who did not reflect, after ten days. Porter (2017) reports on a study of UK commuters and found those who used their travel time to think about and plan for their day were happier, more productive, and less burned out than people who didn't.

Porter (2017) suggests the following process for individual informal reflection.

- Identify some important questions but do not answer them. Examples in the coaching context may include: Why am I not enjoying coaching this client? How could I be more effective with clients that just want to vent?
- Select a reflection process that matches your preferences – for example, a journal, recording a conversation with yourself or reflecting when going on a walk.
- Schedule time – put a regular time in your calendar that you can use to reflect.
- Start small – start with five minutes reflection and extend the time as you can.
- Do it – start with your questions, let your mind quieten down, consider a range of possible perspectives, brainstorm ideas.
- Ask for help – if you get stuck, ask a friend, ask your supervisor, find a coach who can listen and then hold you accountable.

Reflective Practice Case Study: Individual Informal Reflection

Annabelle ran a small but very successful executive coaching practice in the centre of the city. She was in her late fifties and had an established practice mostly with senior executives in the telecommunication sector. Over the last two years she had felt as though she was starting to lose her passion and spark for the business. Her decrease in energy happened so slowly that it crept up on her without warning. She did notice that her commute to work on a Monday morning was the worst time and that she had the persistent thought 'What is the point!' One Monday morning at the start of winter when the weather was gloomy, she reached a low point. To her dismay, she found herself in each coaching session that day, counting down the time rather than engaging with her clients. On her commute home she started to think that she just wanted to close the business down and take early retirement. Perhaps a year or two of travel in the Mediterranean would change her perspective? She had these thoughts every evening for a week and was starting to make some initial plans when she decided that to retire at this stage was to throw many years of hard business development away. Then it hit her that the critical issue was that she needed to find a successor to her business and spend the next few years handing it over. If she did this she could happily retire in a stronger financial position and with the knowledge that her hard work in building the business was going to generate a lasting legacy. At this point she recognised the value of the informal reflection that she was undertaking. Every evening for the next few months she spent her commute thinking about who she knew that could be a potential successor and as the winter months slipped by, she felt her spirits and energy steadily rising. Her informal reflection was making a great deal of difference.

Self-Reflective Exercise: Individual Informal Reflective Practice

Following is a template that can be used as a guide to this reflective practice process.

Individual Informal Reflective Practice Template

What is the topic I want to work on?
Example: How can I help generate better outcomes for my coaching clients?

How will I reflect on this topic – simply think it over, use a journal, draw a flow chart etc?
Example: I will use a journal to help me think through this.

How often will I reflect on this issue over the next month?
Example: I will spend time at the end of each Friday reflecting on my week and reviewing how I could do better.

When will I make the time for this reflection?
Example: I will put a calendar reminder in my phone.

How will I hold myself accountable?
Example: I will tell my supervisor what I am doing and suggest we put it on our monthly meeting agenda.

2. Individual Workbook-based Reflection

The key idea in this second type of reflective practice is to have a self-paced structured learning programme for the individual coach. This workbook can be developed as a basis for building this type of regular professional development practice.

The steps in individual workbook-based reflective practice are:

- Decide on the topic or area of your reflective practice and professional development.
- Find a relevant book, video, training course or other resource that provides the key ideas for you to use in your development.
- Select a reflection process that matches your preferences – for example, a journal, recording a conversation with yourself or writing up reflective practice exercises.
- Decide on how often the reflective practice will be undertaken.
- Find a way to hold yourself accountable.
- Undertake the reflective practice and document the outcomes and lessons learned.
- Apply these lessons in your coaching practice.

Reflective Practice Case Study: Individual Workbook-based Reflection

Billy worked for a large organisational psychology consultancy as a coach. He had gained his Master of Science in Coaching Psychology five years previously and had worked as a professional coach ever since. He really enjoyed the work and found his clients both fascinating and challenging. About a month ago Billy began coaching a senior IT manager whose work performance was being affected by acute anxiety. Billy spent the first session establishing an effective relationship and understanding the background to the problem. He used the popular GROW model of coaching but found that the client was unable to identify any options for alternative ways of dealing with the anxiety. Billy concluded that the client's biggest fear was fear itself and that this cycle greatly intensified the client's feelings. Billy decided that he needed some new ways of dealing with this situation. He had been to a very interesting training course on Acceptance and Commitment Therapy (ACT) for coaches about a year ago but had felt he did not understand the material well enough to apply it in his work. At this point he decided to read Chapter 13 of this book on using ACT techniques and apply an individual workbook-based reflection process. The next weekend he read the material and undertook the reflective practice exercises on Cognitive Defusion, Acceptance and Expansion and The Observing Self. Billy was astonished that by working on his own mild anxiety using these techniques he could stop struggling with the uncomfortable feelings, embrace them and let them go. To Billy, this reflective practice gave him a deep experiential understanding of these techniques. When he next met with his client, he was able to talk in a humble way about his own occasional anxiety and how he had found ACT very helpful. Billy felt that he was now able to speak with conviction and passion about ACT, which had changed from being a very interesting set of ideas to an extremely useful range of techniques that he understood at a deeply personal level. Billy felt that without using the reflective practice approach he would not have been able to apply the techniques in his coaching. The reduction in his own anxiety was an additional and most welcome bonus for him.

Reflective Practice Exercise: Individual Workbook-based Reflection

Following is a template that can be used as a guide to this reflective practice process.

Individual Workbook-based Reflective Practice Template

What is the topic you want to work on?
Example: I want to expand the range of ways I assist my clients and to start to use ACT techniques when appropriate in my coaching.

What resources will you use?
Example: I will start with Chapter 13: Internet Supplemented Acceptance and Commitment Therapy Techniques in this workbook and use the suggested reflective practice exercises.

How will you reflect on this topic – simply think it over, use a journal, draw a flow chart etc?
Example: I will make notes from Chapter 13 and then record my answers to the reflective practice exercises.

How often will you reflect on this issue over the next month?
Example: I will spend one hour early on each Monday morning working on my development.

How will you make the time for this reflection?
Example: I will put a calendar reminder in my phone.

How will you hold yourself accountable?
Example: I will work with my peer supervisor to talk over my reflective practice and my subsequent development.

What is the result of this self-reflection?
Example: I now understand the value of being more fully present in my coaching and sharing my awareness with my client.

How will you apply this refection in your coaching?
Example: Whenever I feel stuck in a coaching session, I will share exactly what I am feeling with my client and see what happens.

3. Workbook-based Reflective Practice in Pairs

This form of reflective practice is very similar to the individual workbook-based approach but involves working in pairs. The key difference is that in this type of reflective practice it is critical to establish psychological safety and confidentiality with the colleague or associate that is being worked with.

The usual steps in workbook-based reflective practice for pairs are:

- Decide on the topic or area of your reflective practice and professional development.
- Identify a colleague or associate to work with.
- Build a psychologically safe confidential relationship with this person – this topic is covered in Chapter 3: Psychological Connection, Safety and Confidentiality.
- Find a relevant book, video, training course or other resource that provides the key ideas for you to use in your development.
- Select a reflection process that matches the preferences of both individuals – for example, a journal, recording a conversation with yourself or writing up reflective practice exercises.
- Decide on how often the reflective practice will be undertaken.
- Find a way to hold yourselves accountable.
- Undertake the reflective practice and document the outcomes and lessons learned.
- Both individuals in the pair can then apply these lessons in their respective coaching practices.

Reflective Practice Case Study: Workbook-based Reflective Practice in Pairs

Caroline was a newly qualified coach who had recently completed an ICF accredited Certificate in Coaching programme. She was very excited about being able to work with the managers in the financial institution that employed her. Her initial work was with first line managers who were her own age and she found that the solution-focused model of coaching that she had learned was very useful. However, about a month ago she had been asked to coach a group of more senior managers that she found rather intimidating. At this point Caroline decided she needed some support in giving constructive but challenging feedback to these clients. She asked her colleague Daniel if they could work together to develop their coaching skills further. Caroline had learned a great deal in the Certificate in Coaching and had a useful supervisor to talk cases over with but still felt she needed more. She worked with Daniel on a weekly basis using a range of self-practice exercises including those on constructive challenging in Chapter 10 of this workbook. Over these months of reflective practice Caroline found that the experiential learning was invaluable and was particularly helpful in dealing with her senior manager clients.

Reflective Practice Exercise: Workbook-based Reflective Practice in Pairs

Following is a template that can be used as a guide to this reflective practice process.

Workbook-based Reflective Practice in Pairs Template

What is the topic I want to work on?
Example: I want to improve my ability to give constructive and challenging feedback to clients.

Who will you work with on this?
Example: I will work with my colleague Daniel.

How will you build a psychologically safe and confidential relationship with this person?
Example: I already know Daniel and trust him so I can talk openly about what I need in order to feel safe in this work together.

What resources will you use?
Example: I will start with Chapter 10: The Critical Skills in this workbook and use the suggested reflective practice exercises.

How will you reflect on this topic – simply think it over, use a journal, draw a flow chart etc?
Example: I will make notes from Chapter 10 and then record my answers to the reflective practice exercises.

How often will you reflect on this issue over the next month?
Example: I will spend one hour on Friday afternoons with Daniel working on our development.

How will you ensure you make the time for this reflection?
Example: I will put a calendar reminder in my phone.

How will you hold yourself accountable?
Example: Daniel and I will be sure to follow up and ensure we are applying the skills we are learning.

What is the result of this self-reflection?
Example: I feel much more confident and skilled as a coach.

How will you apply this refection in your coaching?
Example: I will apply constructive challenging whenever it is needed in my work.

4. Supervision and Reflective Practice

Coaching supervision can be defined as 'a formal and protected time for facilitating a coach's in-depth reflection on their practice with a trained coaching supervisor' (Association for Coaching, 2018, p. 1). The aim of supervision is to assist the coach to build competence, creativity and confidence. Supervision helps to ensure the best possible outcome for coaches, clients and their sponsoring organisations. (Association for Coaching, 2019).

Hawkins and Smith (2013) outline the CLEAR supervision model: contract, listen, explore, action and review. The CLEAR model is based on the following beliefs:

- Each supervision session should start by discovering the work the supervisee wants to do in the session and jointly agreeing how it will be done.
- Next there is a time of listening and exploring the supervisee's issues.
- Then there is the action phase – moving from intellectual understanding to trying out the new ways.
- The final review involves exploration of the relevant people in the supervisee's sphere (client, organisation, etc.) and how these people would value what has happened in supervision and also how this would impact the supervisee–supervisor relationship.

In a systematic literature review of supervision in coaching, Bachkirova et al. (2020) identified 699 publications, excluded 631 based on research quality and focused on 68 selected sources where they identified four main themes:

- There are many definitions of coaching supervision, but no one widely agreed version.

- The development of theory in coaching supervision is piecemeal.
- The value of supervision has been researched using a wide range of methods including qualitative, quantitative and one randomised controlled trial with the value of supervision being its ability to provide a time for thoughtful contemplation, the opportunity to present and explore cases, to be challenged, to validate the supervisee's practice and to provide continuing learning.
- Research into coaching supervision is limited; however, there is recognition of its importance and an increase in its uptake. Further systematic research is needed.

Supervision would normally include an opportunity for in-depth reflection on the client's practice; however, less frequently does it offer the coach the opportunity to be coached and then have time for reflective practice on this. Bisson (2017) in his book *Coach Yourself First: A Coach's Guide to Self-Reflection* suggests that supervision is important in supporting reflective learning and practice for coaches. This practice ensures that the coach is wholeheartedly engaged in the learning and professional development process. Bisson also suggests that creating an opportunity for reflective practice immediately after the supervision phase of the session will help the coach to consolidate their learning.

Reflective Practice Case Study: Supervision and Reflection

David had over 15 years of experience as a coaching supervisor and provided a valuable service for newly graduated coaches from his local university. He thoroughly enjoyed working with the enthusiastic graduates who were thirsty for feedback and insights. However, he had recently started supervising a younger coach who consistently displayed his impatience towards his clients' progress. David and the young coach talked over four different clients during a series of supervision sessions and the young coach's impatience remained stubbornly entrenched. David expressed very clearly his observation about the level of impatience, but it seemed to make little difference. David needed to try something new. He decided to offer the young coach a self-reflective session where rather than providing case-focused supervision, he would provide coaching to the coach. This process was begun in the next session and David felt that at last he was making progress. When the young coach was in the client's seat, he could immediately see just how hard change was and he was able to experience David's empathic confrontation first hand. This helped the young coach to be much less impatient with his own clients.

Reflective Practice Exercise: Supervision with Reflection

Following is a template that can be used as a guide to this reflective practice process.

Supervision with Reflective Practice Template

What is the topic you want to work on?
Example: I chose to work on my impatience with the progress my clients are making.

Did you feel psychologically safe during the coaching experience?
Example: Absolutely, I trust my supervisor a great deal.

What are your reflections on what it is like to be a client?
Example: I was aware of the real care and compassion that my supervisor offered me.

What did the supervisor do in the session that helped to address your issue?
Example: In a very caring way he confronted me with my own impatience and showed me just how hard personal change can feel.

Can you apply the insights from the session to your own coaching practice?
Example: Yes, I think I will be more empathetic with my clients and far less impatient.

What is your action plan?
Example: I have two clients that I am seeing this week where applying more empathy and less impatience could be useful.

How will you follow up?
Example: I will be very keen to discuss my progress with my supervisor in our next session.

Was the opportunity to reflect in this way useful?
Example: It is easy to talk about coaching models and techniques, but it is the actual experience of being coached and dealing with my own personal issues that makes it so useful.

5. Peer Group Reflective Practice

Peer group reflective practice can be defined as a professional development opportunity that involves small groups undertaking reflective practice exercises, sharing their experiences, learning from them and then applying them to their own coaching practices.

The usual steps in peer group reflective practice are:

- Decide on the topic or area of your reflective practice and professional development.
- Identify a small number of colleagues or associates to work with – four or five is an ideal number.
- Build a psychologically safe confidential relationship with these people – this topic is covered in Chapter 3: Psychological Connection, Safety and Confidentiality.
- Find a relevant book, video, training course or other resource that provides the key ideas to use in your development.
- Select a reflection process that matches both your preferences – for example, a journal, recording a conversation with yourself or writing up reflective practice exercises.
- Decide on how often the reflective practice will be undertaken.
- Find a way to hold yourselves accountable.
- Undertake the reflective practice and document the outcomes and lessons learned.
- Apply these lessons in your coaching practices.

Reflective Practice Case Study: Peer Group Self-Reflection

Emma worked for a large hospital as a leadership coach. She spent most of her time with senior medical specialists trying to build high performance teams. As patients were rarely cared for by just one health professional, teamwork was critical for patient safety because it greatly reduced adverse events caused by miscommunication. Emma found that developing teamwork was a challenge because there was typically an overlap in roles played by different team members, the hierarchical nature of the health care system often worked against collaboration, team members were often changing and there was rarely time for reflective practice. Emma was having a very frustrating time with a team on a geriatric ward where several unfortunate discharges had resulted in rapid re-admissions for patients. Emma had a great group of colleagues that she worked with, who often had lunch together or went for a drink after work. While Emma enjoyed the social connection, she felt frustrated that her colleagues rarely spent time together in effective problem solving or in helping each other. Their social time was often dominated with airing complaints and gossip. Emma decided that she wanted to form a small group of people who could effectively use reflective practice to support and develop each other.

The issue Emma wanted to work on was how to exert influence over senior medical practitioners when she clearly had no authority over them. She formed a group of four colleagues and they met on a Tuesday for lunch with a structured reflective practice process. Emma was careful to build a respectful, trusting and supportive atmosphere in the team and to ensure that confidentiality was agreed. Emma asked if one of her colleagues Fiona would act as team coach for the session. Fiona worked skilfully with the team to draw out their experience and insight into medical team development. This really helped to facilitate learning for the whole group. During the session, Emma was struck by the experience of a junior team member who had made considerable progress by working very closely with the head of Oncology Services. By combining the authority of the head of division with the knowledge of this leadership coach, they had made considerable progress in team development, despite all the obstacles.

Towards the end of the session Emma suggested that the group spend time using the Gibbs (1988) reflective practice model to better learn from the experience. She led the group through the five questions: What happened? How did we each feel? What was good and bad about the experience? What insights can I gain from the experience? and What do I want to do next? Overall, the group found the experience to be very helpful, they felt supported and informed in the group, they liked the open sharing of ideas, the insight they gained was that without a structured reflective process they might not have learned anything and they all went on to put their newly gained insights into practice.

Reflective Practice Exercise: Peer Group Self-Reflection

Following is a template that can be used as a guide to this reflective practice process.

Peer Group Reflective Practice Template

What is the topic you want to work on?
Example: I want to learn from my colleagues how they develop effective medical teams.

What happened in the peer group session?
Example: We built a great sense of trust in the group and this led to open sharing of experience.

What did we feel in the session?
Example: We felt supported and cared for.

What was good and bad about the experience?
Example: The high level of trust enabled us to openly share ideas.

What insights did we gain from the session?
Example: We had a wonderful range of shared experience that is a great basis for our learning as professionals.

What will we do next?
Example: We will apply these great ideas in our work and get together again next week to have another session.

6. Classroom and Training-based Reflection

The use of experiential and reflective approaches to improve classroom and academic learning is now well established particularly in the training of therapists (McGinn, 2015; Farrell & Shaw, 2018). Bennett-Levy et al. (2001) have produced a training method for Cognitive Behaviour Therapy (CBT) practitioners that includes using this approach to help therapists deal with their own problems. It also uses reflective practice to identify insights and to develop ways to apply these to their own therapeutic practice. The approach uses a structured workbook to help trainees to learn, reflect and link this learning to their clinical practice.

The empirical evidence for the use of experiential and reflective approaches in training Cognitive Behaviour Therapy (CBT) practitioners is set out in several places, for example, Bennett-Levy et al. (2015) and Haarhoff and Thwaites (2016). In summary, the evidence suggests that for CBT therapists the experiential and reflective programme enhances understanding of the CBT model, builds therapeutic skills, develops confidence as a therapist and improves belief in this therapeutic model. Participants typically report having a deeper sense of what the therapy is all about and better reflective skills, a key competency needed for continuous learning. This approach has also demonstrated improvements in the therapist's attitude towards their clients. This has included both better interpersonal skills and enhanced empathy for clients. Participants report personal insights and changes in their own lives as well as enhanced capability as a therapist (Bennett-Levy et al., 2015).

The meta-synthesis of Gale and Schröder (2014) has been set out in Chapter 1 and suggests that experiential and reflective approaches using CBT can be a useful training and development strategy.

Reflective Practice Case Study: Classroom- and Training-based Self-Reflection

Finn ran a training organisation specialising in workplace coaching. He used a wide range of training methods including presentations, group discussion, coaching demonstrations, role plays and expert panel discussions. Overall, the programme was successful, but Finn felt that somehow he could do more. He wanted to increase the level of engagement and connection that his students had with the topics. After doing a lot of reading he decided that he would introduce a series of reflective elements into each of his topics. He wanted his students to have more than intellectual knowledge and to have powerful experiential learning. Finn recognised that his students had gained a wealth of life experiences that was a rich resource for learning – but how could he harness this? He wanted his students to have a deep personal experience where they worked on their own personal challenges but how could they do this in a classroom where there was an understandable reluctance to share highly personal material?

To overcome this, he developed a simple workbook that enabled each of his students to apply CBT techniques to their own problems or challenges. This became a critical element of homework between training sessions. Students were encouraged to report back each session on their progress in addressing their issues. However, Finn was careful to restrict the classroom sharing just to the *process* of using CBT and not the *content* of their challenges. So, students reported back on how they were able to analyse their own problems using CBT concepts and how they developed strategies to overcoming these, all without having to disclose exactly the nature of their problem. The students were then encouraged to reflect on the experience and find ways to apply what they learned to their own coaching practice. The result was a great success and Finn was very happy with the balance between giving his students a deeply personal experience but in a psychologically safe way. The reflective practice element was reported to be one of the highlights of the programme by the students.

Reflective Practice Exercise: Classroom- and Training-based Learning

Following is a template that can be used as a guide to this reflective practice process. The exercise is designed for students of coaching courses to help them think through the issues involved in this approach.

Classroom- and Training-based Reflective Practice Template

What area of coaching would you like to apply an experiential and self-reflective approach to?
Example: Our course has covered the use of CBT techniques in coaching and I would like to use this.

What personal problem or challenge do you want to work on?
Example: I feel anxious when I start coaching new clients.

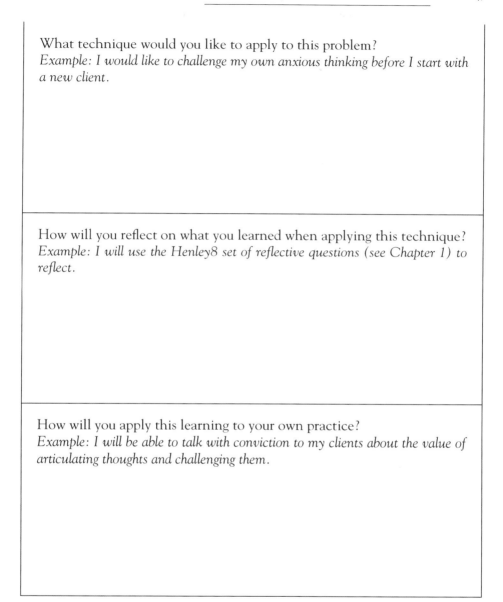

What technique would you like to apply to this problem?
Example: I would like to challenge my own anxious thinking before I start with a new client.

How will you reflect on what you learned when applying this technique?
Example: I will use the Henley8 set of reflective questions (see Chapter 1) to reflect.

How will you apply this learning to your own practice?
Example: I will be able to talk with conviction to my clients about the value of articulating thoughts and challenging them.

7. Intensive Group-based Triple Reflective Practice

A more advanced form of reflective professional development for coaches is the intensive triple reflective practice group method. In this approach four or five coaches meet for a day and each of the participants has an hour of coaching from a senior experienced practitioner, plus the opportunity to reflect on that experience and to have feedback and commentary from their peers (McCormick, 2020, 2021b, 2021c). When participants undertake triple self-reflection:

1. They consider what it is like to be coached rather than to be the coach. Sitting in the client's seat provides an opportunity to understand issues such as how hard it can be to change, how easy it is for others to see issues that we ourselves cannot see.
2. They can think through what they saw when watching the senior coach and consider how they might apply these learnings in their own practice.
3. They receive feedback from the other members of the group and have the chance to reflect on this and learn from it.

The steps in developing this self-reflective group process are as follows.

-   Initially each participant completes a Reflective Practice Personal Questionnaire (based on the Shapiro Personal Questionnaire, Shapiro, 1961) to identify a small number of issues or problems to be coached on in the group session.

-   The group of coaches meets for a day session where they:
    o   review the nature of coaching and the approach that will be used on the day;
    o   receive individual coaching from the senior practitioner;
    o   reflect on what it was like to be coached;
    o   discuss their reflections;
    o   decide on how to apply these insights to their own practice.

-   Finally, each participant repeats their Reflective Practice Personal Questionnaire and completes a Reflective Practice Session Rating Scale (Murphy et al., 2020) to enable the evaluation of the session.

To run successful reflective practice sessions for coaches it is important that all individuals in any group session get on well and trust each other. Rather than simply announcing the running of a reflective practice programme and taking the first to enrol, it is recommended that the session leader find one individual who is keen to start a reflective practice group and ask that person to invite three or four other coaches who they know to join them in the session. The advantage of this process is that the initial individuals pick participants who they know and trust which greatly speeds up the connection and psychological safety formation process (McCormick, 2021c).

It is also important to make clear on any promotional material that participants should only bring moderate level issues to the reflective practice session. Deep-seated and existential problems are obviously not suitable for a format that offers one hour of coaching to each person. If individuals have serious problems, they are not excluded from the reflective practice session but asked to find a clinical psychologist to work with on that issue and only bring their moderate issues to the session (McCormick, 2021c).

One-Day Format for an Intensive Group-based Triple Reflective Practice Session

A typical one-day intensive reflective practice session would consist of the following.

9.00 am	Welcome and introductions by participants including their journey into coaching.
	Discussion about the reflective practice approach.
	Identifying each participant's expectations and learning objectives for the day.
	The importance of keeping a day journal and writing down the insights gained during the day and how these can be applied in a practical way.
	Discussion on creating psychological safety for the session.
9.30 am	Discussion about the nature of coaching.
	Review the coaching model used in the programme.
10.00 am	Break
10.15 am	Discussion of the participants' own topics they wish to cover in the coaching sessions.

10.30 am	Undertake the first coaching session with an individual participant.
	Reflective practice of the coaching by the participant, comments by the coach, feedback from the members of the group.
	Discussion on what the participant learned and how this can be applied to their own coaching practice.
11.30 am	Undertake the second coaching session with reflections.
12.30 pm	Lunch
1.30 pm	Undertake the third coaching session with reflections.
2.30 pm	Break
2.45 pm	Undertake the fourth coaching session with reflections.
3.45 pm	Undertake the fifth coaching session with reflections.
4.45 pm	Review of the day, each participant to undertake the assessment of their progress made in the coaching session, and complete the Reflective Practice Session Rating Scale.
	Offer further coaching assistance if this is needed by any participant after the session.
5.15 pm	Finish of the session.

Useful self-reflective questions for the session include:

• How did it feel to be coached? What thoughts, feelings and sensations were you aware of?
• What did you achieve in this session? What insights did you gain?
• What did the coach do?
• What elements of the coaching process did you observe in the session?
• What did you learn about your clients' experience of being coached?
• What did you learn from being coached that you can apply in your own practice?

The session leader's role is to continuously demonstrate the core behaviours of a coach: committed listening, building trust and rapport, demonstrating positive intent, asking powerful questions, providing reflective feedback and overall building a thinking partnership with the client (Barnes et al., 2017).

The Benefits of Intensive Sessions

It is helpful for the session leader to share some of the benefits of reflective practice sessions, and McCormick (2020, 2021b, 2021c) suggests that these include:

- Enabling coaches to work on their own issues is hugely beneficial and a rare opportunity for self-care.
- As executive coaching is private and confidential it is unusual for anyone to see a range of live sessions.
- The client gains experiential understanding of the coaching process.
- The client gets feedback from multiple sources and this is very valuable and accelerates their professional development.
- Often for the first time, coaches can understand how demanding it can be in the client's seat.
- Seeing the iterative, dynamic and sometimes rather chaotic reality of coaching enables the client to understand it is not a set process as is implied by many coaching models.
- The vulnerability shown by the participants draws them together with a common understanding of their own humanity.

Participants' Comments about the Sessions

McCormick (2021c) has set out some typical comments from participants who have been involved in reflective practice sessions:

- I started the session feeling nervous and rather uncomfortable but the discussion on psychological safety helped me a lot.
- I got a whole new insight into my struggle with work–life balance and came to understand that without adequate self-care I cannot really care for my family or my clients.
- It was so great to see the coaching process live. I have coached for many years and have always wondered if I was 'doing it properly'!
- I really enjoyed seeing how relentlessly positive and solution focused the coach was – that is a real learning that I can apply in my practice.
- I am a much better coach for having seen the dynamic nature of the coaching process unfold in front of my eyes.

- It was just great to spend a day in a supportive caring environment with other respected professional coaches.
- I wanted to find a way to increase my personal fitness and I came to understand that I have been setting huge unrealistic goals in this area and the session helped me to understand that taking a small initial step is the place to start.

Self-Reflective Exercise: Being a Group Reflective Practice Session Leader

Intensive Group-based Triple Reflective Practice Session Template
Would you want to facilitate intensive group reflective practice sessions? *Example: Yes, I would be very interested in doing this.*
Would you feel comfortable having other coaches watch you hold small group coaching sessions? *Example: I am sure it would be a challenge but worth it.*
Do you know coaches that might be interested in this type of professional development? *Example: Yes, I know of one other coach who might be interested.*

Are there other issues or areas you would want to research before undertaking a reflective practice session?

Example: I would want to have an in-depth discussion with a successful session leader about the process before I undertook it.

Summary

This chapter has presented the practical steps needed to run a wide range of reflective practice sessions. The chapter includes:

- How reflective practice fits well with the criteria for adult learning.
- How to design reflective practice sessions.
- The seven types of reflective practice.
- Case studies to illustrate these different types of reflective practice.
- Reflective practice exercises to work on.

The aim of this chapter was to enable coaches to feel knowledgeable, confident and comfortable in running a wide range of reflective practice sessions.

Part II
Connection and Safety

Setting the Stage for Reflective Practice Groups

The purpose of Part II of the book is to present the foundations that are essential to run reflective practice sessions. This part includes material on the importance of psychological connection, safety and confidentiality as well as a section on measuring the outcome of reflective practice sessions.

DOI: 10.4324/9781003285144-4

3
Psychological Connection, Safety and Confidentiality

INTRODUCTION TO THE CHAPTER

This chapter sets out the practical steps necessary to develop the right dynamics for group reflective practice to flourish, that is, the development of psychological connection, safety and confidentiality. Creating the right environment for participants is important when holding reflective practice sessions in pairs, small groups and classroom settings.

The aim of the chapter is to enable participants to feel confident in building the critical foundations necessary for successful reflective practice sessions.

What Psychological Connection Is

Common understanding and connection are critical for any effective team (Katzenbach & Smith, 1993). In the context of reflective practice sessions participants often describe psychological connection as being able to relate to and understand each other. Sharing of personal challenges in this context quickly builds a sense of belonging and empathy.

Two key activities in reflective practice sessions build connection. At the start of any group, the session leader should disclose his or her journey into coaching so demonstrating openness and some vulnerability. The story typically includes both career high and low points and the vulnerability expressed in this type of story builds a common bond. Participants then share their journey into coaching stories, further building the interpersonal 'glue' in the group. The second activity is for participants to share the problems or challenges that they wish to work on in the session. Group members typically find a connection and commonality in these topics as many members have shared experiences.

DOI: 10.4324/9781003285144-5

What Psychological Safety Is

When asked, participants in reflective practice sessions typically say that psychological safety means being accepted without criticism in the group and being able to share their personal thoughts and feelings without fear of disapproval.

A Model of Psychological Safety

Clark (2020) provides a four-stage model of psychological safety in the workplace that is relevant to the reflective practice context. According to the model psychological safety is a condition where people feel:

- Included.
- Safe to learn.
- Safe to contribute.
- Safe to politely challenge the status quo – without fear of being embarrassed or punished in some way.

These four stages of psychological safety reflect the natural progression of participants in reflective practice groups. When these groups progress through the stages, they create deep connection, powerful learning, greater contribution and more innovative ideas. A wide range of empirical studies show that psychological safety plays an important role in team effectiveness (Edmondson & Lei, 2014).

Exercises to Build Psychological Safety

Below are a series of exercises that can be undertaken in any reflective practice group to build and maintain psychological safety.

- Hold a discussion around reflective practice values and behaviours. At the start of the group the session leader can ask, 'What important personal values are associated with building psychological safety in our reflective practice session? These values can be listed on the left-hand side of a white board or flip chart. The session leader can then review the list of values and build a consensus around the top three or four values by asking, 'Which are the most important values as far as each person here is concerned?' Once the top values have been identified the session leader can ask, 'What concrete behaviours would you observe when someone was displaying each of these values?' This behaviours list can be drawn up on the right-hand side of a white board or flip chart.

- Disclosing best and worst psychological safety experiences. The leader can start a discussion by asking, 'Tell us about a time when you felt really safe in a work or other group. What was going on? How did this sense of safety develop?' A summary of the main points is written up on a white board. Then the session leader asks, 'Tell us about a time when you felt really very unsafe in a work or other group. What was going on? How did this lack of safety develop?' Following the discussion, a definition of what psychological safety means to the group can be drawn up and agreed.

- Hold a 'concerns and mitigation' discussion. In this exercise the leader starts by asking, 'What are some of your concerns or fears about a lack of psychological safety? What would you not want to happen?' The leader then writes these concerns on the left-hand side of a white board. Then the session leader asks, 'Let's look at the first concern and think about how this can be mitigated. What can be done to overcome this fear?' The mitigation factors are then written up on the right-hand side of the whiteboard.

The benefits of these types of discussion are:

- Participants understand what is expected of them and each other.
- Group cohesion is built.
- The boundaries of acceptable behaviours are agreed.
- The degree of psychological safety of group members increases.

Assessing Psychological Safety

The informal measurement of psychological safety at the beginning and end of a group reflective practice session can be very helpful in providing a fuller understanding of the concerns of the participants. These assessments can be done using a simple pen and paper survey or by asking participants what they feel.

At the beginning and end of the reflective practice session the leader can ask: 'On a five-point scale, where 1 equals "very low" and 5 equals "very high", how comfortable do you feel about the following?'

- Being able to talk openly about your personal concerns?
- Not talking about matters that are too personal for this group?
- Working with other members of this reflective practice group?
- Being coached in front of your peers?
- Having others comment on you as a client?

- Having the coach comment on your response as a client?
- The overall reflective practice process?

Scores can be collected at the beginning of the session and if they are low then the specific issues can be addressed. Scores obtained at the beginning of a session can be compared with scores at the end and the implications of the changes discussed and action taken if needed to maximise safety.

Reflective Practice Exercise: Creating Psychological Connection and Safety

Creating Psychological Connection and Safety: Reflective Practice Exercise Template

If you were to facilitate a reflective practice session, how would you create psychological connection?
Example: I would resist any temptation to rush into the exercises of the day, relax and allow more time for participants to simply get to know each other.

If you were to facilitate a reflective practice session, how would you create psychological safety?
Example: I now see the critical value of psychological safety and would ensure we take the time to develop this.

How would you measure psychological safety in a reflective practice session?
Example: I would ask each person to rate their feeling of safety on a one to ten scale.

Are there other psychological connection or safety issues that you want to research?
Example: I want to read more about how my clients who are senior executives can build psychological safety in their organisations.

Confidentiality in Reflective Practice Groups

Confidentiality in reflective practice groups involves members keeping others' information private and not disclosing it to others outside the group. Confidentiality can be developed and maintained in a group by holding a discussion on: the definition of confidentiality, the types of disclosure that are not allowed, e.g., face-to-face, text, email, social media and other forums, the consequences of breach of confidentiality, e.g., exclusion from the group. Most confidentiality agreements in reflective practice groups are verbal; however, written and signed agreement can be used if necessary.

Summary

This chapter sets out the practical steps necessary to develop the right dynamics for reflective practice sessions to flourish. That is, the development of psychological connection, safety and confidentiality. The aim of the chapter is to enable participants to build the critical foundations necessary for successful reflective practice sessions.

4
Establishing Effectiveness Measurement

INTRODUCTION TO THE CHAPTER

This chapter sets out ways in which the effectiveness of both group reflective practice sessions and individual coaching can be easily assessed. The outlined measures set out in this chapter are not the only way in which this assessment can take place, but they have been useful to date (McCormick, 2020). There are two assessments discussed in this chapter, the first measures coaching outcome and the second the quality of the relationship between coach and client. The aim of the chapter is to enable anyone planning to run group reflective practice or individual coaching sessions to have a set of simple, clear measures to understand the effectiveness of their work.

Client-Generated Outcome Measures

Every coaching client presents with a different set of issues that are generated by a combination of the individual and their circumstances. Client-generated outcome measures (CGOMs) have been developed to assess this unique set of issues. CGOMs are particularly relevant in assessing change in individual coaching and reflective practice sessions because they provide a sensitive and highly selective measurement of the exact issues the client brings to the session (Elliott et al., 2015).

An early CGOM was developed by Shapiro (1961) and called the Personal Questionnaire. Shapiro developed the measure to assess psychological symptoms that were relevant to the unique issues specific to the person and their circumstances (Shapiro, 1961). The psychometric properties of the Personal Questionnaire have been assessed by Elliott et al. (2015) and they concluded that this measure met the criteria for evidence-based measurement of client psychological distress. In the clinical setting, the Personal Questionnaires are

DOI: 10.4324/9781003285144-6

useful for monitoring a client's symptoms and complaints over the course of therapy and are especially useful because they allow the clinician to assess the presenting problems using the client's own words in a systematic and structured way. The Personal Questionnaire is also ideally suited for those situations where the client's problems are unusual and cannot be adequately captured by any of the standard measures (Morley, 2013). The Personal Questionnaire does not use pre-selected items that have been pre-tested in a larger sample of clients. It is a technique that has several distinguishing features (Morley, 2013):

- The content of each question is determined by the individual client.
- The scale (range) of experience covered in each question is agreed with and calibrated by the client.
- The format of the Personal Questionnaire contains a measure of reliability (in the form of internal consistency) that can be assessed on every occasion of administration.

The steps in the original Personal Questionnaire have been outlined by Morley (2013):

- The clinician asks the client for a series of statements that describe their current problems or distress and complaints.
- Two additional statements are developed for each of the client's problem statements, with one setting out the expected endpoint of therapy and the second the estimated midpoint in therapy. For example, the problem statement may be 'I am fearful of public speaking and totally avoid it', the midpoint statement may be 'I am somewhat afraid of public speaking and rarely do it' and the endpoint statement 'I feel somewhat nervous about public speaking, but I do it anyway'.
- A set of cards is then prepared with all the possible pairings of statements: problem versus midpoint, midpoint versus endpoint, problem versus endpoint.
- The cards are then presented to the client who decides which of the paired statements is closer to their current state.

With repeated administration the clinician can identify shifts in the description of the client's current state and assess how close the client's description is from the endpoint or recovery state.

An alternative CGOM is the PSYCHLOPS (Psychological Outcome Profiles) developed by Ashworth et al. (2004). This is a plain English measure that was based on the MYMOP (Measure Your own Medical Outcome Profile)

(Paterson, 1996) a client- generated questionnaire developed to assess physical illness. It was later re-worked into a before and after assessment for psychotherapy. It seeks the client's own 'world view' by asking what the most important problem is to them, as an individual. It does not prompt, suggest responses or frame possible areas of psychological distress. It is designed to be a highly sensitive indicator of change, documenting the improvement, or otherwise, after therapy (Ashworth et al., 2004).

McCormick (2020) has developed a simple type of a CGOM called the Reflective Practice Outcome Questionnaire that has been used in outcome measurement of individual coaching and group reflective practice sessions for coaches. The approach involves asking each participant to generate their own list of four or five issues or problems that they want to deal with in coaching. The participants then rate these statements on a 7-point scale that measures how much they are bothered by these issues from 1: Not at All, 2: Very Little, 3: Little, 4: Moderately, 5: Considerably, 6: Very Considerably, 7: Maximum Possible. Typical problems or issues identified by clients to work on in individual or group sessions include unhelpful emotions, difficult work relationships, career challenges, work–life navigation and business development challenges. Participants are asked to complete the Reflective Practice Questionnaire at the beginning and end of the session. The difference between the beginning and end scores is a measure of the improvement the client feels that they have made during the session.

Working Alliance Measures

The quality of the relationship between coach and client is a critical factor in the successful outcome of the coaching process and therefore is important to measure (O'Broin & Palmer, 2010). This relationship is called the working or coaching alliance:

> The Coaching Alliance reflects the quality of the coachee's and coach's engagement in collaborative, purposive work within the coaching relationship, and is jointly negotiated, and renegotiated throughout the coaching process over time.
>
> (O'Broin & Palmer, 2007, p. 305)

Graßmann et al. (2020) examined a large number of studies evaluating the impact of the working alliance between the client and the coach on coaching outcome. Their meta-analysis used 27 samples (N = 3563 coaching processes) and found a moderate, consistent relationship between the quality of the working alliance and the client's perception of the coaching outcomes. The strongest positive relationship was between the working alliance and affective and cognitive coaching outcomes. The results apply independently of the number of coaching sessions, the type of clients, the level of coaches' expertise and the clients' or coaches' perspectives.

The quality of the working alliance has been measured by a range of different instruments. One established measure, the Working Alliance Inventory, was developed for psychotherapy research (Horvath & Greenberg, 1989). The inventory is based on the work of Bordin (1979, 1994) who viewed the working alliance as consisting of three elements:

- Agreement between therapist and client on the tasks of therapy.
- Agreement on the goals of therapy.
- The development of an affective bond between the two individuals.

Horvath and Greenberg (1989) examined the psychometric properties of the Working Alliance Inventory and their data suggested that it had adequate reliability. It was also found to be reliably correlated with a range of relevant counsellor and client self-reported outcome measures so there was a preliminary indication of the validity of the Inventory.

The Session Rating Scale was developed in the 1990s after research indicated that a positive alliance relationship between therapist and client was one of the best predictors of therapeutic outcomes (Duncan et al., 2003). This version was a 10-item measure, using a Likert-type scale to measure client perceptions of the quality of the working alliance (Duncan et al., 2003). However, there were ongoing concerns by practitioners that the measure was too long. As a result, a four-item version was developed by Bordin (1979) assessing (1) the bond between therapist and client, (2) goal agreement and (3) task agreement. A fourth item was later added to the scale asking about the fit of the session with the client's needs (Duncan et al., 2003).

Murphy et al. (2020) undertook a review of the psychometric properties of the Session Rating Scale and their findings showed a high internal consistency and other supporting evidence for the scale's value in assessing the therapeutic alliance. Test–retest reliability estimates were reported in 4 of the 12 studies included in this review (ranging from .54 to .70).

Other working alliance measures include the Supervisory Working Alliance Inventory by Efstation et al. (1990). This Inventory has three factors relevant to the supervisor (client focus, rapport and identification) and two supervisee factors (rapport and client focus). The Inventory was found to have adequate scale reliability, and useful convergent and divergent validity when compared with the Supervisory Styles Inventory (Friedlander & Ward, 1984). Validity for the trainee scores was initially established with a significant prediction of scores on the Self-Efficacy Inventory (Friedlander & Snyder, 1983).

Another working alliance measure was produced by Kelley et al. (2010) who developed the Real Relationship Inventory, which consists of two subscales – realism and genuineness. The authors developed and established the validity of the 24-item Inventory using a sample of clients who were in psychotherapy (n = 94). Their findings provide initial confirmation of validity and reliability of the measure. Positive relationships were found between the Inventory and a range of related measures including those of working alliance.

Having reviewed a range of the available working alliance measures, McCormick (2020) used a five-item assessment that was tailored to fit with the development of coaching skills in reflective practice groups. The measure, called the Reflective Practice Coaching Session Assessment included items on the quality of the relationship between coach and coachee, the level of agreement on the aim of the coaching, the fit of the coaching process, the level of assistance in improving the client's coaching practice and the general relevance of the session for the client.

Effectiveness Measurement Case Study

Leila was a very experienced executive coach who had been asked to put in a proposal for coaching with the top eight executives in a major accounting firm. The firm made it very clear that they not only needed coaching for the senior leaders, but they wanted evidence that the coaching programme was delivering results. Leila had completed a Master of Science in Coaching Psychology three years prior, so she felt she was familiar with a range of measurement instruments for coaching. In her discussions with the Head of Human Capital for the firm, it became clear that the firm wanted two types of measures, firstly an assessment of the quality of the relationship between the coach and executive and secondly an evaluation of the impact of the coaching from the executive's perspective.

She initially looked at a range of leadership measures but quickly became overwhelmed by the range of possible areas to measure. These areas included authenticity, caring, collaboration, composure, decisiveness, organisational astuteness, personal productivity, presence, results focus, self-awareness, team building, visionary communication and work–life navigation. The challenge that Leila had was that any of the executives may want to work on areas that were not covered in the leadership dimensions in any chosen measure. Leila readily understood the difference between a leadership development programme that covered a set curriculum and so could easily be assessed and a coaching programme where the starting point was understanding the client's own agenda and undertaking coaching to meet their unique needs. Leila spent a week uncertain about how to address the firm's needs.

In a session with her supervisor, Leila was pointed in the direction of a range of relevant client-generated outcome measures. These measures were based on the idea that each executive had a unique set of problems, issues or concerns that were generated by a combination of their own personality, experience and current circumstances. Leila discovered that these measures were totally different from the usual standardised leadership inventories that aim to place an individual within a larger population of leaders in terms of general factors and norms. Leila was inspired by a quote from a famous psychologist, Gordon Allport, who said, 'as long as psychology deals with universals and not with particulars, it won't deal with much' (Allport, 1960, p. 146). She found that client generated measures had been around for a long time (Pascal & Zax, 1956) but she was not familiar with them. She developed a plan:

- She asked each executive in the initial session to identify a range of problems, issues or concerns that they wanted to work on in the upcoming coaching sessions. She got a very wide range of answers to this question, from dealing with entitled team members, to handling staff from the official government financial regulator, to achieving better work–life balance.
- Leila then asked each executive how much each of their issues bothered them on a 1–7 point scale.
- Leila then used this to draw up a simple client-generated outcome measure.
- Every third session Leila asked each executive to identify how much their own selected issues bothered them at that time.
- She then used this information to draw up a simple graph that showed the progress made by each executive in dealing with each of their individual issues.
- The result was a very comprehensive, systematic and personalised coaching effectiveness report.

This work addressed the firm's issue of how to evaluate the impact of the coaching from the executive's perspective, leaving Leila with the dilemma of how to assess the quality of the coaching relationship.

Leila had learned in her Master's programme the importance of the coaching relationship or alliance as a predictor of programme success. She had also learned that there were several factors that led to an effective coaching alliance and these included the level of trust between coach and executive, the level of agreement on the desired goal of coaching and the clarity of the coaching agreement and process. She checked with the Head of Human Capital that if she measured these factors then this would be an effective way to assess the quality of the relationship between the coach and executive. The Head of Human Capital was delighted by this type of assessment as it was so different from the usual informal coaching relationship evaluation the firm had become used to, which she described as 'coach and hope!'.

At the end of the coaching programme Leila was able to send a report to the Head of Human Capital demonstrating a steady progressive reduction in the level of concern that each executive experienced over the course of the coaching. In addition, Leila was able to show a very high level of coaching relationship alliance for the group with average ratings being 4 out of 5 on the scale.

Leila felt that she had learned a great deal about coaching measurement as a result of the experience and decided to adopt this type of simple assessment in all future coaching sessions. The accounting firm was delighted with the outcome and felt that they wanted to invest more in executive coaching as a result.

Reflective Practice Exercise: Establishing Effectiveness Measurement

What type of measurement do you undertake for your individual or group coaching?
Example: All of my measurement is simply informal 'word of mouth' reporting by clients.

If you wanted to measure the effectiveness of your coaching session, what would you do?
Example: I would use a mix of outcome and working alliance measures.

If you were to facilitate a group reflective practice session, how would you establish the baseline?
Example: The questionnaires set out in this chapter look useful.

Are there other reflective practice baseline measurement issues you want to use in the evaluation of your sessions?
Example: It would be very useful to ask participants to keep a journal during the session and qualitatively analyse the critical or important moments they note down during the sessions.

Summary

This chapter sets out ways in which the effectiveness of both individual coaching and group reflective practice sessions can be easily assessed. The outlined measures set out in this chapter are not the only way in which this assessment can take place, but they have proven to be useful to date (McCormick, 2020). The aim of the chapter is to enable anyone planning to run group reflective practice sessions or individual coaching to have a set of simple, clear measures to understand the issues participants want coaching in and to assess changes over time.

Part III
The Nature of Coaching

This part of the book explores what coaching is, the conceptual models of coaching, how it can be undertaken with executives, how effective it is, and the last chapter explores the solution-focused coaching model. The purpose of this part of the book is to enable readers to have a deeper understanding of what coaching is and the steps that can be taken in any coaching session.

DOI: 10.4324/9781003285144-7

5
What Coaching Is

INTRODUCTION TO THE CHAPTER

This chapter explores what coaching is and the wide range of models that can be used in coaching sessions to provide a clear and visible path through these sessions. It also includes a reflective practice exercise to help coaches think more about the model of coaching they use and why.

Coaching helps individuals identify and work towards their goals using evidence-based psychological methods (Grant & Cavanagh, 2007). Coaching has grown greatly as a business, with the International Coaching Federation stating that in 2019 the estimated revenue from coaching was US$2.849 billion, representing a 21% increase over the 2015 estimate (Pomerantz, 2020).

Coaching in the workplace involves a one-to-one learning and development approach in which a collaborative, reflective, goal-focused relationship is used to achieve the client's professional outcomes (Smither, 2011). The term coaching has been applied to a wide range of one-to-one development activities; however, there is a growing consensus that the core features of coaching are as follows (Bono et al., 2009; Smither, 2011):

- A helping relationship between the coach and client has been developed and is maintained over time.
- There is a formal coaching agreement or contract setting personal development objectives, which has been agreed and documented.
- The coaching aims to achieve the objectives set out in the coaching contract by focusing on interpersonal and intrapersonal issues.
- The client strives to grow using the tools, skills and opportunities he or she needs to develop and become more effective.

DOI: 10.4324/9781003285144-8

The Range of Coaching Models

There is a wide range of coaching models that are designed to help describe the specific phases in the coaching conversation (Grant, 2011). The following models are explored by Edgerton and Palmer (2005).

One of the most popular of these is the GROW model (Whitmore, 1996) which is defined as:

Goal – what the client wants to achieve in coaching.
Reality – helping the client to explore the current situation and be objective about it.
Options – helping the client to maximise the choices.
What next or Way forward or Wrap up – the action plan to follow up and develop accountability.

The CLEAR model which is a five-step process developed by Peter Hawkins (Grant, 2011).

Contracting – clarifying the client's needs and setting the goals.
Listening – becoming aware of the detail and the patterns of client behaviour.
Exploring – enabling the client to generate insights about their situation.
Action – supporting the client to find the best way forward.
Review – closing the session with both coach and client reflecting on their work together.

The ACHIEVE model was developed by Dembkowski and Eldridge (2003). They saw the model as a logical progression from the GROW model that developed the coaching relationship in a systematic manner:

Assess current situation and the issues the client wants to work on.
Creatively brainstorm the alternatives to current situation.
Hone goals to gain clarity.
Initiate options by developing a range of these to move toward the goal.
Evaluate options to find the most effective one.
Valid action programme design – developing an action plan.
Encourage momentum – provide ongoing support and encouragement.

(Dembkowski & Eldridge, 2003 p. 21)

Libri (2004) suggested the POSITIVE model developed from the GROW and ACHIEVE models and aimed to produce an optimum coaching relationship. Examples of key questions in each phase are provided below:

Purpose – what do you want to achieve?
Observations – what have you tried so far and what has worked well?
Strategy – what does success look like from your perspective?
Insight – how committed are you in achieving this goal on a scale of 1 to 10?
Team – who will you share your goal with in order to get support?
Initiate – when will you start to implement these actions ?
Value – how will you celebrate your success and how will you feel about this?
Encourage – how are you going with your goals and what do you need help with?

These models provide the coach with a range of ways of navigating the coaching conversation in a systematic manner.

Reflective Practice Exercise: The Coaching Model You Use

Which coaching model do you generally use? Why?
Example: I use GROW as it seems to be the most widely used.

What are the strengths and weaknesses of the coaching model that you use?
Example: GROW model is simple but it is not so easy to generate good coaching questions using this model.

Are there other coaching model issues that you want to research?
Example: I would like to read some more about the POSITIVE model and try it out.

What is your action plan?
Example: I will research the POSITIVE model in the next week, discuss this with my supervisor and implement it will my clients, where appropriate, after that.

Summary

This chapter explores what coaching is and the wide range of models that can be used in coaching sessions to provide a clear and visible path through these sessions. The chapter also contains a reflective practice exercise to help coaches think more about the model of coaching they use and why.

6
The Conceptual Models of Coaching

INTRODUCTION TO THE CHAPTER

This chapter covers:

- The background to a range of conceptual models of coaching including:
  - o   The Four Key Pillars Model.
  - o   The Six-Category Intervention Model.
  - o   The Coaching Alliance Conceptual Model.
- A reflective practice exercise using each of these three conceptual models.

The aim of the chapter is to help the reader relate to and engage with the concepts of coaching and enjoy a range of self-reflective exercises.

Background to the Conceptual Models of Coaching

The word *coach* was first used in English in the 1500s and it refers to a kind of carriage (Witherspoon & White, 1996). So, the verb *to coach* means to transport a person from one place to where they want to go. That definition resonates today. Coaching helps individuals identify and work towards their goals using evidence-based psychological methods (Grant & Cavanagh, 2007).

The term *executive coaching* means many different things, with some writers suggesting it is a method to learn specific skills, others that it is used to improve performance and some writers suggesting it is a process to prepare for career development (Witherspoon & White, 1996). Still others see it as a method to support wider organisational improvement or change. Despite the different meanings, coaching is typically based on an ongoing, confidential, supportive yet challenging one-on-one relationship between coach and executive (Witherspoon & White, 1996).

DOI: 10.4324/9781003285144-9

The exact origins of executive coaching are unclear, but Harris (1999) suggests that professionals probably used a potent mix of psychological and organisational development techniques when working with leaders long before the term executive coaching was coined. Tobias (1996) suggests the term, *executive coaching*, was first used in the late 1980s and it consisted of a repackaging of consulting and counselling techniques and terms.

McCauley and Hezlett (2001) state that executive coaching was first developed to help talented individuals whose careers were in danger of stalling. Later, it was used with high potential executives as a method of professional development for career advancement.

Executive coaching is most successful as a three-way partnership between coach, executive and the client organisation. Each party needs to contribute to the success of the coaching process. Although the principal work is done between executive and coach, coaching is always conducted in the context of the organisation's goals and objectives (Ennis et al., 2015).

Executive coaching can be defined as:

> a one-on-one individualised process to benefit the leader and his/her organisation. Working with goals defined by both the leader and the organisation, a qualified and trusted coach uses various coaching methods and feedback data to develop the executive's capacity for current and future leadership. This coaching is guided by a coaching partnership to achieve maximum impact and the highest level of learning.
>
> (Ennis et al., 2015, p. 8)

In the solution-focused conceptualisation provided by Szabo and Meier (2008), coaching is the process of creating a frame of reference or a view of the world so that the client can find new solutions.

Executive coaching, like human resource development in general, is an area of practice that is far ahead of its theory (Kampa-Kokesch & Anderson, 2001). There is:

- A lack of a set of agreed philosophical assumptions and a framework to guide theory building.
- A shortage of well-researched methods of theory building.
- Little shared understanding of the core concepts of theory and theory building (Lynham, 2000).

Three conceptual models of coaching will be explored in the next section, the Four Key Pillars model of Joo (2005), the Six Category Intervention model of Heron (1976) and the Coaching Alliance model of O'Broin and Palmer (2010).

The Four Key Pillars Model

Joo (2005) has made progress on building a conceptual model for executive coaching that is based on four key pillars: coaching antecedents, coaching process, initial outcomes and final outcomes.

Antecedents

There are three antecedents to successful coaching:

- The experience, ability and other characteristics of the coach.
- The openness to feedback and willingness to change of the individual client.
- The level of support and investment offered by the organisation or economic client.

Process

There are three elements of the coaching process that are conducive to success:

- The coaching approach or the type of coaching wanted by the client, which might include advice, counsel, teaching, feedback or a sounding board.
- The quality of the coaching relationship, which includes the calibre of personal chemistry between coach and client.
- The availability of client feedback, which may include relevant commentary from the client's peers and manager about their personal style or performance.

Initial Outcomes

Successful coaching will typically enhance the self-awareness of the client into his or her own interpersonal style and relationship building. One common purpose of executive coaching is to provide the client with the opportunity to see themselves as others do, by the coach providing them with a metaphysical mirror.

Coaching not only builds awareness but is a key driver of the learning of new knowledge, skills and mindsets. It also provides the client with insights into their own values and prejudgements.

Coaching typically involves three levels of learning:

- Tactical problem solving – developing options for dealing with day-to-day organisational challenges.
- Developing leadership capabilities and new ways of thinking and acting that generalise to other situations and roles – for example, the idea of leader-as-servant rather than leader-as-master.
- Learning how to learn, that is developing skills and habits of reflective practice that ensure that learning will continue after coaching ends. This is an often overlooked goal of coaching. Its aims are to prevent an executive's long-term dependency on his or her coach and teach habits of learning and reflective practice that will last a lifetime, enabling him or her to keep developing throughout their career (Ennis et al., 2015).

Final Outcomes

Successful coaching leads the individual client to greater problem solving, leadership, interpersonal skills, confidence, resilience and work–life balance. This in turn leads to better team, divisional and organisational performance.

In summary the conceptual model of Joo (2005) provides a comprehensive overview of the major elements in successful coaching.

Reflective Practice Exercise: The Four Pillars Conceptual Model

Think about a recent coaching assignment that you have now completed. Write a brief description of the process and outcome of the coaching. *Example: I finished working with a senior manager from an internet service provider this week. I used the solution-focused coaching model to help her improve her delegation and work–life balance. Overall, the work went very well.*

Now write a brief description of each of the following conceptual elements.

1.   My experience and ability as a coach.
Example: I have a Master of Science in Coaching for Behaviour Change and five years experience. I have now worked with about 100 clients but still feel I have a lot to learn to maximise my coaching.

2.   The openness to feedback and willingness to change of the client.
Example: The client was initially quite resistant to the idea that she could delegate more. She felt her team were already fully stretched and she did not want to stress them further. It took some time for her to accept that delegation was possible.

3.   What is the level of support and investment offered by the organisation or economic client?
Example: The organisation was very supportive and the coaching agreement was to do as much as the client wanted.

4.   What was the coaching approach or the type of coaching wanted by the client, which might include advice, counsel, teaching, feedback or a sounding board?
Example: The client wanted to better manage their work–life balance but initially could not see how more delegation fitted into this. I used solution-focused coaching with some advice and challenge.

5.   What was the quality of the coaching relationship including the calibre of personal chemistry between coach and client?
Example: The client was very open and curious. We got on really well and both clearly enjoyed working together.

6.   What was the willingness of the client to receive feedback including commentary from the client's peers and manager about their personal style or performance?
Example: The client was initially rather resistant to feedback but once she found that her team were willing to take on some of her work, she was very open to delegation.

7.   What was the level of self-awareness of the client at the end of coaching?
Example: At the end of coaching her level of self-awareness was very high.

8. What was the quality and quantity of learning undertaken by the client as seen at the end of coaching?
Example: The client learned a lot about how her assumptions held her back. She assumed her staff could not take on more work so felt stuck at first.

9. What was the success of the coaching as assessed from the perspective of the individual client?
Example: She saw the coaching as very successful and has already referred a member of her team for coaching.

10. What was the success of the coaching as assessed from the perspective of the organisation?
Example: I have been in touch with the People and Culture Manager who said he was pleased with the outcome.

11. Was the outcome of the coaching a product of the coaching antecedents and coaching processes as outlined in the conceptual model of Joo (2005)? How was the outcome driven by the elements in the model?
Example: It is very interesting to use the model to reflect on my work and I can see that so many factors were favourable: the client was willing to learn, the organisation was supportive etc.

12. Now, how can you use your learnings from this reflective practice
     exercise to improve your coaching?
     *Example: This model helps me think broadly about the critical elements in
     coaching and not just feel that I achieved or failed.*

The Six-Category Intervention Model

Heron (1976) developed a six-category intervention analysis that provides a
useful conceptual model relevant to coaching. This intervention categorisa-
tion would usefully fit in the *Coaching Approach* area of the Joo (2005) overall
conceptual model.

The Heron model can assist coaches to assess their session interaction types
in post-session reflective practice. The interventions consist of two types:
authoritative interventions, which are more hierarchical and used when the
coach wants to be more directive, increase awareness, provide advice and make
clear suggestions. The second are facilitative types, which are less hierarchical,
build a sense of self-control, help let go of negative emotions and build insight
(Hamid & Azman 1992).

The following descriptions are adapted from Yürekli (2013).

Authoritative intervention types

Prescriptive

This category includes interactions where the coach provides clear and robust
direction to the client: 'I strongly suggest you do not openly criticise your boss
under those circumstances.'

Informative

This category denotes situations where the coach's aim is to share their experience or knowledge about the circumstance: 'From my experience that would
work really well!'

Confronting

In this category, the intention of the coach is to challenge the client over elements of their performance that may be difficult or below the required standard. The aim is to help the client to build awareness of the consequences of their behaviour: 'If I were your colleague and you said that to me, I would be very angry!'

Facilitative intervention types

Cathartic

This category is the kind of intervention where the client is given the opportunity to talk in depth about their feelings such as sadness, frustration or anxiety. This process allows the client to release negative emotions: 'Tell me more about what happened and why it was so painful.'

Catalytic

In this category, the goal of the coach is to inspire the client's self-discovery by probing important areas and helping them understand the feelings, thoughts and knowledge necessary to gain insight: 'Looking back on the situation, what did you do well, why and what would you change next time?'

Supportive

The aim of this type of intervention is for the coach to support the significance of the client's insights, strengths and actions. This is achieved by increasing their self-confidence and confirming that their efforts are constructive and worthwhile: 'You did really well in being able to express your views in such a constructive and assertive way.'

In summary, the Six-Category Intervention model provides a useful classification of the types of interaction that the coach can have with their clients.

Reflective Practice Exercise: The Six-Category Intervention Model

Think about a recent coaching session and write a summary below.

Use the Six-Category Model as set out below to decide on the frequency of intervention you used in the session.

Prescriptive - where you as coach provided strong direction to the client.

Rate your frequency of use on the scale below:

A lot   10   9   8   7   6   5   4   3   2   1 Not at all

Comments:
Example: I try to ask questions and not be too prescriptive. However when I am tired I can easily slip into prescriptive mode!

Informative – where you aimed to share your knowledge about the situation.

Rate your frequency of use on the scale below:

A lot   10   9   8   7   6   5   4   3   2   1 Not at all

Comments:
Example: I am happy to share my knowledge but I always ask if the client wants my input before I do.

Confronting – where you aimed to challenge the client over aspects of their performance that may be problematic.

Rate your frequency of use on the scale below:

A lot   10   9   8   7   6   5   4   3   2   1 Not at all

Comments:
Example: I never do this but know it is important – it's an area for development.

Cathartic – where you gave the client the opportunity to talk about their feelings such as frustration and anger so they could discharge their negative emotions.

Rate your frequency of use on the scale below:

A lot   10   9   8   7   6   5   4   3   2   1 Not at all

Comments:
Example: I am a good listener so this is a strength.

Supportive – where you affirmed the value of the client's qualities, attitudes, and actions to raise self-esteem and confirm that the client's efforts are constructive.

Rate your frequency of use on the scale below:

A lot   10   9   8   7   6   5   4   3   2   1 Not at all

Comments:
Example: I think this is so important and do it regularly.

Review your ratings and consider the intervention styles you use most and least in coaching.
Example: I use supporting most and confronting least.

How do you want to improve your coaching?
Example: I really want to learn more about empathetic confrontation techniques.

The Coaching Alliance Conceptual Model

O'Broin and Palmer (2010) present a conceptual approach that draws on the best predictor of coaching outcome – the working alliance. This would fit well into the *Coaching Relationship* box of the overall conceptual model of Joo (2005) above. The working alliance is a concept that has been applied across a range of sport and exercise psychology concepts (Katz & Hemmings, 2009) and coaching psychology (Palmer & McDowall, 2010).

A working definition is:

> The Coaching Alliance reflects the quality of the coachee's and coach's engagement in collaborative, purposive work within the coaching relationship, and is jointly negotiated, and renegotiated throughout the coaching process over time.
>
> (O'Broin & Palmer, 2010, p. 4)

This type of alliance is seen as applicable across a range of conceptual approaches. It provides a framework for assessing the quality of the collaborative work of the coach and coachee. Bordin (1994) identified three key features of the alliance: common goals, tasks and bonds. For the Coaching Alliance to work:

- Goals about the outcomes of coaching must be mutually agreed.
- A common understanding of the tasks to be undertaken between sessions needs to be decided.

- The bonds or mutual empathy and respect between coach and coachee need to be strong.

In summary the Coaching Alliance conceptual model provides a way to think about and understand the ongoing relationship between coach and client. It enables the coach to consider the key factors that allows a high-quality coaching relationship.

Reflective Practice Exercise: The Coaching Alliance

Write a brief description of a recent coaching session.
Example: I have just finished a coaching session working on building authentic leadership. My client is socially awkward and so I was quite unsure if I added value or not.

In this session, did you mutually agree goals about the outcomes of coaching? Please describe what happened below.
Example: Yes, this was the easy part of the session.

Did you reach a common understanding of the tasks to be undertaken between sessions? Please describe what happened below.
Example: Yes, this also went well.

Did you build mutual empathy and respect between yourself and the client? Please describe what happened below.
Example: This was the challenging part of the session. I was put off by his awkward manner and struggled to engage with him.

Overall, how well did you develop the coaching alliance with your client?
Example: I would give myself a 5 out of 10.

Given this reflective practice what did you learn about your coaching practice?
Example: I was unsure how well I was doing in the coaching session, yet at the end the client said the session was very helpful. I need to be careful that my inner critic does not get too loud in my sessions.

How do you want to improve your coaching?
Example: I want to accept my client's awkward manner, not be put off by it, focus less on myself and more on his development.

Summary

This chapter has covered:

- The background to a range of conceptual models of coaching including:
    - o   The Four Key Pillars Model.
    - o   The Six-Category Intervention Model.
    - o   The Coaching Alliance Conceptual Model.
- A reflective practice exercise using each of these three conceptual models.

The aim of the chapter was to set out the models of coaching and a range of self-reflective exercises to help the reader relate to and engage further with the content.

7
Executive Coaching

INTRODUCTION TO THE CHAPTER

This chapter will provide:

- A range of definitions of executive coaching.
- The principles that enable it to operate effectively.
- The conditions necessary for the executive to learn.
- The core competencies of an executive coach.
- How executive coaching can be contrasted with supervisory coaching, mentoring and psychotherapy.
- The experience of executive coaching.
- A self-reflective exercise.

The aim of the chapter is to provide the reader with an overview of what executive coaching is and how it operates.

Definition of Executive Coaching

Baron & Morin (2009) suggest executive coaching can variously be defined as:

- The practice of providing senior people in the workplace with the tools, knowledge and opportunities they need to develop and be more effective (Peterson, 1996).
- The teaching of skills within a personal relationship with the executive and providing feedback on interpersonal relationships and skills (Sperry, 1993).
- An ongoing series of meetings designed around the person's current issues or relevant problem to assist the executive to improve their consistent and confident focus by enhancing strengths and manages shortcomings (Tobias, 1996).

DOI: 10.4324/9781003285144-10

Peterson (2010) suggests that executive coaching has the following defining criteria:

- It is a one-on-one activity, as contrasted to group or team coaching. Although some authors see individual and group coaching as very similar (e.g., Kampa & White, 2002), Peterson (2010) sees them as significantly different and suggests that it is not clear how group coaching differs from related practices such as team building or similar activities.
- It is relationship based, requiring a sound level of trust, understanding and rapport as contrasted with content-based processes such as training, which require less of these variables.
- It is methodology based and uses specific tools and techniques as part of a structured overall process, as opposed to more free-flowing conversations with a trusted advisor.
- It is provided by a professional coach rather than a manager, peer or human resources (HR) professional.
- It uses multiple sessions over time, which permits for follow-up and accountability, as opposed to one or two free-flowing conversations.
- It involves important stakeholders beyond the coach and participant. The goals of both the participant and the organisation are important.
- It is customised to the individual with differences in the content, style, goals, scheduling and the techniques seen between different sessions.
- It improves the executive's ability to learn and develop independently.

Overarching Principles

The Executive Coaching Forum (ECF, 2015) suggests that there are seven overarching principles for executive coaching:

- A *systems perspective* in which the goal of developing a single executive is always undertaken within the context and overall goal of organisational success.
- *Results orientation* with the coaching having a clear focus on specific agreed results.
- *Business focus* with the development of the executive undertaken within the context of the business's needs.
- *Partnership*, with the coach primarily focusing on the work of an individual but within the context of a collaborative relationship with other stakeholders such as the HR Department.
- *Competence* with the executive coach needing to maintain a high degree of capability to work effectively with senior leaders.

- *Integrity* with trust, sensitivity and confidentiality being at the heart of the effective coaching relationship.
- *Judgement* within effective executive coaching being a delicate balance between art, science and relevant improvisation.

Conditions for Learning

In executive coaching there are five conditions necessary for learning (Hicks & Peterson, 1999):

- Insight: The extent to which the executive understands the areas he or she needs to develop in to be more effective.
- Motivation: The degree to which the individual is willing to invest the time and energy required to develop the necessary competence.
- Capabilities: The extent to which the executive has the necessary core skills and knowledge.
- Real-world practice: The degree to which the executive applies his or her skills and knowledge at work.
- Accountability: The extent to which the person's development has meaningful consequences.

Types of Executive Coaching

Peterson (2010) suggests that there are four major types of executive coach:

- Feedback coaches who provide insights generated from interviews with peers and other relevant stakeholders, psychometric instruments and multi-rater surveys. Typically feedback coaches meet with the client for one or two sessions and generate a development plan with them.
- Insight, motivation and accountability coaches who help the client clarify goals, values, aspirations and generate action plans to improve performance. The coach then follows up with the client to provide support and accountability.
- Content coaches who are experts in particular areas such as presentation and communication skills or selling skills.
- Development-process coaches who are experts in learning and the psychology of human behaviour. They help the person to develop without being an expert in the technical area of interest to the client. They provide motivation, problem solving and capability building skills and help the client transfer these into real-world settings.

Core Competencies

The International Coaching Federation (ICF 2019, updated 30 July 2021) core competencies are:

A. Foundation.

   1. Demonstrates ethical practice.
   2. Embodies a coaching mindset.

B. Co-creating the relationship.

   3. Establishes and maintains agreements.
   4. Cultivates trust and safety.
   5. Maintains presence.

C. Communicating effectively.

   6. Listens actively.
   7. Evokes awareness.

D. Cultivating learning and growth.

   8. Facilitates client growth.

The Executive Coaching Forum (ECF, 2015) defines the core competencies of executive coaches as:

- 'Psychological knowledge: knowledge of psychological theories and concepts relevant to the practice of executive coaching as well as social intelligence or emotional intelligence' (ECF, 2015, p. 50).
- 'Business acumen: knowledge of how different types of businesses work, their functional areas, business models, industry knowledge along with specifics about a given company' (ECF, 2015, p. 51).
- 'Organizational knowledge: understanding the context of organization(s), organizational structures, systems, processes, and how to assess all of these elements of the organization' (ECF, 2015, p. 52).
- 'Coaching knowledge: knowledge of theory, research and practice in the field of executive coaching' (ECF, 2015, p. 53).

Contrasted Coaching with Supervisory Coaching, Mentoring and Psychotherapy

Baron & Morin (2009) argue that executive coaching can be contrasted with supervisory coaching and mentoring. They suggest that supervisory coaching involves the use of coaching behaviours by managers to supervise subordinates, and contrast mentoring can be defined as 'a relationship between an older, more experienced mentor and a younger, less experienced protégé for the purpose of helping and developing the protégé's career' (Ragins & Kram, 2007, p. 5).

Several authors refer to the similarities between executive coaching and psychotherapy as both these two types of relationships aim to help individuals understand how their emotional and cognitive responses interfere with their self-efficacy (Hodgetts, 2002). However, the differences outlined by Baron and Morin (2009, p. 51) are:

- Executive coaching which aims to develop professional skills, is much more specific to the work setting than is the psychotherapy process (Peltier, 2001).
- Coaching focuses on the present and future, where therapy places more emphasis on the past (Gray, 2006).
- Coaching is more directive and action oriented than therapy (Levinson, 1996).
- The organisation almost always pays for the coaching so there is a joint responsibility to both the client and the organisation (Kilburg & Lowman, 2002).
- Therapy explores deep personal issues such as behaviour patterns and dysfunctional personality traits while executive coaching explores work behaviours and capability (Kilburg, 2000, Peltier, 2001).
- Therapeutic work requires clinical expertise that few coaches have (Ting & Hart, 2004).

The Experience of Coaching

de Haan (2019), in his book *Critical Moments in Executive Coaching: Understanding the Coaching Process through Research and Evidence-Based Theory*, describes the qualitative research he undertook into executive coaching. In one phase of this research 75 coaches with more than eight years' experience were asked to describe critical moments in their coaching. These moments were obtained by asking the question: 'Describe briefly one critical moment (an exciting, tense or significant moment) with one of your coachees. Think about what was critical in the coaching journey, or a moment when you did not quite know what to do.' (p. 21)

Analysis of the critical moments revealed several specific anxieties felt by these experienced coaches. These included anxieties about:

- The boundaries of coaching.
- The coach's role.

- The coach's use of their own intuition.
- What the coach contributed or did not contribute.
- The specific behaviour of the coachee in the session.
- The coach's view of themselves.

The research indicated that positive change in coaching occurred when:

- There was sufficient trust to allow intuition to work.
- The intuition of the coach led to unbiased observations.
- The coach had the ability to put things into perspective.
- The coach had the courage to put forward their observations in a way that the client could hear them.
- The coach had a clear well-defined coaching relationship with the client, yet this also allowed for 'room to move'.
- The well-defined relationship allowed more trust which in turn allowed intuition to work.

Reflective Practice Exercise: Executive Coaching Competencies

Rate yourself on each of the following competencies using the scale 1 = little or no experience to 10 = expert level and able to teach others.

- Psychological Knowledge: knowledge of psychological theories and concepts relevant to the practice of executive coaching as well as social intelligence or emotional intelligence.

1   2   3   4   5   6   7   8   9   10

Comments:
Example: I have a Master of Science in Psychology, so this is an area of strength for me.

- Business Acumen: knowledge of how different types of businesses work, their functional areas, business models, industry knowledge along with specifics about a given company.

1   2   3   4   5   6   7   8   9   10

Comments:
Example: I spent five years in a major consulting firm, so my knowledge is good, but not great.

- Organisational Knowledge: understanding the context of organisations, organisational structures, systems, processes, and how to assess all of these elements of the organisation.

1   2   3   4   5   6   7   8   9   10

Comments:
Example: This is an area that I need to develop in.

What areas of coaching do you want to improve in first?
Example: I would like to improve my organisational knowledge.

What areas of coaching are you able to assist others to learn?
Example: I have a sound psychological knowledge.

What is your key professional goal this year?
Example: I get a business mentor so I can understand more about organisational politics.

How will you hold yourself accountable?
Example: I will talk to my coaching supervisor about my progress on a regular basis.

Summary

This chapter provided:

- A range of definitions of executive coaching.
- The principles that enable it to operate effectively.
- The conditions necessary for the executive to learn.
- The core competencies of an executive coach.
- How executive coaching can be contrasted with supervisory coaching, mentoring and psychotherapy.
- The experience of executive coaching.
- A self-reflective exercise.

The aim of the chapter was to provide the reader with an overview of what executive coaching is and how it operates.

8
Coaching Effectiveness

INTRODUCTION TO THE CHAPTER

This chapter sets out the research findings on the effectiveness of coaching in achieving positive change for clients and organisations. It looks at the active ingredients in coaching that predict effectiveness and provides a reflective practice exercise. The aim of the chapter is for the reader to feel confident that coaching is an effective, evidence-based approach.

Systematic Reviews and Meta-analytic Studies

There are many anecdotal and uncontrolled studies in the coaching effectiveness literature, so poor research design and criterion measurement is a frequently cited problem (Grant et al., 2010). Despite this, research quality is improving and a number of meta-analytic studies have been published (e.g., Theeboom et al., 2014; Jones et al., 2016).

Some of the more important research is reviewed in more detail below. Theeboom et al. (2014) included 18 studies and reported positive overall effects of coaching with aggregated outcome measures and with significant improvements observed in performance and skills, well-being, coping, work attitudes and goal-directed self-regulation. They also concluded that the number of coaching sessions is not related to the effectiveness of the intervention. This meta-analysis was criticised by Jones et al. (2016) as it utilised a mix of studies using organisational samples with other studies based on educational and general non-organisational samples (e.g., 7 out of the 18 studies included used non-organisational samples such as students or general population samples). Consequently, the implications of the meta-analysis for organisations applying coaching for performance improvement at work are confounded and therefore inconclusive.

DOI: 10.4324/9781003285144-11

Table 8.1 Sample of coaching efficacy research studies

Research authors	Summary of findings
Lai & McDowall (2014)	A systematic review of workplace, life and personal coaching, finding that a positive coaching relationship was important for a successful outcome – this positive relationship included building trust, two-way communication and a transparent contracting process.
Theeboom et al. (2014)	A meta-analysis that examined workplace coaching and found a positive relationship with coping and goal directed self-regulation.
Sonesh et al. (2015)	A meta-analysis that reviewed executive, leadership and business coaching and found the impact of coaching on overall relationship outcomes was significant.
Blackman et al. (2016)	A systematic review of the use of external business coaches that found it had a positive impact on individual learning and development outcomes.
Grover & Furnham (2016)	A systematic review that examined executive, leadership and business coaching and found that coaching had a positive outcome on self-efficacy, stress, anxiety and well-being.
Jones et al. (2016)	A meta-analysis that assessed workplace coaching using both external and internal coaches and found that coaching had a positive effect on all outcome measures.
Burt & Talati (2017)	A meta-analysis that examined workplace coaching and found moderately significant positive effects for clients.

(Continued)

Table 8.1 (Continued)

Research authors	Summary of findings
Bozer & Jones (2018)	A systematic review of workplace coaching that found seven factors were important for success: self-efficacy, coaching motivation, goal orientation, trust, interpersonal attraction, feedback intervention and supervisory support.
Graßmann et al. (2020)	A meta-analysis that assessed workplace coaching and found a moderate and consistent impact of high-quality working alliance relationships and coaching outcomes.
Brown et al. (2021)	A study that researched the impact of coaching on emerging leaders and found that these clients showed improvements in leader identity, clarity of self-concept, humility, sense of purpose, satisfaction with life, and lower psychological distress.
Wang et al. (2022)	A meta-analysis that examined psychologically informed coaching for impact in the workplace and found positive effects on goal attainment and self-efficacy, with greater impact being seen in others' ratings of clients' performance than self-rating.

Jones et al. (2016) provided a more focused meta-analysis of the effectiveness of workplace coaching on learning and performance outcomes. This analysis excluded studies that involved the use of managers as coaches as well as peer coaching. They found 54 relevant studies from their literature search and 17 met their inclusion criteria (n = 2,267 individuals). The average sample size of these studies was 133 with seven studies from the United States; two in the United Kingdom; three in Australia, two in Norway; one in Egypt; one in Israel; and one in Denmark. These studies were conducted in service, manufacturing, construction and public/government sectors. Their analyses indicate that coaching had positive effects on organisational outcomes overall as well as on skill development, affective control and individual level performance.

Once again, they concluded that the number of coaching sessions is not related to the effectiveness of the intervention. They found that coaching was more effective when multi-source feedback systems were not used, and that coaching was effective whether conducted face-to-face or using blended techniques such as combining face-to-face with e-coaching. Overall, the authors concluded that coaching has utility in improving individual performance in organisations.

While the above meta-analyses found that coaching had positive effects for individuals, less research has focused on 'how' coaching works from a psychological perspective (Bono et al., 2009; Smither, 2011). Graßmann et al. (2020) addressed this issue and found 548 relevant studies but after applying their selection criteria undertook a meta-analysis of 23 studies with a focus on the relationship between the working alliance of coach and clients and a broad range of coaching outcomes. A working alliance means that coaches and clients mutually agree on their goals, the tasks to get to those goals, and they create a bond that entails trust, respect and liking for each other (Baron & Morin, 2009; Bordin, 1979; Horvath & Greenberg, 1989). The results indicate a moderate and consistent overall relationship between a high-quality working alliance and coaching outcomes for clients. The strongest relationship was between the working alliance and affective and cognitive coaching outcomes. Interestingly, working alliance was negatively related to any unintended detrimental effects of coaching. Results revealed no differences regarding the type of clients, coaches' expertise, number of coaching sessions, and clients' or coaches' perspectives. These results are like the outcomes for other helping relationships like psychotherapy or mentoring and support the importance of a high-quality working alliance in coaching (Graßmann et al., 2020).

McInerney et al. (2021) used a meta-synthesis of 16 studies to examine the enduring effects from executive coaching on managers. They suggested that the cognitive, behavioural and affective benefits of coaching persist in the months following coaching and that some client benefits only emerge after the coaching has finished. They call for more research on how the effects of executive coaching unfold over time.

Graf and Dionne (2021) indicate that the growing professionalism of coaching has resulted in a substantial gain in the level of high-quality research. They reviewed eight international meta-analyses of coaching outcome research published since 2020. The authors concluded that the research has moved beyond the question of whether coaching works, as the answer is clearly yes. Research is now exploring what the success and risk factors in coaching are, as well as the level of impact coaching has on the client and the organisation.

Wang et al. (2022) undertook a meta-analysis using 20 studies and confirmed that coaching that utilised psychological approaches improved work-related outcomes, particularly goal attainment and self-efficacy. Coaching produced a greater impact on objective work performance as rated by others (e.g., 360 feedback) than on client self-reported performance. Cognitive behavioural-oriented coaching improved self-regulation and awareness while promoting work satisfaction and sustainable changes. The authors advocate an integrative approach that combines coaching techniques (e.g., cognitive behavioural and solution-focused techniques), a strength-based approach and contextual approach that considers the clients' values, motivators and the level and type of organisational resources available.

Coaching is a widely used developmental approach for senior leaders, but its impact has been little researched with young, emerging leaders. Brown et al. (2021) examined the effect of leadership coaching on university students. They used an experimental design and showed that students who worked with a professional coach, compared to those in the waitlist control, showed greater changes in leader identity, clarity of self-concept, humility, sense of purpose, satisfaction with life, and lower psychological distress. In a second study they used peer observations to support the validity of these positive findings.

The Active Ingredients in Coaching

Page and de Haan (2014) looked at the active ingredients in executive coaching that predicted effectiveness. They reviewed studies that examined the impact of:

- The personality profiles of both coach and client.
- The strength of the coaching relationship.
- The type of coaching intervention.

Each of these factors is examined in more detail below.

Personality and Coaching

Page and de Haan (2014) found that personality had a significant influence in coaching effectiveness. Stewart et al. (2008) examined the impact of client personality and client self-efficacy on coaching outcome. They measured the 'Big-Five' personality traits and general self-efficacy with 110 coaching clients. They found the clients scoring higher in the personality traits conscientiousness, openness, emotional stability had more positive coaching outcomes and that general self-efficacy was positively correlated with outcome.

Scoular and Linley (2006) found that when the coach and client differed *more* on their Myers-Briggs Type Indicator profiles, the outcome scores were significantly higher. This suggests that personality differences between coach and client lead to better coaching outcomes.

Relationship

Baron and Morin (2012) examined 30 internal coach/client pairs and found that the coaching relationship, as measured by the Working Alliance Inventory (Horvath & Greenberg, 1986), predicted the coaching outcome of client self-efficacy. The coaches' ratings of the working alliance were not a significant predictor. Boyce et al. (2010) found that coach credibility and client–coach compatibility positively impact the coaching outcome by enhancing the coaching relationship.

Type of intervention

Specific coaching techniques or interventions do not predict positive outcomes that are more closely linked to factors such as the quality of the coaching relationship, empathic understanding and positive expectations (de Haan et al., 2011). The client–coach relationship is the key factor in how clients perceive the outcome of coaching (de Haan et al. 2013).

In a later study, de Haan et al. (2020) reviewed two large-scale, randomised controlled trials and both demonstrated that the coaching relationship or working alliance was an important determinant of effectiveness. The first trial conducted in a global health care company found that executive coaching is an effective intervention as assessed by both clients and their line managers. In the second trial, one group of business-school students were coached by qualified coaches while a second same-sized group formed the control group. Longitudinal data was collected over eight occasions from both students and coaches showing a positive relationship to effectiveness over the six-month coaching programme.

Reflective Exercise: Executive Coaching Effectiveness

What information did you learn or was reinforced from reading this section?
Example: There really is a lot of research on coaching effectiveness. The large-scale, randomised controlled trials are very important.

What can you do to improve the effectiveness of your coaching?
Example: I would like to learn more about improving the quality of the coaching relationship with challenging clients.

Summary

This chapter sets out the research findings on the effectiveness of coaching in achieving positive change for clients and organisations. It looks at the active ingredients in coaching that predict effectiveness and provides a reflective practice exercise. The aim of the chapter is for the reader to feel confident that coaching is an effective, evidence-based approach.

9
Solution-Focused Coaching

INTRODUCTION TO THE CHAPTER

Given the research finding in the last chapter that the number of coaching sessions is not related to the effectiveness of the intervention, there is logic in focusing on models of coaching that assume that positive change can occur rapidly (Grant, 2019). This chapter aims to provide the reader with a clear view of how to implement rapid solution-focused coaching.

Background to Solution-Focused Coaching

Solution-focused coaching grew out of solution-focused brief therapy (Szabo & Meier, 2008). Solution-focused brief therapy is a strengths-based approach founded on over 20 years of theoretical development, clinical practice, and empirical research (de Shazer et al. 1986). It is different from traditional approaches to treatment in that it minimises the emphasis on past failings and problems and focuses on clients' strengths and previous successes. Solution-focused coaching is based on the same core assumptions as solution-focused brief therapy.

Core Assumptions

The core assumptions of this type of coaching as summarised from Grant (2019) are:

- *Positive change can happen rapidly.* This assumption contrasts with many traditional schools that assume that change takes a considerable period.
- *A non-pathological model.* Problems are defined by the client in his or her own terms and are not indications of pathology.

DOI: 10.4324/9781003285144-12

- *Focusing on solutions is better than focusing on problems.* The coach facilitates the development of solutions rather than trying to understand the origin of the problem.
- *Use of existing client resources.* The coach helps the client recognise and utilise their own resources which at the time they may be unaware of.
- *Positive change will occur.* Positive change is viewed as inevitable in coaching with the expectation that the client will participate in change-related activity outside of the coaching session.
- *Each client is unique, so all interventions are individualised.* Coaching processes and actions are all designed specifically for each client.
- *The future focus.* The emphasis is more on looking forward (what the client wants to have happen) than the past.

Core Techniques

Solution-focused coaching has a group of core techniques that most involved practitioners agree are essential (Grant, 2019). These are:

- *Reframing presenting problems as potential solutions.* Reframing is the process of looking at a situation from a different perspective and so providing a new 'lens' or 'frame of reference' to foster a different understanding and to open up new ways of thinking and behaving.
- *The use of scaling.* Scaling is a way of subjectively measuring experience, for example, asking the client to rate on a 1-to-10 scale how close to their goal they are, and then asking them what would take them to the next point on the scale.
- *The use of the* 'what-if?' *or* 'magic question'. This starts the discovery of potential new solutions. In the 'magic question' the coach can ask: 'Imagine that you went to bed tonight, and when you woke up the problem had somehow magically disappeared, and the solution was present . . . what is the first thing that you'd notice?' The question needs to be phrased in a way that makes sense to the client in his or her own world view. A useful variation is the 'what if' question – 'If things were going a lot better, what would be different?'
- *Highlighting exceptions.* In coaching there is always an 'exception' to any problem – a time or context where the presenting problem is not quite as bad. The coach helps the client identify exceptions and so do more of what is already working and less of what is not.
- *The use of clear, specific goal setting.* Using small attainable goals within a specific time frame is critical.

The Solution-Focused Coaching Framework

Grant (2019) outlines a simple systematic process that coaches can work through using this approach.

- *Listen for solutions*. At the start of coaching the client typically talks about their problems (hopes or aspirations) and the coach's role is to actively listen, communicate to the client that they have been heard, and to become aware of possible solutions in the presenting story. The key skill here is not 'buying into the problem' but reframing problems in a way that allows for a range of solutions.
- *Probe for solutions*. Next, the coach asks questions that increase the client's awareness of possible solutions, by using curiosity and not accepting the client's (often pessimistic) assumptions as inevitable.
- *Talk about solutions*. The interaction then explores further growth options or concrete actions. The aim is to help the client to construct a vision of a likely positive future, highlighting undiscovered strengths and developing practical solutions.
- *Plan for solutions*. By the end of the session, both parties will have a specific action plan that will enable the client to move towards their goal. The action plan and target times for completion should be written down by both parties whenever possible. Scaling is very important for the coach to better understand the client confidence level. This may involve the coach asking the client to rate their confidence of completing these action plan on a scale from 1 (not likely) to 10 (very likely). This scaling is a clear reality that allows the coach to assess the effectiveness of the session and, if the confidence rating is low (say 7 or below), to agree changes to the action plans. Low confidence levels are often caused by the action plan being misdirected or overly ambitious.

The Steps in Solution-focused Coaching

An easy-to-read and very useful approach to solution focused coaching can be found in the book by Szabo and Meier (2008) *Coaching Plain & Simple: Solution-focused Brief Coaching Essentials*. They outline the following elements that are the key steps in the coaching process.

Step 1: The Coaching Agreement

Solution-focused coaching starts with the end in mind according to Szabo and Meier (2008). The initial step involves the coach and client coming to a joint understanding and agreement about what a successful coaching outcome looks like.

Relevant initial questions include:

- 'What do you want to achieve in this first session?'
- 'What do you want to achieve by the end of our coaching sessions?'
- 'What will the first step be that will tell you that you can manage on your own?'
- 'How will you notice that things are good enough and that it is time to finish our coaching?'

For clients who don't know what they want – a relevant question can be 'What would you rather do instead?' So, for a client who does not know what they want in their career, the coach can ask 'So what is it you do not want to do?' A list of what the client does not want to do can then easily be turned into a list of what they want – 'I do not want to stay in this current job' can become 'I want to move to another job'.

For clients who bring big complex multiple issues it is important to find a manageable place to start and relevant questions can be:

- 'You have talked about a range of challenges – what should we start working on now?'
- 'After we finish this session, what will the first sign be that you are moving towards your goal?'

The coach and client may draw up a *coaching agreement* together, which can consist of writing up:

- The issues the client wants to work on.
- The issues the organisation wants the client to work on.
- The context of the issue – a brief statement about the current circumstances.
- The overall outcomes or goals the client wants to achieve.
- The first issue that the coach and client will work on.
- How the coach and client will monitor progress.
- How frequently the coach and client will meet.
- The reporting back to the organisation if this is needed.

Step 2: The Preferred Future

Many clients come to coaching with an overwhelming focus on their problem, obstacle or challenge and without a clear view of what they want. The art of solution-focused coaching is to 'jump over' the obstacles and help the client to start seeing solutions. As stated in the Core Techniques above, the coach can do this by asking the 'magic question'. This starts the discovery of potential new solutions. The coach can ask: 'Imagine that all the issues you have brought to coaching resolved themselves overnight and the solution was present . . . what is the first thing that you'd do?' This question helps to uncover what the client really wants out of coaching. A related question is 'What would your friends notice after the miracle had happened?'

This phase of the coaching helps the client to experience something about what the world would be like if the problem went away. It provides an important sense of hope and future focus rather than an exploration of the causes and misery of the problem. Also, it starts a more detailed discussion on the consequences of the miracle for daily actions. The coach will often spend time to explore the preferred future by asking 'What else would you notice?' The coach explores the actions that the client would do after the problem went away. At the end of this phase of coaching the client has typically articulated a whole range of actions that they could do. This provides an important path towards future success.

Some coaches may feel uncomfortable asking the rather fanciful 'miracle question' and prefer the alternative 'what if' question – 'Suppose things were going a lot better, what would be different?' Related questions are – 'Suppose after some time you had managed to reach your goal – what would you be doing differently then?' or 'Suppose your boss suddenly started behaving the way you wanted – what would you do differently?'

It is important to use the word *suppose* at the start of these questions as this avoids a discussion about the obstacles such as lack of time or resources or the personality of the boss. The aim of this phase is to connect the client with all the good things that are waiting when the solution is reached.

Step 3: Precursors of the Solution

This third step is designed to build the confidence of the client in the planned future. Once the client is clear what they want and how they wish to live they can start to move forward. Precursors are small helpful things that the client is already doing that can be built upon to create a better future. For example, the client who is struggling to exercise as they want, is almost certainly doing some exercise such as walking from their car park to their office. The coach can help them build upon this by suggesting that an improvement might be parking further away from the office and walking more. Related questions to look for precursors at this step are:

- 'What was the most recent time when you did something that was at least a little like the miracle?'

- 'What are some other examples of the small steps you have already taken?'
- 'When you made one of those small steps – how did you do it?'

Some clients resist talking about any form of progress and prefer to spend the session talking about how difficult things are. When this happens, the coach can reinforce their coping and resilience by asking:

- 'How did you cope in such a difficult time?'
- 'How do you maintain the resilience needed to cope with all that?'
- 'How do you find the confidence to go on?'

Authentic and genuine compliments are also important in this phase. Clients are typically coping valiantly with life but seeing themselves as failing. The coach can compliment them on many things such as their determination, resilience and fortitude. These compliments are very powerful as they show the client that the coach sees success and strengths embedded in the client's suffering. These strengths can then be built upon in the coaching session.

Scaling questions are also important in this step of coaching. The coach can ask 'On a scale from 1 being no progress to 10 being the total solution – where are you now?' The client will typically say 2 or 3 on the scale. The coach can then explore what the client is doing to have reached that point rather than being at 1.

Clients who come to coaching are often not taking care of themselves in terms of getting adequate exercise, having a good diet and sleeping well. If this is the case, the coach can ask them to keep a simple diary of self-care – for example recording a short note on their phones when they have eaten a home-cooked healthy dinner. This helps to reinforce the small steps that are so important to building a better future.

Step 4: Clues for Upcoming Progress

This involves building on the scaling question by asking – 'If you are currently 3 on the scale what would it take to get you to a 4?' or 'What would other people notice if you moved one point further up the scale?'

The language used by the coach is critical. Asking the client – 'Can you move from step 3 to step 4?' is not useful as the client may feel that they simply cannot do this. By contrast, asking, 'How would it feel if you were at step 4?'

is much more likely to generate a positive response. When clients start to think about what could work, they are in a much stronger position to move forward.

Clients often set impossible goals for themselves such as defining fitness as going to the gym four times a week for one hour or deciding to *never* eat chocolate again! Such goals typically result in failure. The coach can encourage the client to take small steps and define success in a pragmatic way. For example, a realistic goal may be to go to the gym one day a week for half an hour or only eating chocolate after eating a piece of fruit. Creating a pattern of achievement of taking small steps is critical in building confidence and avoiding failure.

Another important technique at this stage of coaching is to increase the choice or options that the client has. This is critical as it provides a range of different ways the client can reach his or her goals. For example, if the client wants to delay having a glass of wine in the evening, they may decide that they can either go for a walk, read a chapter of a book or have a snack at 5pm rather than drinking wine at this time. The range of options helps as the client may not feel like going for a walk in the rain but he or she may enjoy one of the other paths to success. In the long term, building a range of options is an important step in changing unwanted behaviours.

Step 5: Session Conclusion

Szabo and Meier (2008) have a range of suggestions for the coach to undertake towards the end of the coaching session.

- Asking open questions such as, 'Before we finish today what else do you want to talk about?' or 'How can we best close the session today, to bring it to a helpful finish for you?'
- Rechecking the session goal by asking, 'On a scale of 1 to 10 how close are we to reaching our session goal?'
- Having a thinking break by suggesting, 'I just want to give you a few minutes to think through what we have achieved in the session today – I will come back shortly and we can talk this over'.
- Offering compliments by saying, 'Today I was really impressed by your ability to . . .'
- Trying experiments by asking, 'How about ending each day at work by spending two minutes writing down the good things that happened that day? Then we can review these in our next session'.

- Agreeing on the next session by asking, 'Would you like to make a time for another session?'.

At this stage it is also important to finalise the action plan developed in the session and make sure the client and coach both write this down. The coach can ask 'What actions are you going to take as a result of this session and shall we both write these down so we can review them next time?'

Solution-focused Coaching Case Study

Step 1: Coaching Agreement

Adam was a well-built accountant in his forties who was referred to the Executive Coaching Centre as part of the firm's wellness programme. When the coach asked what he wanted to work on in coaching, Adam said he wanted to improve his lifestyle. In exploring this, it became clear that Adam had had a very demanding year with lots of stress at work and real problems recruiting staff at the calibre needed. He had recently been to his doctor for an annual check-up and was told that he had not only put on 5kg since his last visit but that his blood cholesterol levels had risen sharply. When asked what he wanted to achieve in this first session he replied he wanted a better lifestyle. When the coach asked for more detail Adam said he wanted to lose weight, improve his exercise, reduce his cholesterol and sleep better. 'Which one of these four issues shall we work on first?' asked the coach. Adam felt that if he increased his exercise that would help with weight control and sleep so that was a useful place to start.

'What would you like to achieve by the end of our coaching sessions?' asked the coach to which Adam said he wanted a greater sense of control over his life and particularly his lifestyle.

Step 2: The Preferred Future

The coach then asked the 'miracle question': 'Suppose you woke up tomorrow and you did have that greater sense of control and your lifestyle was largely as you wanted it – what would you be doing differently? Adam said that he would wake up in the morning feeling refreshed, would go for a run or use his home gym for 30 minutes each morning and would stop eating junk food snacks after work. 'What is the most important part of the change?' the coach asked, and Adam said it was getting the exercise.

Step 3: Precursors of the Solution

'When was the last time you were exercising regularly?' asked the coach. Adam started on a long story of how he had been a promising athlete in his early twenties and had competed at a national level in running at that time. However, he had been forced to stop for many months due to a serious ankle injury that resulted in surgery. After this he had slowly built up his fitness but was never again able to gain his initial performance levels.

'What sort of exercise did you do as part of your recovery?' asked the coach. Adam said he had been guided by his sports coach and started very gradually with a routine of walking for 30 metres, running for 30 metres, walking for 30 metres and so on, every other day for the first three months. Then he had progressed to 20-minute slow running, then 30 minutes, until he built up to being able to run for an hour without undue fatigue.

'So, you really understand a great deal about how to get fit in a progressive way!' said the coach. Adam agreed that his approach worked years ago but building fitness now was much more difficult due to his weight gain and lack of motivation.

'Reflecting on what worked so well for you in the past, what do you think you need to do now to build up your fitness?' asked the coach. 'Well, I had never really considered the way I recovered from my surgery all those years ago as important, but it does provide a path forward that I should have figured out myself' was the response.

Step 4: Clues for Upcoming Progress

'So, on a 1 to 10 scale where 1 equals very unfit and 10 equals very fit, where are you now?' asked the coach. About 2 was the reply. 'What would it take to get you to 3 or 4 on the scale?' asked the coach. 'Well, if I repeated the routine given to me by my sports coach, I would walk and run, three times a week for three months', Adam replied.

'That sounds like a plan! Shall we both write that down and see how you get on between now and our next session?' said the coach. Adam agreed and wrote down the plan.

Step 5: Session Conclusion

The coach asked 'Adam, reflecting back on our session today, what have you been able to achieve?' 'Well, I came today feeling very frustrated at myself and kind of stuck, but I can see that by looking at my past recovery programme I now know how I can move forward, it really is quite simple,' said Adam.

'On a scale of 1 to 10 how confident are you that you can exercise as we discussed?' the coach asked. 'About 5', replied Adam, 'As I have a lot of work-related travel over the next month and that is likely to make it hard. There will be client dinners and a lot of other entertaining'. 'Does that mean we should alter our action plan?' asked the coach. 'Well, if we had another coaching session in a month, and I had been able to have two weeks of exercise in that time, that would be OK, not great, but OK' Adam replied.

'Well done, Adam, I think that the revised plan is credible and it shows me you really want to be practical and realistic' was the response.

The coach then asked, 'Before we finish today is there anything else you want to talk about?' Adam said that he also really wanted to learn how to improve his sleep. 'We can certainly cover that in the next session', the coach responded.

'That sounds great to me and I will see you in a month', said Adam. The coach said 'It has been a great session today, Adam, and I really look forward to hearing about your progress next time. If you can achieve the plan, that is fantastic, but if life gets complicated and it is just not possible, then that is OK too and we can learn some useful lessons about overcoming obstacles next time'.

Coaching Challenges

The above case study was written to illustrate a relatively simple coaching challenge. However, coaching is often not this simple. Examples of some of the complexity that can be encountered in sessions is set out below.

Step 1: Coaching Agreement

Sometimes clients have a seemingly endless list of issues they want to work on and before they have made any progress on one issue, they want to move to another. If the client does this repeatedly the coach needs to ask, 'I see we have now moved to a different problem, which of these issues shall we deal with first?'

Step 2: The Preferred Future

Occasionally, clients will suddenly burst into tears or look very distressed after being asked what their life would look like if their problems went away. Under these circumstances, the coach needs to allow them time to express their emotions fully before asking this type of question again.

Step 3: Precursors of the Solution

Occasionally, clients have no previous behaviours or ideas that have helped with the presenting problems. Under these circumstances it can be useful for the coach to ask, 'Would you like me to tell you how some of my other clients have dealt with these challenges?'

Step 4: Clues for Upcoming Progress

Some clients are unaware how to progress further and may need guidance from the coach at this point.

Step 5: Session Conclusion

Getting some clients to be specific about actions they will undertake between coaching sessions can be difficult. These clients are often anxious about trying anything in case they fail. Under these circumstances it can be useful for the coach to suggest very small, easy to achieve steps that the client can feel comfortable about achieving.

When Solution-focused Coaching Is Not Enough

Solution-focused coaching is a very useful approach for many clients. However, sometimes clients have very entrenched problems that may require techniques from other areas of psychology such as Acceptance and Commitment Therapy (Harris, 2007, 2009) or Gestalt Therapy (Perls et al., 1951; Perls, 1969). As coaches move through their careers it can be very useful for them to explore a range of therapeutic models so they can pick up useful techniques and approaches.

Reflective Practice Exercise: Solution-focused Coaching

When you review the solution-focused coaching model what do you find useful about it?
Example: The model seems to be a useful means of generating great coaching questions.

Are there disadvantages in the solution-focused coaching model for you?
Example: I would need to do a lot more reading and study before I felt comfortable with the model.

Are there particular clients that would seem very suited to the solution-focused coaching approach?
Example: Yes, I coach a number of executives who seem very impatient for progress and this approach seems very relevant to them.

Based on what you have read in this chapter, what do you want to do differently?
Example: I will try out solution-focused coaching.

The Effectiveness of Solution-focused Coaching

Grant (2012) undertook a randomised control trial study comparing the effectiveness of coaches asking problem-focused versus solution-focused questions on positive or negative affect, self-efficacy, goal attainment and action planning. The study involved 225 participants who were randomly assigned to either the problem- or solution-focused question group. Both coaching conditions were effective at moving the clients towards the goal approach, but the solution-focused group did significantly better. Problem-focused questions did not impact on affect or self-efficacy. Solution-focused questions significantly increased positive affect, decreased negative affect and increased self-efficacy. The solution-focused group also generated more actions steps to help achieve their goal. Grant recommends that coaches should aim for a solution focus if they want effective goal-focused sessions.

Grant and Gerrard (2020) compared the result of using three different question sets: solution-focused questions, problem-focused questions and combined problem-focused and solution-focused coaching questions. A total of 80 participants were randomly allocated to one of either of the three groups. Solution-focused questions were more effective than problem-focused questions on all measures. Solution-focused questions increased self-efficacy and decreased negative affect compared to a combined problem- and solution-focused approach.

The Limits of Solution-focused Coaching

While solution-focused coaching can be useful for many clients, it can also be overdone. In her book *Coach the Person Not the Problem: A Guide to using Reflective Inquiry*, Marcia Reynolds (2020) argues that coaches need to take care they do not spend too much of their time thinking up great questions if this means they are not connecting with their clients. She advocates the reflective inquiry approach, which involves coaches making reflective statements and then asking questions. Reflective statements include paraphrasing, recapping, identifying key or conflicting issues, using metaphors and identifying emotional shifts. Reynolds suggests that using both reflective statements and questions free the coach from the burden of having to find exactly the right question. She states that questions seek answers, but reflective inquiry provokes insight. An example of a reflective inquiry may involve the coach saying, 'I see you are finding it difficult to identify any good options for moving a step closer to your solution – if you talked to a good friend about your problem, what would they suggest you do?'

Summary

In summary the solution-focused approach to coaching provides a rapid, practical and systematic way to assist many clients to address their issues and reach their goals. The model has a range of clear assumptions and techniques as well as a very clear process that can help the coach guide the client to a better life. However, like any approach it needs to be used with sensitivity and mature judgement. Having read this chapter, the trained coach should have enough information to try this approach in future.

10
The Critical Skills

INTRODUCTION TO THE CHAPTER

In this chapter a wide range of coaching skills is explored including:

- Growing a thinking partnership.
- Committed listening.
- Rapport and trust.
- Paraphrasing.
- Presuming positive intent.
- Asking powerful questions.
- Providing reflective feedback.
- Constructive challenging.
- Holding to account.
- Reframing and seeing different perspectives.
- Using intuition.

Self-reflective exercises are presented for each of these skills and that can be used as a basis of self-improvement. The aim of this part of the book is to increase awareness and capability in coaching.

Coaching Skills

A range of critical psychological skills lie at the heart of coaching and these help clients to become more effective managers and leaders. Coaching skills are typically applied to a specific work-related issue so they can be incorporated into the person's permanent management or leadership repertoire (Peltier, 2010). A range of important coaching skills is presented below.

DOI: 10.4324/9781003285144-13

Growing a Thinking Partnership

A partnership is a collaborative relationship between two or more parties who work towards joint goals in a mutually agreed manner. In executive coaching the partnership is three way, between the coach, client and the organisation (Kilburg & Lowman, 2002). A thinking partnership is a collaborative relationship between equals that generates a supportive environment that helps the client gain insight, understanding and knowledge. This partnership enables the client to build awareness of themselves and others, so developing greater choice and freedom to act. The development of the client will then have an impact on the productivity of the client's team and so the organisation. To grow the thinking partnership the coach should know and respect the client, both personally and professionally. This allows the coach to gain greater insight or awareness into who the client is as a person and not just the way they present in one setting. A coach should endeavour to understand the client's values and beliefs, as well as their personality traits (Barnes et al., 2017). This deep understanding allows the collaborative and creative partnership to flourish.

Reflective Practice Exercise: Growing a Thinking Partnership

Recall a recent coaching session and write a summary below.
Example: Last week I worked with a senior executive who was stuck for ideas on how to motivate her team.

If a thinking partnership is a collaborative relationship that aims to help the client gain insight, understanding and knowledge by building awareness of themselves and others – how well did you achieve this in the recent session? Circle the number that is your answer on the scale below.

Not at all 1   2   3   4   5   6   7   8   9   10 A great deal

What process did you use to build this partnership?
Example: I started by asking her about the most motivational managers she had ever worked for.

What content was developed?
Example: The executive came up with the importance of showing individual personal attention as the key to motivation.

What was the impact on the client?
Example: She said she felt a sense of relief having thought about this idea.

What was the impact on you as coach?
Example: I was pleased that she come up with the idea so clearly as now she is highly motivated to put it into action.

What improvements would you like to make?
Example: I could be a bit more patient with my clients and give them more time to come up with their own ideas.

What strengths do you wish to build on?
Example: My questioning skills are a strength that I can build upon.

After you make these changes how well will you be able to build a thinking partnership in future?

Not at all 1   2   3   4   5   6   7   8   9   10 A great deal

---

Comments

Committed Listening

Listening is critical in coaching as it enables the client to feel valued, understood and cared about. A committed listener displays the following behaviours:

- Focusing on what the client is saying.
- Putting aside instantaneous judgement and permitting the client to complete their thoughts before speaking.
- Listening for the full message, both verbal and nonverbal.
- Recognising that the same words have different meanings to different people.
- Respecting the client's views even when these are different from one's own.
- Searching for a solution.
- Not providing advice (Barnes et al., 2017).

Julie Starr in her book, *The Coaching Manual* (Starr, 2016), outlines four levels of listening:

1. Cosmetic listening – this is a passive form of listening when the person looks like they are listening, but they are thinking about something else.
2. Conversational listening – also a passive form of listening when the person is engaged in both listening and talking.
3. Active listening – an active form of listening when the person is focused on what the other individual is saying and giving them their full attention.
4. Deep listening – a more potent form of active listening where the person is more intensely focused on the words, meanings and patterns expressed by the other and not on what they will say next.

Effective coaches strive for deep listening and often need to resist being distracted by their own internal dialogue.

Reflective Practice Exercise: Committed Listening

Recall a recent coaching session and write a summary below.

How well were you listening to your client in this session? Estimate the percentage of time you spend in each level of listening.

Level of listening	Percentage of time
Cosmetic listening – this is a passive form of listening when the person looks like they are listening, but they are thinking about something else.	
Conversational listening – also a passive form of listening when the person is engaged in both listening and talking.	
Active listening – an active form of listening when the person is focused on what the other individual is saying and giving them their attention.	
Deep listening – a more potent form of active listening where the person is more intensely focused on the words, meanings and patterns expressed by the other and not on what they will say next.	
Total	100%

How do you want to change the percentage time spent in each different level of listening?
Example: I do a lot of Active Listening, but I want to do more Deep Listening.

How will you action these changes?
Example: I have a client next Monday morning who I want to listen more to and will put a note in my calendar to do this.

Rapport and Trust

Rapport is the ability to develop a relationship that is characterised by mutual understanding and easy communication. Trust is the capacity to rely on the character, ability, strength or truth of someone else. To build rapport and trust the coach needs to know the person he or she is working with, make them feel comfortable and use a range of skills to facilitate an effective learning relationship. The coach should also encourage the client to share what they believe and value about learning and their work. Also, to respect the client as a thinking partner, not just as a receiver of good advice. The coach should directly discuss the areas the client wants to enhance and help the client identify and reflect upon their goals and successes in coaching (Barnes et al., 2017).

Great coaches are warm, attentive and easy to relate to – they have rapport. Rapport is built by identifying the 'sameness' between two individuals. This sameness may include:

- Similar physical appearance and clothes – if one person looks similar in age, height, weight and features they tend to be more comfortable with the other person.
- Body language and physical gestures – people with good rapport tend to mirror the posture of each other.
- Qualities of voice – the tone, speed of speech and timbre or pitch of the voice is often similar when rapport is high.
- Language or words used – the nature of the words used are often related to the profession of the individual and using a common jargon is typically found in individuals with high levels of rapport.
- Beliefs and values – finding common ground in terms of beliefs and values is an important method to build rapport (Starr, 2016).

Starr (2016) suggests several ways to build trust and openness in coaching:

- Share personal facts and details occasionally, e.g., mention your family circumstances.
- Occasionally disclose your thoughts and feelings about events outside of coaching.
- Keep any confidences between you and the client.
- Support the client in conversation outside the coaching sessions if this is relevant.

Reflective Practice Exercise: Rapport and Trust

Recall a recent coaching session and rate the level of rapport and trust you achieved in the session using the following scale:

5   Very strong support, trust, sense of being positively connected.
4   Strong sense of knowing, the familiar.
3   Genuine warmth.
2   Comfortable, familiar.
1   Some warmth.
0   Neutral.
−1   Some hesitation.
−2   Some discomfort, detachment.
−3   Awareness of dislike, disassociation.
−4   Genuine aversion, antipathy, real dislike.
−5   Stronger hostility, even loathing.
      (Adapted from Laborde, 1983, cited in Starr, 2016)

My score

Comments

How can you improve the level of rapport and trust in your sessions? What will you do differently?
Example: I scored a 3 on the scale but I want to work towards a 4.

When will you reassess your level of rapport and trust?
Example: I will reassess my level at the end of the week.

Paraphrasing

Paraphrasing involves the coach expressing the client's meaning using different words. The purpose of paraphrasing is to bring greater clarity to the client's perspectives. It allows the coach to communicate to the client that he or she is being listened to, cared for and understood (Barnes et al., 2017).

Paraphrasing is closely aligned with committed listening as it involves taking what has just been said and attempting to articulate the true intention of the words spoken. Quality paraphrasing includes being fully attentive by setting aside competing distractors, listening with the intent to understand, capturing the essence of the message, reflecting on the essence of voice tone and gestures and paraphrasing before asking questions (Costa & Garmston, 2002; Barnes et al., 2017).

Reflective Practice Exercise: Paraphrasing

Recall a recent coaching session and assess your ability and frequency of paraphrasing.

Example: I worked with an impatient and talkative CEO last week and felt it difficult to say anything, let alone paraphrasing.

How well are you able to express the client's meaning using different words?

Not at all well 1   2   3   4   5   6   7   8   9   10 Very well

Comments

How would you like to improve your paraphrasing skill?
Example: I would like to be able to find a gap in the conversation to let my CEO client know that I am listening and can paraphrase her words.

How frequently did you paraphrase the client's meaning in the coaching session you recalled? Rate yourself on the scale below.
Example: Not at all.

Not at all 1   2   3   4   5   6   7   8   9   10 Very frequently

---

How would you like to improve your paraphrasing frequency?
Example: I will attempt to paraphrase the content with my client at least twice in a session.

Presuming Positive Intent

Barnes et al. (2017) suggest that to be effective the coach should avoid assumptions based on their impressions, personality or prior experiences with similar clients. Positive coaching requires the coach to:

- Assume the client has positive intentions in both their actions and behaviours.

- Presume the client has already thought about or done what the coach is discussing.
- Use positive language to communicate a genuine belief in the client.

Presuming positive intent provides the client with a sense of hope for the future.

Reflective Practice Exercise: Presuming Positive Intent

Recall a recent coaching session and assess your presumption of positive intent.

Summarise your session below.

Example: Yesterday I had a distressed and burned-out client who was very tearful. I struggled to communicate positive intent.

How much did you assume the client had positive intentions in their actions and behaviours? Rate yourself on the scale below.

Not at all 1   2   3   4   5   6   7   8   9   10 A great deal

Why did you make this rating?

Example: I struggled to communicate positive intent because the client was so pessimistic.

How would you like to improve?

Example: I want to be able to tell my sad distressed client that I think he is doing well coping with very difficult situations.

How much did you assume that the client had previously thought about or done what you as coach were discussing? Rate yourself on the scale below.

Not at all 1   2   3   4   5   6   7   8   9   10 A great deal

Why did you make this rating?

How would you like to improve?
Example: I need to do some mental rehearsal, so I am better prepared for sad and distressed clients.

How much did you use positive language to communicate a genuine belief in the client? Rate yourself on the scale below.

Not at all 1   2   3   4   5   6   7   8   9   10 A great deal

Why did you make this rating?

How would you like to improve?
Example: I could use more impactful language when being positive with my clients.

Asking Powerful Questions

Good coaching questions are simple, have a clear purpose and are influential without being controlling (Starr, 2016).

Kowalski and Casper (2007) suggest that the most important tool in coaching is the ability to ask powerful, thought-provoking questions. These questions should aim to discover what the client is thinking and how they see their future.

Types of coaching questions

Coaching employs a wide range of questions including those set out in Table 10.1.

Table 10.1 Types of coaching questions and their purpose

Type	Purpose	Example
Rapport-building questions	These questions are used at the beginning of a session to build trust and mutual understanding.	Tell me about why that is so important to you?
Open questions	These begin with 'what' 'how' 'where' 'who' 'when' and these enable the client to provide a free-form response. These are compared to closed questions which can be answered with 'yes' or 'no'.	How did you become so resilient?
Clarifying questions	These help the coach to get a better understanding of a situation.	Can you tell me what happened after that?

(Continued)

Table 10.1 (Continued)

Type	Purpose	Example
Scale questions	These help the coach to assess progress or gauge importance.	On a scale of 1–10 with 1 being low and 10 being high, how confident are you that you can do this?
Solution-focused questions	These ask how a goal can be achieved or opportunity created.	What would you like to achieve in that area?
Hypothetical questions	These help the client to be open and imagine the possibilities of a better future.	What could you achieve if your boss started to respect you more?
Focus questions	These help to move the conversation to a more positive place.	What have you achieved already?
Paradoxical questions	These contradictory questions help the client to make sense of puzzling situations.	Do you think that if you try to do less at work you will achieve more?
Miracle questions	These encourage the client to 'step beyond' the problems and move towards solutions.	Suppose you woke up tomorrow and all these difficulties were over, what is the first thing you would do?

Source: Adapted from Animas, 2021.

There is evidence that solution-focused questions, which ask how a goal can be achieved or opportunity created, increase positive affect, decrease negative affect and increase self-efficacy as compared to problem-focused questions, which ask about what went wrong and why (Grant, 2012).

Reflective Practice Exercise: Asking Powerful Questions

Recall a recent coaching session and assess the types of questions that you asked. Write a summary of the session below then complete the rating scale.

Type	Frequency of asking (Circle your response)
Rapport-building questions	Not at all – A little – Quite a lot – A Great deal
Open questions	Not at all – A little – Quite a lot – A Great deal
Clarifying questions	Not at all – A little – Quite a lot – A Great deal
Scale questions	Not at all – A little – Quite a lot – A Great deal
Solution-focused questions	Not at all – A little – Quite a lot – A Great deal
Hypothetical questions	Not at all – A little – Quite a lot – A Great deal
Focus questions	Not at all – A little – Quite a lot – A Great deal
Paradoxical questions	Not at all – A little – Quite a lot – A Great deal
Miracle questions	Not at all – A little – Quite a lot – A Great deal

What types of questions do you use a lot of?
Example: I do a lot of rapport building and open questions.

What types of questions do you use least?
Example: I almost never use paradoxical questions.

How would you like to improve your asking of powerful questions?
Example: I want to ask more scaling and solution-focused questions.

Providing Reflective Feedback

Jug et al. (2019) define feedback as providing personalised information based on direct observation, crafted and delivered so receivers can use the information to achieve their best potential.

The requirements for reflective feedback are for the coach to be specific, positive, generous whenever possible, ask permission before giving feedback, keep in mind that the goal is self-reliant learning and generally avoid negative or insensitive feedback. Reflective feedback allows the coach to integrate concepts, skills and knowledge so helping the client to reframe their thinking and use these new perspectives to improve (Barnes et al., 2017).

Effective feedback conversations should be bidirectional, conducted within a committed learning alliance to create shared understanding of goals, performance and a mutually agreed-upon action plan (Telio et al., 2015). The client needs to have time to reflect on the feedback, to ask questions of clarification and to assess the validity and applicability of the feedback and to respond to the coach.

Feedback should be a formative assessment used to promote further development from the client. It is different from evaluation, which is summative, so intended to summarise a client's achievement at a particular time. Ideally, feedback provides timely, descriptive information regarding direct observations of the coach in the coaching environment. Feedback should be descriptive, constructive and non-judgemental. Word choice should be deliberate and avoid judgement. The tone of the message should promote dialogue, reinforce the positive environment, which in turn fosters learning (Jug et al., 2019).

Writers in the educational sector suggest that there is often a mismatch between the perceived amount of feedback received versus feedback given. When asked, learners frequently say they receive insufficient feedback, whereas educators say they are giving feedback frequently (Adcroft, 2011). This is relevant in the coaching context and the situation needs to be monitored with the coach from time to time asking, 'Would you like some feedback on that issue?' and 'Are you getting enough feedback from me?'

The coach should avoid language attributing feedback to the client or their personality rather than to directly observed behaviour. Feedback should always be about behaviour that the client can change; for example, 'You had an angry tone when you described the discussion with your boss, is that how it happened at the time?' rather than 'You're an angry person!' (Jug et al., 2019).

One useful feedback method in coaching is Ask–Tell–Ask. This consists of:

- Ask – the coach asks the client for a self-assessment on how they handled a situation.
- Tell – the coach gives the client feedback on their performance, as the coach saw it.
- Ask – the coach asks the client for commentary on the accuracy of the feedback and on the actions they want to take as a result of the conversation (adapted from Jug et al., 2019).

Reflective Practice Exercise: Providing Reflective Feedback

Recall a recent coaching session and assess the quality and quantity of feedback you gave. Write a summary of the session below.

Write down a range of specific examples of feedback you gave in this session.
Example: Now I think about this issue I realise that I do not give a lot of feedback in my sessions.

Assess the quality of the feedback you give. Were you specific, generous, did you ask permission before providing feedback, did you remember that the goal of feedback is self-directed learning, and did you generally avoid negative feedback?

Rate the overall quality of your feedback using the scale below.

Poor quality 1   2   3   4   5   6   7   8   9   10 Excellent quality

Comments:

How would you like to improve?
Example: I have a client who can get quite angry in sessions and I want to sensitively tell him that this is how he comes across to me.

Assess the quantity of feedback you gave in this session. Rate yourself on the scale below.

Too little 1   2   3   4   5   6   7   8   9   10 Too much

Comments

How would you like to improve?
Example: I want to be more direct, frank and clear in my feedback.

Constructive Challenging

Constructive challenging involves the coach being positively confrontational and taking risks to challenge assumptions (Blakey & Day, 2012). Finlay (2015) outlines several key principles of effective challenging:

- Coaches should believe in the value of challenging clients and understand that often real progress is not made when the client remains in his or her comfort zone.
- Challenges need to be used in the client's best interests and not out of annoyance, impatience or irritation.

- There should be a balance between empathy and confrontation as too much challenge will generate defensiveness and too little will not maximise growth and change.
- If in doubt about the client's ability to handle a challenge the coach should ask for permission – 'Would you like me to challenge you on this point. Do you feel up to it?'
- Coaches can also encourage self-challenging by asking 'If you are going to push yourself to achieve more, what would that look like?'
- It is often more useful to challenge underused strengths rather than weaknesses. For example, to challenge the client to exercise more rather than asking how they can stop mentally 'beating themselves up'.
- Gentle humour can be helpful, for example the coach might say to the client in a light-hearted way 'I bet you can achieve more than that!'

Coaches, too, need to stay open to being challenged by clients. This can be facilitated by asking clients questions such as, 'Are you happy with the progress we are making to date in coaching?'

Reflective Practice Exercise: Constructive Challenging

Recall a recent coaching session and assess the quality and quantity of the constructive challenging. Summarise the session below.

Write down any examples of challenges that you made in this session. *Example: I have an older male client who can be dismissive of the women in his team. I have let his comments go, up until this point. I am not proud of that.*

Rate the overall quality of your challenging. Use the scale below.

Poor quality 1   2   3   4   5   6   7   8   9   10 Excellent quality

Comments

How would you like to improve?
Example: I want to be better prepared with the right challenge when I hear this type of disparaging set of comments towards women.

Assess the quantity of challenges you gave in this session using the scale below.

Too little 1   2   3   4   5   6   7   8   9   10 Too much

Comments

How would you like to improve?
Example: I need to find the courage to speak out more.

Holding to Account

Machin (2010) suggests in the coaching context, holding the client to account means expecting that the client will do what they say they will do. It is an important part of the coaching relationship and clients appreciate it when it is present.

Experience shows that many clients enter coaching because they are frustrated with the progress they are making to achieve their goals. This may be frustration with not being fit, not delegating work, not completing board papers and so on. These types of clients greatly value the coach holding them to account. This is best done after the client has both agreed a clear, achievable action plan and has had a reasonable amount of time to put this into action. Accountability in coaching terms is about:

- Enabling the client to write a clear, realistic action plan with completion times.
- Getting agreement that the client wants the coach to follow up and ask about progress.
- Generously congratulating clients about the progress they have made.
- Empathetically exploring the reasons why the client was not able to achieve their action plan and learning the lessons to apply the next time an action plan is developed (Machin, 2010).

Reflective Practice Exercise: Holding to Account

Recall a recent coaching session and think about whether and how you held your client to account – if this was relevant. Write a summary below. *Example: I was working with a client, who has procrastination issues, on how to develop his new business.*

Did the client write a clear, realistic action plan with completion times? *Example: I now realise that the client and I talked about a range of great ideas but did not end with a concrete plan.*

Did you get agreement that the client wants you to follow up and ask about progress?
Example: No, I did not but I will next time. I will hold myself to account!

When you did the follow up – did you generously congratulate the client about the progress made?
Example: No, I did not but will do so next time.

If the client was not able to implement the action plan, did you empathetically explore the reasons for this and learn the lessons to apply the next time an action plan is developed?
Example: I will explain the logic of learning lessons to my clients in future.

What do you want to improve? By when?
Example: I will aim to have an agreed action plan and follow-up date with all clients, starting today.

Reframing and Seeing Different Perspectives

Mattila (2001) suggests that reframing is both important and the most basic technique in both family therapy and brief therapy. It is also critical in coaching (Grant, 2019). The term reframing was first used in the 1960s and meant the reinterpretation of client messages to present the positive side of difficulties or problematic behaviour. The psychiatrist Milton H. Erickson helped explain the skill of reframing by building on the methods he used in hypnosis. The reframe involved carefully observing the client and defining whatever they did, or did not do, as success and evidence that the hypnotic trance is deepening. For example, if in a trance the client raised their hand this is an obvious sign of the success of hypnosis. But if the client did not raise their hand, as it felt heavy, this could prove that they were deeply relaxed and would go into deeper trance levels (Haley, 1973). So, if the client tried and failed, Erickson would point out their determination. If a client behaved passively, he would comment on their endurance. Erickson had the ability to state a positive view without it appearing trite or just reassuring. He was consistently able to demonstrate a positive and realistic reframe (Haley, 1973). The most important element of reframing is the use of questions, comments, reinterpretations and so on to help the client see their situation in different ways (Mattila, 2001).

Here are some examples of reframing:

- Lazy reframed to laid back, mellow, gentle, relaxed, taking it easy.
- Pushy reframed to assertive, go-get-them, in a hurry, action oriented.
- Impatient reframed to results-focused, action-oriented, has high standards.
- Uncaring reframed to wanting others to drive their own actions, detached, allowing room for others.
- Depressed reframed to needing to rest, overwhelmed, quiet, slowing down.
- Aggressive reframed to vigorous, forceful, unaware of his own strength.
- Nagging reframed to loving interest, concerned, trying to bring out the best in someone.
- Withdrawn reframed to unselfish, deep thinker, thoughtful, shy, quiet (Adapted from Mattila, 2001, p. 54).

Dilts (1996) (cited in Mattila, 2001, p. 68) outlines a six-step reframing process as a self-help process:

1. Decide on the problem you want to work on, e.g., I feel uncomfortable selling my coaching services.
2. Identify with that part of yourself that is responsible for this, e.g., I have a part of me, like a little child, that feels vulnerable and unsure.
3. Find the positive purpose/intention behind the problem, e.g., that inner child is telling me that I need to be very well prepared for these types of discussions and find ways to build my confidence.
4. Find three other ways to satisfy that positive intention without the negative outcome, e.g., I could work out what is my unique coaching value. I could write and practise a short selling pitch. I could practise this pitch with a colleague and get some support.
5. Have the part of yourself that creates the symptoms agree to implement the new choices. My inner child feels fearful about facing this issue head on but agrees it is essential for my business.
6. Ecology check – does any other part of you, as coach, dislike the choices? For example, 'My critical parent thinks that I just need to toughen up and sell – but I can easily talk back to his voice in my head'.

Szabo and Meier (2008) suggest that coaching is the process of creating a frame of reference or view of the world so that the client can see different perspectives and so find new solutions.

Cavanagh and Grant (2010) propose that reframing is a central tool in solution-focused coaching and defined it as a method the coach uses to open possibilities and to focus the client's resources. They outline several reframing examples inlcuding:

- Reframing problems to solutions – Client, 'I feel totally lost'. Coach, 'So you want to get a sense of control over your life'. Client, 'I have been struggling with this issue for the last two years'. Coach, 'What have you done to maintain your resilience for such a long time?'
- Reframing to highlight positive exceptions in a group of negative comments – Client, 'I just detest my work'. Coach 'That sounds really bad . . . but tell me, which parts of your job are the least undesirable?'
- Reframing to clarify previously unclear goals – Client, 'I really want to improve my management capability'. Coach, 'So what does good management look like to you?'

Reflective Practice Exercise: Reframing and Seeing Different Perspectives

Recall a recent coaching session and summarise it below.
Example: I had a client with a difficult relationship with her mother.

Did you reframe the client's problems into solutions?
Example: Yes, I did towards the end of the session.

How did you do this?
Example: I asked my client what her mother most respected about her and she said it was her caring sensitive nature.

How could you improve this type of reframing?
Example: I want to be less drawn into my client's sadness and better able to step back and find a compassionate way to reframe sadness.

Did you reframe to highlight positive exceptions or negative perceptions/ frame?
Example: Yes, the client saw sadness as bad but later came to see her sensitivity as a real strength.

How did you do this?
Example: Asking her what her mother valued about her. This enabled her to see her sadness through a different and positive lens.

Did you reframe to clarify previously unclear goals? How did you do this?
Example: Not in this case.

How could you improve your reframing?
Example: I want to read more in this area, particularly about Milton H. Erickson.

To be successful, reframing needs to fit with the way the client is thinking. The client will not 'buy' the story unless they have been heard, felt cared for and are ready to listen. The successful reframe lifts the problem out of the *symptom* frame and puts it in the *clear, positive solution* frame (Mattila, 2001).

Using Intuition

Effective coaches are often called intuitive (Starr, 2016). Intuition calls upon the wisdom that is acquired over a lifetime. It is a speedy, creative and subconscious process that can reveal the nature of thoughts, emotions or insights without reasoning or analysis. It works sufficiently often to be taken seriously (Murray, 2004).

In their research on intuition, Ambady and Rosenthal (1992) found that humans can instantly perceive nonverbal cues in response to novel situations. This instant impression is often as powerful as information gained by getting to know a situation or person over a longer period. They coined the term 'thin slices' to refer to such instantaneous non-verbal cues. Later, author Malcolm Gladwell referred extensively to Ambady's work in his popular book, *Blink: The Power of Thinking Without Thinking* (Gladwell, 2005).

These intuitive approaches carry risks that need to be managed through honest assessment and review. Not using intuition is also risky because intuitive insights are at the root of holistic thinking and innovation (Murray, 2004).

Learning to improve intuition involves deep listening where the coach is focusing their full attention on the client and what they are saying rather than listening to their own internal dialogue (Starr, 2016).

Reflective Practice Exercise: Using Intuition

Recall a recent coaching session and summarise it below.
Example: I was working with a very unhappy client.

Think about whether and how you used your intuition to jump to a creative insight, option or solution.
Example: The client spent a lot of time in the session complaining about others and their lack of performance.

Describe the situation and the creative insight, option or solution that you developed.
Example: During the session I asked him if he felt sad about how other people could not be relied on. This comment had a profound effect and the client started talking about his underlying and longstanding problems, which was very helpful in the coaching process.

Describe your level of listening (cosmetic, conversational, active or deep) at the time of your intuitive response?
Example: I was listening very actively.

How much do you trust yourself and your inner wisdom to make the most of your intuition?
Example: I am getting better at this with experience.

How do you want to improve in this area?
Example: I want to find the confidence to believe in myself and my intuition more.

Summary

In conclusion, effective coaching requires the use of a wide range of skills that build a strong thinking partnership between coach and client. This chapter covered a variety of skills, including:

- Growing a thinking partnership.
- Committed listening.
- Rapport and trust.
- Paraphrasing.
- Presuming positive intent.
- Asking powerful questions.
- Providing reflective feedback.
- Constructive challenging.
- Holding to account.
- Reframing and seeing different perspectives.
- Using intuition.

Self-reflective exercises were presented for each of these skills to facilitate self-improvement. The aim of this part of the book was to increase awareness and capability in coaching.

Part IV

Using Innovative Therapeutic Techniques in Coaching and Reflective Practice Sessions

Part IV sets out how coaches can increase their impact by using a wide range of approaches and techniques from psychotherapy and clinical psychology. The section draws on innovative therapeutic approaches that have either been more recently developed or are used less frequently but are highly relevant to many forms of coaching.

DOI: 10.4324/9781003285144-14

11

An Eclectic versus Integrated Approach to Using Therapeutic Techniques in Coaching

INTRODUCTION TO THE CHAPTER

This chapter introduces the eclectic and integrative approaches to using psychotherapeutic techniques in coaching. It illustrates the difference between the two approaches and argues that coaches need a range of different techniques to be effective but that these techniques need to be used in a thoughtful, planned and systematic manner.

The Eclectic Coaching Approach

Coaching psychologists report using a range of theories and techniques from psychodynamic, humanistic, problem-focused, behavioural and cognitive approaches (Whybrow & Palmer, 2006). One common issue raised in group reflective practice sessions run for coaches is, 'I have learned a number of new techniques to apply in coaching over the last year or so. Now I find myself jumping between approaches frequently in my sessions. Is this eclectic approach the best way to help my clients?'

Eclectic means the use of a method or approach that is composed of elements drawn from various sources (Merriam-Webster, 2021). The eclectic coach typically draws on a range of theories and techniques with no theoretical concepts underpinning the practice, with the choice based on the individual's belief that the combination is effective. The practice and experience of the coach helps to identify the pathways the individual adopts. At the extreme, new coaches or therapists can fall into syncretism, a random combination without cohesion that can be hazardous to the client (Benito, 2018).

DOI: 10.4324/9781003285144-15

The eclectic approach to coaching is illustrated in Figure 11.1 with the coach starting by gaining agreement from the client about what he or she wants to work on in the session. Then the coach moves between coaching models, for example solution-focused (Szabo & Meier 2008), GROW (Whitmore, 1996), CLEAR (Hawkins & Smith, 2013) and between therapeutic techniques, for example ACT (Harris, 2009) or Rational Emotive Behaviour Therapy (Ellis, 1994). The moves between coaching models and therapeutic techniques are determined in a largely spontaneous manner depending on the issues raised by the client and without a systematic or thoughtful approach.

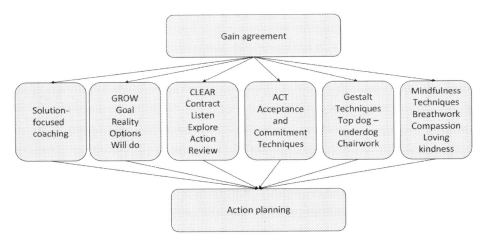

Figure 11.1 The eclectic coaching approach

The Integrated Coaching Approach

By contrast, integrative means to form, coordinate or blend into a functioning or unified whole (Merriam-Webster, 2021). Cooper and McLeod (2007) suggest that the underlying principle of an integrative approach is that client problems have multiple causes and so using only one therapeutic method is unlikely to be successful. Nothing is appropriate in all situations as different clients are helped by different processes at different times. In practice integrative coaching means in any one session the coach will primarily adhere to one coaching model but supplement this with the use of a small number of other therapeutic techniques as needed. This aims to produce a coherent, clear and unified approach to coaching, which can be easily explained to the client if needed (Erskine & Moursund, 1988; Erskine & Trautmann, 1996). The integrative approach is supported by research that suggests that a diverse range of therapeutic methods can be beneficial to clients, even when their underlying models or theories are not directly compatible, provided the coach can understand and explain the approach to the client if this is needed (Castonguay & Beutler, 2006; Cooper, 2008).

An example of integrative coaching is presented below. The coach has chosen to use the solution-focused approach (Szabo & Meier, 2008) and works systematically through the model until they reach a point where the client is stuck and unable to generate their own solutions. At this point the coach asks if the client would like to try a therapeutic approach and explains the background and logic behind the change. If the client agrees the coach will use the technique, then having undertaken this, the coach will move back to the solution-focused approach by asking, for example, 'If you use this approach regularly how much of the problem will that solve on a scale of 1, not at all solved, to 10, the problem is totally solved?' If the client provides a rating of 7 or 8 the coach can move on to action planning. If the client provides a low rating the coach can explore why this approach is not very successful and what needs to be done to improve its impact. Towards the end of the session the coach will encourage the client to draw up an action plan and set goals to be achieved before the next coaching session.

The process is illustrated in Figure 11.2.

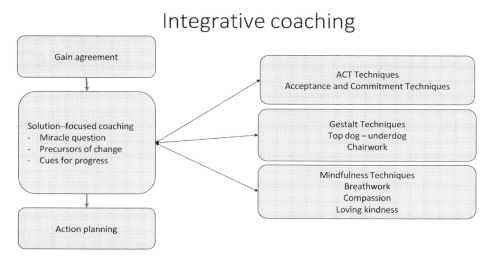

Figure 11.2 Integrative coaching approach

Reflective Practice: Eclectic Versus an Integrated Approach

The differences between these two types of coaching are presented in Table 11.1.

While it can be easy for the coach to take different techniques from different therapies it may not be so easy to integrate the approaches. The experienced coach should be able to use a wide variety of approaches and interventions. The key challenge is how to move from one approach to another while retaining structure and coherence and not falling into haphazard syncretism (Benito, 2018). The model of integrative coaching presented in this chapter is designed to provide a useful structure and coherence.

The implication for training is that the individual coach should be well grounded and fluent in a small number of modes of practice, knowing the strengths and limitations of each to be able to create his or her own coaching style. Understanding that there is a thin line that separates integration from eclecticism and syncretism is critical (Benito, 2018).

Table 11.1 Eclectic versus integrative coaching

Eclectic coaching	Integrative coaching
Uses a range of approaches in a spontaneous manner.	Uses a range of approaches in a planned systematic manner.
The approach is not planned out before the session.	Is a planned but flexible approach.
Can use several coaching models in one session.	Uses only one coaching model in one session.
Can seem confusing for the client as the coach moves between approaches.	Less likely to be confusing for the client as the coach can easily explain the change in approach.
This approach can generate confusion for the coach as they move from one conceptual model to another.	Less likely to cause confusion as the coach has an integrated conceptual model in mind to guide them during the session.

Summary

This chapter introduced the eclectic and integrative approaches to coaching. It illustrated the difference between the two approaches and argued that coaches need a range of different techniques to be effective, but that these techniques need to be used in a thoughtful, planned and systematic manner.

12

Using Unified Protocol Cognitive Behaviour Therapy Techniques

INTRODUCTION TO THE CHAPTER

This chapter:

- Introduces Cognitive Behaviour Therapy (CBT).
- Discusses the recently developed Unified Protocol Cognitive Behaviour Therapy (UP CBT).
- Summarises the elements of the Unified Protocol.
- Discusses the effectiveness of CBT and UP CBT.
- Introduces UP Cognitive Behaviour Coaching (UP CBC).
- Provides a case study to illustrate the value of UP CBC.
- Sets out two reflective practice exercises for coaches using these techniques.

Introduction to Cognitive Behaviour Therapy

Cognitive Behaviour Therapy (CBT) has its origins in the 1950s with a clinical psychologist named Albert Ellis, who was trained as a psychoanalyst, and became frustrated at the slow progress of his clients. He noted that his clients often got better when they altered the ways they thought about themselves, their problems and their environment. He found that his clients made more progress when he focused directly on their beliefs and he went on to use this approach to develop Rational Emotive Behaviour Therapy (Ellis, 1994). In the 1960s, a psychiatrist, Aaron Beck, developed a related approach called Cognitive Therapy (Beck, 1995). Both these approaches were based on the idea that changing how people think can change their dysfunctional emotions and behaviours (Froggatt, 2006).

CBT has progressed a great deal since its inception and new, evidence-based interventions have been developed to assist with a wide range of psychological

DOI: 10.4324/9781003285144-16

distress using a unified protocol of interventions. This approach contrasts to the diagnosis-specific CBT approaches such as CBT for phobias, for anxiety or for depression (Khakpoor & Omid, 2018). These transdiagnostic interventions address issues such as emotional avoidance, rather than individual symptoms such as generalised worry or feelings of worthlessness in depression. This approach better treats the range of comorbid disorders that are not targeted in diagnosis-specific treatments. It also has the advantage that providers can be trained in one unified protocol for use with a wide range of clients in different settings, thus increasing efficiency and providing cost savings.

Unified Protocol CBT (UP CBT) is based on the idea that a significant proportion of the variance in effectiveness of psychotherapy is due to the common factors such as client expectation, structured regular sessions and the quality of the therapist–client relationship. Therefore, a single protocol of interventions can be developed to address a wide range of conditions (Dalgleish et al., 2020).

The Unified Protocol for Cognitive Behaviour Therapy

Barlow et al. (2011), in their book *The Unified Protocol for Transdiagnostic Treatment of Emotional Disorders: Therapist Guide*, set out the detail of the protocol for UP CBT which is summarised below.

The protocol aims to assist people struggling with intensely painful emotions such as anger, anxiety, guilt and sadness. Emotional disorders are characterised by frequent strong emotions, negative reactions to these emotions and the vain attempt to avoid the pain. The unified protocol programme is designed to treat a wide range of emotional disorders including generalised anxiety, social anxiety, post-traumatic stress, depression and eating disorders.

The core of the protocol consists of the following steps:

- Setting goals and maintaining motivation.
- Understanding the nature and purpose of emotions.
- Mindful emotional awareness, mindful mood induction and anchoring in the present.
- Cognitive flexibility, countering emotional behaviours and facing physical sensations.
- The final step is emotional exposure.

Initially the client is asked to record their experiences and keep track of their progress throughout the treatment. There are a range of assessment scales that can be used at this stage including an anxiety, a depression, a general emotional experience or a positive emotion scale (Barlow et al., 2011). The client is encouraged to plot their scores on their chosen scale over time to monitor progress.

Setting Goals and Maintaining Motivation

This step involves the client clarifying their difficulties by identifying their top two problems, setting two concrete improvement goals for both of these and then developing a series of steps to reach each goal. Motivation is developed by the client undertaking an exercise to identify the benefits and costs of changing versus staying the same.

Understanding Emotions

This step starts with a review of progress as recorded by the client using a relevant assessment scale; for example, for anger or anxiety. The protocol then explains that the aim of the programme is not to get rid of negative emotions but to help the client respond differently to them when they arise. There is a description of the range of emotions, e.g., sadness, anxiety, anger etc. and their necessary role in the client's life. For example, the purpose of sadness is to enable the client to withdraw and recuperate after a time of loss while the purpose of anxiety is to raise an internal alarm to a possible danger. The client is taught that emotions consist of three components, what they think, how they feel and how they behave. The homework for the session is to practise monitoring emotional states and breaking them down into their component thoughts, physical sensations and behaviours.

Next the client is taught the ARC model and that all emotions follow a path from Antecedents (something that triggers the emotion) to Responses (the thoughts, physical sensations and behaviours that occur during the emotional experience) to Consequences (what happens as a result of the emotional response). The homework involves tracking emotional experiences by using the ARC model.

Mindful Emotional Management

The next step starts with a review of progress and their use of the ARC model. The client is then taught that although they have been very aware of their emotions up to this point in time, they now can learn to be mindfully aware in the present moment in a non-judgemental way. This *mindful emotional awareness* means moving from 'I feel sad and hopeless' to 'I accept that I have a heavy feeling in my chest right now'. The client is taught a guided meditation process that includes:

- Being grounded in the here and now.
- Attending to the breath.
- Describing sensations that arise in a non-judgemental way.
- Understanding that thoughts that arise are just thoughts and not facts.
- Noticing the ebb and flow of emotions.
- Remembering the exercise is not about trying to relax but about mindful awareness of emotions.

When the client is comfortable with *mindful emotional awareness*, they can move on to *mindful mood induction*. They are asked to find a piece of music, or some other stimulus, that brings back memories. They listen to the music or view the stimulus and practise describing their feelings in a non-judgemental manner. They watch their emotions ebb and flow and do not push them away or hang on to them. They then move on to use a range of different music or other stimuli to bring up a variety of emotions that they learn to be more comfortable with.

After practising these exercises for about a week the client is encouraged to build mindful awareness into their daily life in an exercise called *anchoring in the present*. The steps in this are:

- Using a cue, e.g., the feeling of the feet on the floor, to be grounded in the present moment.
- Checking what the person is thinking, feeling and doing at this moment.
- Asking if the person's current response is consistent with what is happening right now or if it is a reaction to some past event or prediction about the future?
- If needed, altering the response to bring it in line with the current moment rather than to a post event or prediction.

The homework is to monitor progress, to practise mindfulness awareness and *anchoring in the present*.

Building Thinking Flexibility

Building thinking flexibility is the next step in the protocol and this starts by understanding thoughts and how to counter them. Thoughts are important as they help produce emotions, e.g., if the client thinks, 'That stranger might attack me', they will feel afraid, while if they think, 'That person looks strange so I will not make eye contact', they feel very different. The client is also taught that thoughts arrive instantly and automatically. If they see a face in a crowd they may automatically think that they look like, for example, an old friend, a dangerous criminal, a caring mother, etc. Because thoughts happen so quickly clients can easily jump to incorrect conclusions. People with troublesome emotions often fall into thinking traps that include jumping to conclusions without reviewing the facts, e.g., turbulence while flying in an aircraft means it will crash, or spilling some milk at breakfast means the day will be a disaster. A common thinking trap is automatically thinking the worst, e.g., if you do not get any likes to your social media post, then automatically thinking your friends no longer like you. The client can build cognitive flexibility by challenging their automatic negative thoughts with questions such as:

- Do I really know this is true?
- What else could be going on here?
- What is the concrete evidence for this?
- Even if this were true, how would I handle it?

The client is encouraged to complete the Practicing Thinking Flexibility Form – an adapted version of this is set out in the following table.

What is the antecedent situation?	What are my automatic thoughts?	Have I fallen into a thinking trap?	What is an alternative view?
Example: My friend at work has not said 'Good Morning' to me.	He does not like me anymore!	Yes, this could be a thinking trap – I do not really know why this has happened.	He may be upset about something that happened on the way to work and so be distracted.

If the client finds that under some circumstances the Practicing Thinking Flexibility exercise does not work well, there are other options. The Downward

Arrow exercise can help many clients. The exercise starts with the client picking an automatic thought that they have had recently. The client then asks 'What would it mean if this was true? Why? If it were true what would happen?' This question typically helps the client to identify another related automatic thought. Once this thought has been identified the client again asks 'What would it mean if this was true? Why? If it were true what would happen?' Again, this typically leads to another automatic thought. The process is repeated until a core belief is uncovered that does not lead to further automatic thoughts. The aim of the exercise is to identify the core or enduring beliefs that the client has about themselves, others and the world around them. These core beliefs are absolute statements and assumptions (e.g., 'You cannot trust other people') that often develop in childhood and are largely unconscious. Once core beliefs have been identified they can be challenged but if they remain unknown no challenge is possible. Greenberger and Padesky (2016, p. 156) have a fuller explanation of the exercise.

An example may be as follows:

1. The initial Automatic Thought: *My boss does not respect me.*
2. Question: *What would it mean if this was true? Why? If it were true what would happen?*
3. Next Automatic Thought: *I may be fired and then I would not be able to pay my home loan.*
4. Question: *What would it mean if this was true? Why? If it were true what would happen?*
5. Next Automatic Thought: *I would lose my home.*
6. Question: *What would it mean if this was true? Why? If it were true what would happen?*
7. Next Automatic Thought and Core Belief: *I would be homeless and hopeless!*
8. The Challenge: *I know that I think and feel that I am hopeless, but I do have a good job working with great people so perhaps I am being overly sensitive about that one comment my boss made. My problem is my reaction to these comments by the boss. I am okay!*

Countering Emotional Behaviours

The next step involves understanding emotional behaviours which are the things the client does to manage their emotions. These behaviours can be useful, e.g., getting out of the way of real danger, or unhelpful, e.g., avoiding a meeting because of apprehension. Unhelpful emotional behaviours are particularly troublesome because they often have short-term advantages, e.g., a sense of relief, but long-term disadvantages, e.g., not facing difficult situations and getting into a spiral of worry. The client is encouraged to think about their troublesome emotions, the short- and long-term consequences and then alternative ways of behaving and the benefits of behaving in this new way. A modified version of the Countering Emotional Behaviours exercise is presented in the following table:

My behaviour	Short-term impact	Long-term impact	Alternative option	Benefits of this
Example: Worrying for hours on end.	*I feel like I am trying to solve the problem.*	*I don't solve the problem and get very tired.*	*Set a time limit for worrying and then go for a run to get some exercise.*	*I see if I can solve the problem and if not, I find a useful alternative.*
Anger and expressing this without thinking.	*Yell at my work colleague.*	*My colleague will not interact with me at work.*	*Walk away from a situation before I say anything hurtful.*	*I build good relationships at work.*

Facing Physical Sensations

The client is taught that most emotions not only include thoughts but also physical sensations. For example, distress can involve a high heartrate, shortness of breath, dizziness or disoriented feelings, a lot of muscle tension including tightness in the chest, and sweating. These physical sensations intensify emotional states because clients worry, for example, that a racing heart rate will lead to a heart attack or panic attack. These intense feelings often result in a desire to avoid emotions. This typically leads to short-term relief but to long-term distress because avoiding a situation or feeling teaches the client they cannot cope with it.

The protocol involves telling the client that facing physical sensations, although painful in the short term, makes them easier to tolerate in the long term. Practicing *mindful emotional awareness* and observing physical sensations without judgement helps them to reduce in intensity and minimises the powerfully destructive fear of them.

To better tolerate uncomfortable physical sensations, the client is taught to induce mild versions of these feared feelings, then to be aware of them in a mindful way. Uncomfortable sensations can be induced by hyperventilating or breathing through a drinking straw or running rapidly on the spot for 60 seconds. These activities induce uncomfortable sensations, which the client can practise tolerating, which builds an experiential understanding that these are unpleasant but not catastrophic feelings. The client can practise inducing and tolerating unpleasant sensations between sessions until they feel able to tolerate these without distress.

Emotional Exposure

The final step in the protocol is to ask the client to undertake specific real-life activities that generate uncomfortable emotions. This *emotional exposure* enables the client to test out their unhelpful beliefs about their emotions and to learn to face them in a controlled and safe way. It also enables the client to practise the skills they have learned and to become more confident in tolerating strong emotions.

The most effective forms of *emotional exposure* are real life situations such as deliberately telling a colleague that his or her sexual advances are inappropriate or completing a project to a satisfactory but not perfect level. However, there are some circumstances in which real-life exposure is not possible or practical, e.g., taking multiple aeroplane flights in bad weather. In these cases, the *emotional exposure* is best undertaken using imagery. This type of *emotional exposure* can involve an emotional exposure hierarchy or ladder of fear or frustration. An example of a fear ladder for needles and blood taking is set out below.

1. Looking at a picture of a needle on a table.
2. Watching an orange being injected.
3. Looking at a picture of a needle sticking into an arm.
4. Looking at a video of someone getting an injection.
5. Seeing a syringe and needle on a table.
6. Holding a needle in my hand.
7. Resting a needle against my arm.
8. Slightly pricking my skin with a needle.

9. Getting an injection in my upper arm.
10. Watching as my blood is drawn from my vein.

Over a series of homework sessions, the client can imagine these exposure events, starting with the least default and slowly progressing to the more challenging, until they can learn to tolerate the uncomfortable feelings without avoidance. The client is taught to only move up the next step of the hierarchy when they can tolerate the current step without undue concern.

Before any type of *emotional exposure*, the client is encouraged to prepare themselves by completing the following chart adapted from Barlow et al. (2011).

Reflective Practice Exercise: Emotional Exposure Preparation Form
Describe the *emotional exposure* you are going to undertake. *Example: I want to practise being more assertive with my intimidating boss.*
What automatic thoughts will arise when you undertake this exposure event? *Example: I could ruin my career if I get offside with my boss.*
How can you challenge these automatic unhelpful thoughts and develop other interpretations? *Example: As I am never offensive, it is very unlikely my boss will fire me.*

What emotionals and behaviours will arise?
Example: Sweaty hands and I want to back off quickly.

What other more helpful ways can you behave?
Example: I need to prepare my ideas beforehand and make measured but clear comments.

How can you describe this event and the sensations that arise in a non-judgemental way as you stay in the present moment?
Example: I have sweaty hands as I look at my boss's face. I have the idea that I want to run away but I have a choice about what I do.

After practising the *emotional exposure*, the client can complete a debrief form adapted from Barlow et al. (2011).

Emotional Exposure Debrief Form

What thoughts, physical sensations and emotional behaviours did you experience during this event?
Example: I did feel nervous and intimidated but said what I had prepared in a clear way.

How willing were you to experience these emotions using the scale from 1 = not at all, to 10 = extremely?
Example: I would rate my willingness 7 but I would have withdrawn if my boss got angry.

Rate your thinking flexibility during the event using the scale from 1 = not at all, to, 10 = extremely?
Example: I would rate it 3 as I seemed to have no control over my thinking at the time.

Rate your ability to counter your emotional behaviours during the event using the scale from 1 = not at all, to 10 = extremely?
Example: I would rate myself an 8 as I said what I wanted and did not back off.

What did you learn from this exercise?
Example: Standing up to difficult people is hard for me, but if I am prepared and challenge my automatic thinking, I can do it.

How can you do better in your next exposure exercise?
Example: Having done this once, I feel like next time I could say more about what I think to my boss.

In summary, the UP CBT treatment programme provides clients with a great deal of information about how to cope with unhelpful emotions. The client is taught that:

• Both uncomfortable and comfortable emotions provide important motivation for action.
• Staying in the present moment and being non-judgemental about emotions helps to prevent them from getting more intense.
• How the client thinks about a situation impacts on how they feel, and this then influences how they see the situation.
• Avoiding uncomfortable experiences may help in the short term, but it will make matters worse in the long term.

After completing the programme, the client is asked to draw up an action plan to practise the most useful techniques, to evaluate their ongoing practice and to gain more help if this is required in future.

The Effectiveness of CBT and UP CBT

CBT has been extensively researched with many meta-analytic studies having been undertaken to the point where Hofmann et al. (2012) have produced a review of meta-analyses. They identified 269 meta-analytic studies and reviewed a representative sample of 106 analyses evaluating the impact of CBT for the following problems: anger and aggression, anxiety disorders, bipolar disorder, chronic pain and fatigue, criminal behaviours, depression and dysthymia, distress due to general medical conditions, distress related to pregnancy complications and female hormonal conditions, eating disorders, general stress, insomnia, personality disorders, schizophrenia and other psychotic disorders, somatoform disorders and substance use disorder. Other meta-analytic reviews explored by the authors included the effectiveness of CBT for a range of problems in children and elderly adults. The strongest support for the effectiveness for CBT was for anger control problems, anxiety disorders, bulimia, general stress and somatoform disorders. The authors identified 11 studies that compared the response rates between CBT and other therapies or control conditions. They found that CBT showed higher effectiveness rates than the comparison treatments in seven of these reviews with just one review reporting CBT having lower response rates than the comparison therapy. They concluded that the evidence base for the effectiveness of CBT is very strong. They recommended more effectiveness research be carried out using randomised-controlled trials. In addition they suggested that more research was needed on the effectiveness of CBT with specific subgroups, such as ethnic minorities and low income clients.

Reinholt and Krogh (2014) examined evidence of the overall efficacy of unified protocol transdiagnostic treatment approaches to CBT for anxiety disorders. They reviewed a total of 11 studies (n = 1,933) found these approaches generally had a positive outcome and that these clients did better than wait-list and treatment-as-usual clients with gains being maintained through follow-up. They concluded that there was cautious support for UP approaches and that these treatments offered great promise as an affordable and pragmatic treatment for anxiety disorders.

Carlucci et al. (2021) undertook a meta-analysis to evaluate whether the UP CBT results in significant improvements in anxiety and depression symptoms in children, adolescents and adults. They used 19 random controlled trials and 13 uncontrolled pre-post trials with 2,183 clients in the meta-analysis. They found large to moderate overall effect sizes for both depression and anxiety in the uncontrolled pre-post studies (g = 0.756) and in random controlled trials (g = 0.452), respectively. At a 3–6-month follow-up, large effect sizes were found for combined depression plus anxiety (g = 1.113). UP CBT treatment outperformed both passive and active control groups in dealing with negative affect. They concluded that the manualised UP treatments have potential to improve mental health outcomes, particularly of anxiety and depression.

Unified Protocol Cognitive Behaviour Coaching

Palmer (2009) indicates that Cognitive Behavioural Coaching (also known as Rational Coaching) is firmly based on the work of Albert Ellis and his Rational Emotive Behavioural approach (Ellis, 1994). Like Rational Emotive Behaviour Therapy, Cognitive Behavioural Coaching (CBC) focuses on the identification and disputation of a range of irrational beliefs that are based on rigid, dogmatic, illogical and unhelpful thinking which leads to poor psychological and behavioural performance.

Williams et al. (2010) suggest that the main goals of CBC are to:

- Facilitate the client in achieving their realistic goals.
- Facilitate self-awareness of underlying cognitive and emotional barriers to goal attainment.
- Equip the individual with more effective thinking and behavioural skills.
- Build internal resources, stability and self-acceptance to help the client undertake their choice of actions.
- Enable the client to become their own self-coach.

(Williams et al., 2010, p. 38)

Unified Protocol Cognitive Behaviour Coaching (UP CBC) uses the techniques of UP CBT to assist participants in the workforce to achieve productivity and fulfilment.

Unified Protocol Cognitive Behaviour Coaching Case Study

Mike was a partner in a large accounting firm who had successfully used executive coaching to improve his ability to handle pressure and stress. Mike then asked his executive coach to undertake a coaching programme for his six direct reports. Mike wanted them all to learn a range of techniques to improve their performance under pressure. He also wanted the coaching to be undertaken on a one-on-one basis and for it to last for no more than six sessions. The coach decided that given these constraints, it would be useful to use the UP CBT approach. The structured session plan for the coaching, approved by Mike, was:

- Session 1: explanation of the UP CBT coaching process, building trust and understanding with the client, explaining the nature of pressure and stress.
- Session 2: setting individual coaching goals and building motivation, learning to understand the nature of emotions and following the ARC method of analysis.
- Session 3: learning mindful emotional awareness and practising it, learning about thinking flexibility and practising this.
- Session 4: Countering emotional behaviours and confronting physical sensations.
- Session 5: Putting emotional exposure into practice.
- Session 6: Developing an ongoing action plan to counter stress and maintain performance under pressure.

The coach received excellent feedback from the clients at the end of the programme as they felt much more able to effectively deal with pressure. Mike reported that the coaching had provided good value-for-money.

Reflective Practice Exercise: Unified Protocol Cognitive Behaviour Coaching

Reflective Practice Exercise: Unified Protocol Cognitive Behaviour Coaching

Identify a relevant emotional issue you want to work on and describe it below.
Example: I want to do less binge eating when I come home from work and feel distressed.

Read the book *The Unified Protocol for Transdiagnostic Treatment of Emotional Disorders: Therapist Guide* by Barlow et al. (2011) and identify the key points relevant to your emotional problem.
Example: I understand now that feelings have a purpose and my seeking comfort is a sensible thing to do. What I need is an alternative to binge eating.

Set your own UP CBT coaching goals.
Example: To go for a brisk walk after work when I am stressed and to binge eat less often.

Build your motivation by identifying the benefits and costs of changing versus staying the same.

The benefits of changing are:
Example: I will be healthy and control my weight better.

The costs of changing are:
Example: I will have to exercise a lot of will power to walk rather then eat.

The benefits of staying the same are:
Example: It takes no effort to stay the same.

The costs of staying the same are:
Example: I will end up hating myself.

Review the ARC model, which suggests that all emotions follow a path from Antecedents (something that triggers the emotion) to Responses (the thoughts, physical sensations, and behaviours that occur during the emotional experience) to Consequences (what happens as a result of the emotional response). Use your emotional coaching problem and apply the ARC model.

The Antecedent situation is:
Example: I come home from a stressful day at work.

My Responses are:
Example: I go to the fridge and get out the ice cream and binge eat.

The Consequences are:
Example: I feel bloated and horrible.

Practise mindful emotional awareness and describe what happened in a *non-judgemental* way below.
Example: When I practised mindfulness after work today, I felt my mind was racing and I had a hunger pain in my gut.

Practise thinking flexibly by identifying your automatic thoughts; if these are a result of a thinking trap develop an alternative way to think about the situation. Write this below.
Example: I think 'The only option now is to binge' but I am an adult and I can do lots of different things when stressed.

Practise countering emotional behaviours by:

Summarising your problem emotion.
Example: Binge eating when stressed.

Describing the short-term consequences of this emotion.
Example: Feeling better for a moment, then feeling guilty and weak.

Describe the long-term unhelpful consequences of this emotion.
Example: I will get worse and put on lots of weight.

Identify a range of alternative ways you can behave under these circumstances.
Example: I could go for a walk, ring a friend or do some meditation.

Describe the benefits of behaving in these new alternative ways.
Example: I would feel more in control and more like an adult.

Using These Workbook Exercises in Professional Development

The reflective practice exercises in this chapter are designed to be used:

- In individual reflective practice sessions for students or coaches who want to develop their capability.
- With coaches who want to work with peers in pairs to build their skills.
- For supervisors who want to use experiential learning in their work.
- With classroom instructors or academics teaching coaching skills.
- By senior practitioners who want to run professional development sessions for executive coaches.

Summary

This chapter has

- Introduced Cognitive Behaviour Therapy (CBT).
- Discussed the recently developed Unified Protocol Cognitive Behaviour Therapy (UP CBT).
- Summarised the elements of the Unified Protocol.
- Discussed the effectiveness of CBT and UP CBT.
- Introduced Unified Protocol Cognitive Behavioural Coaching (UP CBC).
- Presented a UP CBC case study.
- Set out several reflective practice exercises using these techniques.

13
Internet Supplemented Acceptance and Commitment Therapy Techniques

INTRODUCTION TO THE CHAPTER

This chapter presents a brief outline of Acceptance and Commitment Therapy (ACT), then shows how the internet is providing a useful platform to supplement ACT therapy and coaching. The focus is then on the specific approaches and techniques that can be used effectively in coaching and reflective practice sessions. The chapter does not aim to make the reader an Acceptance and Commitment therapist but simply to give any competent coach a range of additional approaches they can use if needed. For a fuller explanation of Acceptance and Commitment Therapy see Hayes et al. (1999), Hayes and Harris (2000), Harris (2006, 2007, 2009).

Background to ACT

Acceptance and Commitment Therapy, known as 'ACT' (pronounced as the word 'act') is a mindfulness-based behavioural therapy that uses a wide range of experiential and values-based exercises to help clients. The goal of ACT is to create a rich and meaningful life, while accepting the pain that inevitably goes with it (Harris 2006, 2009).

The Effectiveness of ACT and Internet-Supplemented ACT

ACT has proven effective with a diverse range of clinical conditions including depression, OCD, workplace stress, chronic pain, the stress of terminal cancer, anxiety, PTSD, anorexia, heroin abuse, marijuana abuse, and even schizophrenia (see for example, Zettle & Raines, 1989; Twohig et al., 2006; Bond & Bunce, 2000; Dahl et al., 2004).

DOI: 10.4324/9781003285144-17

In a review of meta-analyses, Gloster et al. (2020) evaluated a wide range of randomised controlled trials examining the effectiveness of ACT on a broad range of conditions. They identified 53 relevant studies but after applying their screening for sound research methodologies they included 20 meta-analyses that reported on 100 controlled effect size studies with 12,477 participants. Their results showed that ACT is an effective treatment for a wide range of conditions, including anxiety, depression, pain, substance use and transdiagnostic groups. They found that ACT was generally more effective than inactive control conditions such as waitlist or placebo, as well as more effective than treatment-as-usual, and most other active therapies excluding CBT.

Recently, ACT has been adapted for internet-based delivery, assisting clients by providing information and exercises in a structured and easily accessed manner. This type of delivery has been documented for a wide range of clients including family carers of people with dementia (Kishita et al., 2021), adults with anxiety (Kelson et al., 2019) and working mothers with preschool children (Sasaki, 2021). There are a wide range of internet-based resources that can be used by executive coaching clients including the US Department of Veterans Administration free ACT Coach app (https://mobile.va.gov/app/act-coach) and on-line training available at (www.actmindfully.com.au) and (https://wise mind.com/series/act-therapy-training/).

Initial evidence suggests that this internet-supplemented approach is useful. Kelson et al. (2019) undertook a systematic review using a total of 20 relevant studies that met research quality criteria. The research included 11 randomized controlled trials and nine uncontrolled pilot studies. The studies examined adult clients with generalized anxiety, social anxiety, illness anxiety and general anxiety symptoms. Eighteen studies reported significant anxiety reduction after internet-based ACT treatment with 13 studies using therapist guidance and five without it. The average attrition rate was 19%. Thirteen studies assessed treatment satisfaction and participants on average rated their internet-based ACT experience above average to high satisfaction. The authors concluded that internet-based ACT can be an effective and acceptable treatment for adults with anxiety symptoms.

Assumptions of ACT

ACT assumes that the processing of the human mind is often destructive and creates psychological suffering and argues that the cause of this suffering is human language. On the positive side, language helps people to share knowledge, learn from the past, predict, plan and imagine things that never existed. On the negative side, language is used to lie, deceive and manipulate, to judge, criticise and attack and to create suffering for ourselves and others (Harris, 2006). Language creates human suffering by setting up a psychological struggle called *experiential avoidance* which involves the vain attempts to avoid thoughts, feelings, memories and physical sensations even when this creates harm in the long run. The more effort individuals spend trying to avoid unwanted private experiences the more they suffer.

The ACT Experiential and Values-based Exercises

Harris (2006) outlines the range of approaches ACT uses to help clients live better lives.

- *Cognitive defusion*: this involves learning to view thoughts, images, memories and sensations as nothing more than words, pictures and bodily sensations. It also involves not seeing them as frightening events, rules to be obeyed or objective facts.
- *Acceptance and expansion*: this involves opening up and allowing the full force of feelings, thoughts and sensations to come and go without struggle, understanding they are an inevitable but temporary part of life, not running from them, or focusing upon them.
- *Contact with the present moment*: this involves being fully aware of the here-and-now with uncritical openness and interest. It allows us to see the flow of thoughts, feelings, sensations and sights as they are, without labels of good or bad, desirable or undesirable.
- *Observing self*: this involves that part of us that is always thinking – generating thoughts, memories, judgements and so on. It is the part of us that can notice and stand above life and observe our thinking and feelings. Connecting to this *Observing self* can help us feel a sense of stillness that allows us to gently distance ourselves from suffering.
- *Defining values*: this involves clarifying what is most important to us, what sort of person we want to be, what we want to stand for in life.
- *Committed Action*: this involves setting goals, based on our values, and taking effective action to live a rich and fulfilling life.

Each of these approaches is considered in more detail below with a focus on the elements that are most relevant to coaching.

Cognitive Defusion

Cognitive defusion involves learning to de-power and see thoughts, images, memories and sensations as nothing more than words, pictures and bodily sensations. It also involves not seeing them as frightening events, rules to be obeyed or objective facts. Achieving this shift in perspective is important in many coaching situations and can greatly reduce the suffering caused by *experiential avoidance* (Harris, 2009).

Cognitive Defusion Case Study

Abdul is a Senior Partner in a major law firm. Over the years he had written many important legal opinions and was widely respected for his views. He came to executive coaching after making a significant but not disastrous error in an opinion. Abdul had become increasingly anxious about the possibility of making another similar error. In discussions it appeared that Abdul had found the error before the client did, had corrected it and sent another draft and had not had any adverse client comments. Despite this, the error tormented him and he would lie awake at night worrying about things going wrong. The coach started with a solution-focused approach and worked with Abdul to identify ways to improve error detection and removal. However, this did nothing to decrease his distress. The coach then introduced him to a range of ideas from ACT and in particular cognitive defusion. At first Abdul resisted seeing his fearful thoughts and feelings as just neurological activity and not things to struggle with. However, he could see that the pain he was suffering from was exacerbated by the struggle he was fuelling. He could also see that the pain and upset over the error was unavoidable, but the extended suffering was self-generated. The coach taught Abdul to identify his fearful thought: 'I stuffed that up and may even do it again'. He was then asked to practise repeating this thought to himself but then adding a new phrase at the beginning 'I am having the thought that – I stuffed that up and may even do it again'. Abdul thought that this could be useful if he really practised it. He chose to do this practice every time he was in a lift alone or walking up the stairs by himself. In addition, Abdul undertook an internet-based training programme of ACT techniques to supplement and reinforce the coaching.

In a coaching session one month later, Abdul said he was feeling and sleeping a lot better but was astonished to understand how he could now get some distance from his thoughts and feelings which had up until that point just seemed like an inseparable part of himself.

Reflective Practice Exercise: Cognitive Defusion

Write down an unhelpful or self-critical thought. Try to capture the essence of the critical thought in a short sentence.
Examples: I am hopeless, I am an idiot for doing that, I am a fraud and will soon be found out.

In a quiet place where you will not be disturbed try repeating this thought four or five times with real feeling and intensity. Place a strong emphasis on the most self-critical part of the sentence.
Example: 'I am an *idiot* for doing that'.

Then repeat the sentence but place the phrase 'I am having the thought that . . .' in front of the self-criticism. Say the new sentence six or seven times.
Example: 'I am having the thought that – I am an *idiot* for doing that'.

Spend a few minutes reflecting on how different it feels to use cognitive defusion and feel what it is like to label your self-criticism as just a thought that you are having.
Example: It is strange to label it like this and see how it reduces the impact of the thought.

Think about how you are going to practise this. Try to find a regular activity that can become a cue for your cognitive defusion practice.
Example: I will practise this sentence every time I have a cup of coffee for the next week and see the impact that this has.

Acceptance and Expansion

Acceptance and expansion involves allowing feelings, thoughts and sensations to come and go without struggle, understanding they are an inevitable but temporary part of life. It includes not running from them or focusing upon them. Acceptance is different to apathy. Apathy is giving up and doing nothing while acceptance is allowing feelings to come and go. Acceptance can free us from impossible burdens such as always having to do things perfectly. Expansion is the idea of giving ourselves the time and opening up to painful feelings when they arise. Expansion allows feelings to flow in, and then almost inevitably, flow away (Harris, 2009). Acceptance and expansion are very powerful techniques that can usefully be used in coaching with clients who are struggling with painful thoughts, feelings, images or sensations.

Acceptance and Expansion Case Study

James came to executive coaching after the sudden death of two very close friends in a motor vehicle accident. He was finding it hard to concentrate at work and could not enjoy time with his family like he used to. He had very intrusive images of the wrecked car that he had first seen in a news website the day of the accident. He kept replaying in his mind the scenes of his friends skidding off the road in very wet weather and hitting a lamppost. He wondered what their last thoughts were before the moment of fatal impact. The funerals of the men had been gut wrenching and the raw grief of their widows and young children almost unbearable.

During the initial coaching session James spent most of the time fighting back tears and repeatedly saying the phrase 'It is what it is'. Towards the end of the session the coach introduced the ACT notion of acceptance and expansion to which James said he really needed to try something new. They set up a two-hour session and the coach asked James to bring along a photo of his two deceased friends. At the start of this second session the coach talked about the idea that the more open we are to our feelings the less they trouble us. James could understand that the fear of pain from his grief was keeping him from really experiencing his feelings. James said he felt he had a good understanding of the concept of expansion and then he talked about how he had initially met his two friends and how they had all had a great time at university together. It did not take long for James to start sobbing deeply. The coach encouraged him to stay with the feelings and let them flow. After about an hour of being able to freely express his distress, James was starting to feel a lot better. The coach then encouraged James to reflect back on the last hour and understand what had happened. James said he found the session very helpful. The coach then explained that feelings of grief come in waves and that it was likely that unexpectedly James would have periods of deep sadness over the coming months. Having experienced expansion and not 'having gone mad with grief', James felt able to make the time to allow his grief to flow as needed. James supplemented his coaching with on-line ACT training on acceptance and expansion. A follow-up session one month later found James feeling much better and having joined a national road safety charity that worked to prevent road deaths and injuries and supports bereaved and injured people.

Reflective Practice Exercise: Acceptance and Expansion

Think about a painful loss in your life such as the death of a parent, loved one, friend or the loss of a house or job. Write a summary of the situation.
Example: I lost my Dad four years ago and I still miss him.

See if you can find a photo of your loved one or some other reminder of your loss. In a quiet place where you will not be disturbed, spend an hour or two thinking about the person, 'talking' to them, telling them about your pain and allow your feelings to flow.
Example: I miss you so much Dad and I see your likeness in my eldest son every day.

When you feel ready and the intensity of the feeling has subsided somewhat, reflect on the value of acceptance and expansion.
*Example: I have not thought about my Dad for some time, but I now under-
stand that the grief is just below the surface. I have experienced the flow of
sadness, which reached a peak and then slowly subsided.*

Are you prepared to be more open and accepting of your feelings?
Example: It is not easy to do but I do see the value of it.

Contact with the Present Moment

Contact with the present moment involves being fully aware of the here-
and-now with uncritical openness and interest. It allows us to see the flow of
thoughts, feelings, sensations and sights as they are and without labels of good
or bad, desirable or undesirable (Harris, 2009).

Contact with the Present Moment Case Study

Abby was a water quality expert in a civil engineering firm. She was a very
bright and able professional who described herself as someone who 'did not
tolerate fools'. She had developed a reputation for being arrogant and dismissive to both clients and staff. This was particularly noticeable in meetings when
Abby was bored and felt the others in the meeting were not understanding
the technical implications of issues. In the coaching, Abby explained that she
was often invited to meetings where very little of the content was relevant
to her but that she needed to be there because there were sometimes critical
technical questions that came up that she had to answer. Getting answers to

these questions was important because the input from Abby would often have a major impact on the scope and cost of the work.

The problem for Abby was that, when she was bored, she would get frustrated, then angry and then frustrated about being angry and a nasty spiral would start. Under these circumstances she recognised that she could become dismissive and sarcastic toward others. Abby was now at the point where she needed to address this problem as there had been several staff complaints about her behaviour. The coach talked with her about the ACT ideas that our own thinking can often be destructive and that getting frustrated at being angry was an unhelpful struggle. Abby told the coach she knew all that already and what she wanted was a solution! The coach suggested she try the ACT *Notice Five Things* exercise (Harris, 2009, p. 171). The coach explained the exercise and talked about the importance of making contact with the present moment as a method to reduce the struggle against anger. He explained that to be in the present moment Abby would need to stop, pay attention, become aware of the realities in the moment and not judge what she saw or heard as good or bad. The coach explained that the exercise had the following steps:

- Pause for a moment.
- Look around and notice five things you can see.
- Listen carefully and notice five things you can hear.
- Notice five things you can feel in contact with your body (e.g., your clothing against your legs, your feet upon the floor, your back against the chair, etc.).
- Finally, do all the above simultaneously if you can.

Abby said she thought this exercise sounded 'weird' but would give it a try. She agreed to try it out in each boring meeting she was in during the next week and then come back to see the coach. Abby supplemented the coaching with the ACT Coach app and on-line ACT training in contact with the present moment. In the follow-up session Anny said that to her surprise the *Notice Five Things* exercise had been effective and that she now understood about the importance of not struggling against her anger but just letting it go.

Reflective Practice Exercise: Contact with the Present Moment

Try this exercise yourself and see what happens.

- Pause for a moment.
- Look around and notice five things you can see.

- Listen carefully and notice five things you can hear.
- Notice five things you can feel in contact with your body (e.g., your clothing against your legs, your feet upon the floor, your back against the chair, etc.).
- Finally, do all the above simultaneously if you can.

What did you experience?
Example: I noticed the chair opposite, the table, the bookshelf, the carpet and the light. I heard Claire speak, Peter respond, Jim argue, Claire argue back and the sound of the air conditioning. I noticed the feel of my feet on the floor, the feel of the chair I am sitting in, the softness of the shirt I am wearing, the feel of my trousers on my legs and the sensations in my hands.

In what circumstances do you think the *Notice Five Things* exercise would be useful to you?
Example: This would be useful to do when I feel anxious in a glass-fronted lift that is moving fast.

In what circumstances do you think the *Notice Five Things* exercise would be useful to your coaching clients?
Example: I have clients whose job requires them to attend their boss's monthly presentation, this would be a better thing for them to do than to get resentful.

The Observing Self

This ACT technique makes an important distinction between the Thinking Self and the Observing Self. The Thinking Self generates thoughts, judgements and memories. As people go through life their views change, their roles change but the sense of 'you' is still the same. All sorts of things change over time but they are not the essence of who the individual is. The Thinking Self is that part of the person that sees and can describe the changes, while the Observing Self is the stable essential 'you'. Linking with this *Observing Self* can help clients feel a sense of connection and stillness that allows them to gently distance themselves from the vicious cycle of suffering (Harris, 2009; Mudd, 2021).

A simple way to describe the Thinking Self and the Observing Self is to compare them to the weather and the sky. The Thinking Self is like the everchanging pattern of sun, clouds and wind that is the weather while the Observing Self is the unchanging sky. The everchanging weather exists below the unchanging sky. No matter how severe the thunderstorm or intensity the sunshine, the sky sits above all this and cannot be damaged in any way by it. Finding the stable, undisturbed self is an important part of ACT (Harris, 2009, Mudd, 2021; Nikolic, 2021). This Observing Self is a safe place that any client can learn to connect with at any time. The client can contact their Observing Self by watching their thoughts and emotions like they were watching a thunderstorm from a window. There is nothing the client can do about the thunderstorm but to simply wait it out, and at some point, the skies will clear and the sun will return. Connecting with the Thinking Self most of the time accentuates the struggle, while connecting with the Observing Self offers distance and respite (Harris, 2009).

ACT also uses the chess metaphor to explain the Observing Self. The chessboard has two opposing teams – black and white. The two teams are at war with each other just like the mind often is – the client struggles with their positive and negative thoughts in their mental war. The more the client fights, the more they come to believe that their thoughts are who they are – this is cognitive fusion. The Observing Self approach suggests that the individual can get some distance from this war by taking the position of the chessboard. The black and white pieces are still at war – the individual can see and feel this; however, if they take the position of the chessboard, it is not the self that is fighting, it is only the thoughts that are. The idea is to recognise that if the client sees themself as at war, they fuse with the content, so they will be in pain. However, if the person observes the war they can perceive it as a temporary experience that is happening and it will pass (Harris, 2009; Nikolic, 2021).

The Observing Self Case Study

Alexis was a very successful business broker who had worked for the same firm for nearly 20 years. She was a very dedicated team member who had an almost obsessional concern for her clients and getting the best deal she could for them. About a year ago her husband was diagnosed with a slow growing inoperable brain tumour. Alexis wanted to care for him and understood that it would be a long and at times very painful process for both of them. The first few months went well and with additional home care Alexis was able to continue at work but also spend a lot of precious time with her husband. However, after about a year her husband started to experience personality changes and the loving, kind man slowly became irritable, aggressive and started to behave in an unconstrained, socially inappropriate manner. He started to accuse her of not caring for him and of having an affair. Alexis tolerated this for some months but slowly she started to secretly resent him. She came to coaching wanting to stop this resentment and wanting to find a sense of peace with the inevitability of his death. The coach used the ACT techniques of Cognitive Defusion and Expansion to help Alexis get some distance from her struggle. However, Alexis still felt torn to the point where she was unable to concentrate at work and at times felt like resigning even though she knew being a full-time carer for her husband would be even more painful for her.

In the next session the coach introduced the chessboard metaphor. She could immediately see the logic of the explanation but felt utterly unable to apply it in any useful way. She worked with the coach to write down the dialogue between her 'caring self' and her 'resentful self'. This was not easy as Alexis was hesitant about saying out loud that she hated both the things her husband said to her and the tone of his accusations. 'After all it is not my loving husband that is talking, it's the brain tumour', she said. The coach was able to explain that just as it was not really her husband who was horrible, so it was not really her that was resentful, it was her 'resentful self'. This separation of 'selves' freed up the process a lot. The coach then introduced the 'observing self' and they were able to talk about the war between the 'caring self' and the 'resentful self'. Alexis learned to step back and observe this dialogue from a more distant standpoint. The coach then asked Alexis how she could use this chessboard approach on a regular basis. Alexis said she would book a meeting room at work every day at 5.30pm and before going home she would spend 15 minutes quietly exploring the internal battle from the observing-self perspective. This helped a lot and Alexis gradually distanced herself from both her internal struggle and her husband's brutal comments. Alexis supplemented her coaching by using the ACT Coach app and found this very helpful to refer to between coaching sessions. Six months later at her husband's funeral she was able to give a speech about what a wonderful man he had been but how sad it was that the tumour had robbed him of this. She felt a deep sense of pride at having been able to be caring to the very end.

Reflective Practice Exercise: The Observing Self

Think about a dilemma in your life that involves an internal struggle for you.
Example: At work I really want to be collaborative with everyone on the team but Peter is so competitive it makes this very difficult.

Identify the Thinking Self and what it is saying.
Example: My Thinking Self is saying that Peter is a jerk and is always telling people about how he is better than everyone else.

This is part of your internal dialogue, how does your mind answer back?
Example: Peter is just immature and his competitiveness is fuelled by his inadequacy. I need to be the mature collaborative one.

What is the nature of your internal struggle?
Example: The struggle is between my sense of resentment and my desire to rise above it.

What would your Observing Self say to your Thinking Self?
Example: Hey, Thinking Self you are having a ding dong battle and it is really unhelpful. I am going to sit back and watch the fireworks!

How can you apply this in your daily life?
Example: Once a week I will take ten minutes to sit down quietly and get in touch with my Observing Self.

How can you apply this in my coaching practice?
Example: I have several unhappy clients who have this internal struggle. I will introduce the weather and sky metaphor to them and see what happens.

Understanding Your Values

Helping the client understand their values involves clarifying what is most important to them, what sort of person they want to be, what they want to stand for in life. ACT places a great deal of importance on values, as one of its main outcomes is for the client to live a rich and meaningful life. To do this the client must know what matters most to them – that is, their values (Harris, 2009).

Steven Hayes in his 'My ACT Tool Kit' (Hayes, 2021) suggests that writing about values has more impact on behaviour and health than just asking people to pick their values from a list. Values writing involves answering a few simple questions. This process can reduce defensiveness and help clients to be more receptive to change. Hayes (2021) suggests clients spend about ten minutes and address the following questions about how they want to live their life. The instructions are, start by selecting an area of your life, for example, you at work, you at home, you as a friend, you as a member of your community. Think about this area and answer the following six questions from Hayes (2021):

- What do I care about in this area?
- What do I want to *do* in this area that reflects that caring?
- When in my life has this value been important?
- What have I seen in my life when others pursue this value, or not?
- What might I do to manifest this value more in my life?
- When have I violated this value and has that been costly?

(https://stevenchayes.com/wp-content/uploads/
2019/05/Values-Writing.pdf)

Understanding Your Values Case Study

Jill was a senior manager in a telecommunications company. She had had a stellar career up until two months ago when she was asked to apply for a very senior role but then did not get the promotion. She felt bitter and betrayed. When she asked her manager about the situation, she was told that the competition from candidates outside the company was very strong and while she was a great candidate, she was not the best. She came to coaching wanting to understand whether she should leave the company and get another job or stay and continue in her current role. The situation was made complex because she really loved the team of people she worked with, felt a close bond and socialised a lot with them. She feared that leaving the job could jeopardise these relationships. She told the coach that she just could not decide what was best. The coach asked her to undertake the Values Writing exercise and it became clear that she had a small number of very strong values. These were: trust, teamwork, connection and inclusion. When she examined these values, she came to understand that her relationships at work were more important than the role she had. While missing out on the promotion was a blow, it was not worth leaving the company and risking losing the connections she had at work. Jill felt more settled knowing that her decision to stay with the company was based on these deeply held values.

Reflective Practice Exercise: Understanding Your Values

Hayes (2021) has a simple but very effective reflective practice exercise called Writing Your Story. The instructions are quoted below.

> Imagine that the next year is going to be a key year in defining who you are in your life. If you were to become more fully you during this year, while at the same time still supporting those you care about, what would your process of 'becoming more fully you' look like over this time? In what areas do you wish to grow? What kind of person are you yearning to be? If you were writing the chapter of the next year of your life, what would the theme be?
>
> (Hayes, https://stevenchayes.com/wp-content/uploads/2019/05/Writing-Your-Story.pdf)

Taking Committed Action

This involves the client setting goals, based on their values, and taking effective action to live a richer and more fulfilling life. Over time they can ensure larger and larger parts of their life are guided and motivated by their values (Harris, 2009).

The steps in committed action are (Harris, 2009):

- Pick an area of your life that is a high priority for action.
- Select the values you want to live by in this area.
- Develop a set of goals and the steps to gradually get there, guided by your values.
- Take small, mindful and consistent steps to move towards a rich and meaningful life.

Hayes (2021) suggests that the best way to create new habits is to anchor these to regular activities as it is far easier to combine habits than to start a new one. For example, if the client wants to eat more fruit and less refined sugar but they regularly eat a cookie with their morning coffee, they could focus on creating a habit of taking an apple as they pick up their coffee and taking a small bite of it before taking the first sip of coffee.

To strengthen commitment to changing their life for the better, the client can start to make small changes 'just because they choose to'. As they make these changes, they build up their willpower which can then be applied to more important areas (Hayes, 2021). For example:

- The client might choose to go for a week without their favourite TV show just to prove they can.
- Go to bed earlier than usual and get up earlier to build a new habit and generate more time in the morning.
- Wear new and different clothes, eat different food, go a different way to work.

Hayes (2021) reports that when he was dealing with a panic disorder, he built up his commitment to change by taking longer and longer walks. Then as a final commitment he gave up dessert for a year – not because that was important, but precisely because it helped him to build his confidence. When he met this goal, he began to trust that he could do what he said he would and this proved to be a huge benefit to him in the long term.

Taking Committed Action Case Study

Daisy came to executive coaching as she was very unhappy in her office manager role at a large accounting firm. She was a solo mother and had a large mortgage so knew she had to work for many years to come. This combination made her feel trapped and unhappy. In her first session, she and the coach talked about what she really valued and wanted in her life. After a long discussion it appeared that she really valued giving to children and her ideal job was an office manager in a children's charity. Knowing this helped Daisy but she lacked the confidence to apply for such roles. The coach suggested that she try and break down the change into small steps. They agreed upon a range of things, which started by selecting a children's charity and giving a regular donation once a month. Next, Daisy went along to the charity's annual general meeting and made a point of having a conversation with several of the senior leaders. Daisy supplemented her coaching with on-line ACT training and found the exercises on taking committed action very helpful. Over the next six months she invited several of these leaders out for a coffee catch-up and talked about her office management capability and her desire to work in the children's charity sector. She was careful not to directly ask for a job or put any pressure on the other person in the coffee meeting.

Finally, Daisy had a call from the CEO of the charity asking if she knew anyone who was interested in an office manager role at their organisation. Daisy said she was interested and in due course was delighted to get the job. It paid a little less than her accounting firm role but there was less travel, so Daisy was happy to take it. The CEO said that she was impressed with Daisy's commitment to the charity, with her regular donations and her personal interest in the leaders of the organisation. Daisy moved to live a life that was far more meaningful and did it in a way that did not threaten her need for financial stability.

Reflective Practice Exercise: Taking Committed Action

Choose an area of your life where you want to make a change for the better. This might be an improvement in your lifestyle, e.g., exercising more, eating less, spending more time with friends, a change in career. Whatever it is, write it in the space below.
Example: I want to exercise more frequently.

Choose the values you want to live by in this area. Use the Values Writing exercise in the previous section to identify the values you want to live by. Write these below.
Example: The value is Good Health.

Develop a set of goals and the steps to gradually get there, guided by these values.

The goals are:
Example: To be able to run from my house to the beach and back without feeling exhausted.

The small steps to get to the goals are:
Example: I will start by running about a quarter of the way, then walking the rest, so I build up my fitness slowly.

The timeframe to get to the goals is:
Example: I want to be able to run all the way within eight weeks.

The people I will get support from in taking these steps are:
Example: I will text my friend Zac each week with a progress report. Zac is very supportive.

Internet Supplemented ACT tools

There are a wide range of internet-based resources that can be used by clients including the US Department of Veterans Administration free ACT Coach app (https://mobile.va.gov/app/act-coach).

The ACT Coach app was developed for veterans, service members, and other people who are in Acceptance and Commitment Therapy in consultation with a therapist. It offers five types of assistance to clients.

- Psychoeducation – there are a wide range of short articles on ACT including topics such as: What is ACT? What is defusion? What is a value? What are actions?

- Mindfulness – there are a range of audio-guided and self-guided exercises including mindful breathing, observing thoughts and observing emotions.
- Values exercises – these enable clients to record their values within categories such as career/employment, citizenship and family relationships.
- Track your ACT moments – where clients can produce logs of their mindfulness, coping and willingness to experience feelings rather than avoid them.
- Take ACTion – which includes a range of tips, metaphors and ideas to overcome barriers.

Using these Workbook Exercises in Professional Development

The reflective practice exercises in this chapter are designed to be used:

- In individual reflective practice sessions for students or coaches who want to develop their capability.
- With coaches who want to work in pairs to build their skills.
- For supervisors who want to use experiential learning in their work.
- With classroom instructors or academics teaching coaching skills.
- By senior practitioners who want to run professional development sessions for coaches.

Summary

This chapter presented an outline of Acceptance and Commitment Therapy (ACT), then showed how the internet has proven to be a useful platform to supplement ACT therapy and coaching. The focus was on the specific approaches and techniques that can be used effectively in coaching and reflective practice sessions. The chapter does not aim to make the reader an ACT therapist but simply to give any competent coach a range of additional approaches they can use if needed.

14
Using Buddhist Psychology Techniques

INTRODUCTION TO THE CHAPTER

This chapter presents a brief outline of Buddhist psychology based on the work of Trungpa (2005), then explores the use of this contemplative approach in therapy (Wegela, 2014). Research on the effectiveness of Buddhism and its techniques in counselling and psychotherapy is set out. The chapter then focuses on how coaches can use Buddhist psychology to improve their practice. After reading the chapter, any trained coach should be able to use a range of Buddhist psychology techniques in coaching and reflective practice sessions. The chapter does not aim to make the reader a contemplative therapist but to simply give any competent coach a range of additional approaches they can use if needed. For a fuller explanation of contemplative therapy using Buddhist psychology techniques see Brazier (1995, 2003), Trungpa (2005), Siegel (2010, 2012), Wegela (2014) and Strong (2021).

The Nature of Buddhist Psychology

'Buddhist psychology is based on the notion that human beings are fundamentally good. Their most basic qualities are positive ones: openness, intelligence, and warmth' (Trungpa, 2005, p. 8). Therefore, the aim of therapy is to help clients connect back to their basic well-being and goodness. Rather than give them a set of techniques to overcome their problems, Buddhist or contemplative therapy offers a fundamentally different perspective on life and so helps clients experience their intrinsic well-being (Trungpa, 2005).

For the contemplative therapist, one obstacle in helping is the client's typical preoccupation with the past. Many clients want to dwell on and unravel their past, but this can be unhelpful if overdone. The Buddhist perspective emphasises that 'the past is gone, and the future has not yet happened, so we work

DOI: 10.4324/9781003285144-18

with the present situation' (Trungpa, 2005, p. 11). This helps the therapist not to diagnose or categorise but to be fully present and listen empathetically. The Buddhist notions of the impermanence and the transitory nature of things are powerful ideas for moving forward from the current difficulties (Trungpa, 2005). For example, the client may feel deep pain about being treated unfairly about not gaining a promotion. After listening empathetically, the contemplative therapist may introduce the idea of the transitory nature of things and that this matter is now past, so helping the client to move on from the pain and to use their abilities to find other opportunities.

Helping the client develop their fundamental well-being is based on building three main qualities: openness, clarity and compassion (Wegela, 2014). As compassion is a substantial topic in both therapy and coaching it has been dealt with in a chapter of its own in this book. The present chapter focuses on the other important elements of Buddhist psychology.

Openness means quietly allowing your thoughts, feelings and sensations to flow without resistance or defence and to know all that is going on in your life (Wegela, 2014).

> Our path is sometimes rough and sometimes smooth; nonetheless, life is a constant journey. Whether we sleep, eat, dress, study, meditate, attend class . . . whatever we do is regarded as our journey, our path. That path consists of opening oneself to the road, opening oneself to the steps we are about to take. The energy which allows us to go on such a journey is known as discipline. It is the discipline of educating oneself without ego, and it is also known as training one's mind.
>
> (Trungpa, 2005, p. 15)

The second quality is clarity, which is the ability to directly experience our perceptions of taste, smell, touch, hearing and sight without classification or interpretation. It is to 'recognise the contents of our thoughts and mental images without distortion' (Wegela, 2014, p. 7). Buddhist psychology promotes examining the mind, that is, to watch it like we watch a busy city street streaming with cars, trucks, vans, cyclists and pedestrians. This quality of clarity is often called 'mindfulness' which is our ability to note things directly without adding thoughts, evaluations or associated noise (Wegela, 2014).

The Effectiveness of Buddhist Psychology Techniques

Cheng and Tse (2013) report that a range of studies have demonstrated positive outcomes on the use of Buddhism and its techniques in counselling and psychotherapy. Studies documented the use of Buddhist teachings in psychoanalysis and CBT as well as combining Buddhist meditation and mindfulness techniques into psychotherapy. They conducted an integrative review starting with 14,328 references and after screening they selected 146 references – 89% in English and 11% in Chinese. Qualitative and quantitative studies examined the use of Mahayana Buddhism philosophy in hospice care, logotherapy, contemporary psychotherapy, psychoanalysis, Morita therapy, meditation and use in the therapeutic relationship. Other studies included the integrating of śūnyata, or ideas of emptiness, loving-kindness, compassion, empathetic joy and equanimity into therapy. They concluded that these techniques demonstrated positive outcomes but that there was a need for more qualitative research that investigated how best to apply Chinese Buddhist philosophy to therapy and counselling.

Coaching Using Buddhist Psychology

To provide practical insights, Table 14.1 contrasts how a typical client perspective might contrast with the Buddhist perspective.

Table 14.1 Contrasting typical client perspectives with a Buddhist psychology perspective

Typical client perspective	Buddhist psychology perspective
I just want to talk about my problem and the past events that caused it.	I will listen carefully to you and then I would like to encourage you to focus on what is happening now more than what happened then – the past is gone.
I have this problem and I just want it to go away.	Everything in life is impermanent so we can be sure this problem will pass.
I am useless.	I understand how you feel and I want to help you on the path to fundamental well-being and happiness.
I do not want to feel like this.	Tell me more about how you feel right now.
I really do not want to feel this way again.	The path to well-being is to be open to the highs and lows of life, knowing that the feeling will certainly pass.
He made me very angry and upset when he said that.	I can see you became very angry and you still feel upset at this moment.
I have felt this way for so long.	How would you like to feel right now?

The Four Noble Truths

Fundamental to the teaching of the Buddha are the Four Noble Truths.

> Though many people think Buddhism is concerned mainly with mystical enlightenment, Buddhism is based on the idea that we all feel confusion, neurosis, and pain, as Buddha emphasized in his Four Noble Truths. It is from the ground of neurosis that Buddhist psychology has developed.
>
> (Trungpa, 2005, p. 166)

The first Noble Truth is the idea that we all suffer. We can suffer when we get what we do not want, when we do not get what we do want, and even when we get what we want, as it can change (Wegela, 2014).

The second Nobel Truth is the idea that we all suffer because we attempt to 'defend our mistaken sense of who we are and what we feel'(Wegela, 2014, p. 10). We suffer more when we invest our energy in vainly protecting ourselves from impermanence and change, not wanting to experience the reality of inescapable pain. We often maintain our mistaken view that 'this should not be happening' or 'this cannot happen to me' or 'management needs to do something' by pushing away those things that undermine or challenge our beliefs. We find friends or social media posts to support our view of how the world ought to be (Rothberg, 2006).

The third Nobel Truth is that the suffering can stop. Rather than being lost in confusion and the fight with the reality of life, we can accept the real pain that comes with the loss of a career, a job, a loved one or a friend. In contemplative therapy the client is encouraged to wholeheartedly express any pain that they feel but not to get into blaming others or shifting responsibility. Resisting the inevitable pain of life extends the suffering while experiencing the pain directly allows us to get through it and move on.

The fourth Noble Truth is the Eightfold Path to living a good life and achieving well-being. It involves finding the 'right view, right intention, right speech, right action, right livelihood, right effort, right mindfulness and right samadhi' [concentration] (Brazier, 2003, p. 15). In summary, it means living a life guided by the ideas of compassionately looking after ourselves and others.

Using the Four Noble Truths in Coaching: A Case Study

Zac was a talented engineer who was in the middle of a very messy divorce. His wife had had an affair with a good friend of his and then left him, saying she no longer loved him. This was very painful for Zac who was shocked by the suddenness and bitterness of the separation. To make matters worse his wife seemed to be trying to turn their two boys against him and the youngest would often come home from a weekend with his mother saying, 'Mummy loves me more than you do'. Zac came to coaching because the grief and distress of his life was interfering with his ability to concentrate at work. For the first three sessions Zac told and retold his story with heartfelt grief and pain. In the fourth session he told the coach, 'I know I have been kicked in the guts, but when I lie awake at night going over and over and over the same stuff, I know I am not doing myself any good'. At this point the coach introduced the idea that suffering equals pain plus resistance, which means that if you resist the inevitable pain in life you suffer more. Zac could see that his struggle was adding to his suffering. The coach encouraged Zac to express his pain fully. Zac asked the coach what he should do instead of struggling. The coach asked Zac what sort of father he wanted to be. Zac answered, 'I want to spend time with my boys, that is the greatest gift I can give them'. The coach asked Zac to spell out what specifically he wanted to do this weekend with his boys. Zac said his oldest was really into making pancakes and he wanted to do this with him, and then clean up the mess without complaining. His youngest had often asked him to be taken to the local amusement park and often in the past Zac had said he was too busy with work. In the next coaching session Zac seemed much more content, saying he enjoyed a great weekend with his boys and that focusing on living his life right was much more important than reliving his grievances.

Reflective Practice Exercise: The Four Noble Truths

Spend some time to think about and write down an area of your life where you struggle or have difficulties.
Example: I struggle with the fact that my dear old mentor and friend Tina is dying.

Close your eyes and think about the reality of pain and suffering in your and other peoples' lives.
Example: When I do this, I feel the suffering of my friend and my own too.

Next try to make a distinction in your mind between the inevitable pain of loss and the suffering that you generate by struggling with the inevitable and wanting things that will never be.
Example: Death is sad but inevitable, so I do feel this pain. However, I am also struggling with the fact that I will not see Tina again.

Now try to accept the inevitable pain but let go of the suffering caused by your own struggles.
Example: I accept the pain of Tina's death but I want to let go of my own suffering, I accept that Tina will be gone soon – fighting this reality is pointless.

Finally, think about some changes you may want to make in your life to live in a more caring way towards yourself and others.
Example: I will make the most of the limited time I have with Tina to gain as much wisdom as I can.

How did you feel doing this exercise?
Example: I can really see how my own struggling makes things worse and that acceptance of what I cannot change is a difficult but powerful thing.

Is there a way in which you can apply the ideas in the Four Noble Truths to your own coaching practice?
Example: This is a very important set of ideas that I can see myself using in coaching when it is appropriate.

Using Buddhist Psychology to Deal with Difficult Emotions

Szczygiel (2014) presents a conceptual framework for assisting clients with difficult emotions that draws upon Buddhist thinking. The four techniques involve: sitting with, middle path, healthy interdependency, and compassion. McCormick and Forsyth (2019) used this framework in a coaching context as set out below.

Sitting with means that the coaching client feels courageous enough to experience and be present with their, typically painful, emotional experience. This may take place during the coaching session, or more importantly on regular occasions between sessions. Sitting with is closely related to mindfulness (being in the moment) and is an important step in dealing with difficult emotions because it helps to overcome the powerful reinforcing but ultimately futile aspects of avoidance. This not wanting to feel difficult emotions is sometimes called experiential avoidance and it involves trying to escape from unpleasant thoughts, feelings, memories and sensations even when doing so causes harm in the long run (Harris, 2009). For example, in coaching, a client may talk about being given extra work because they are very capable but may feel deeply resentful and angry about this. Just sitting with this resentment and anger will often enable them to feel the full intensity of the emotion but then over a period of 15 to 20 minutes they may be able to watch as the emotion subsides. This may allow the client to see that the extra work is not a punishment but a vote of confidence by their boss. It may also free up enough energy to enable the client to speak to their boss about how they are happy to do this extra work but have little current capacity to take on other things at his stage.

When the coach uses the idea of the *middle path*, he or she is encouraging the client to find a balance or middle ground between *holding on* and *letting go*, between rigidity and flexibility, between hating and loving, between embracing and avoiding. This approach challenges the client to give up their range of false dichotomies such as good or bad, positive or negative. This is helpful when the difficult emotions the client is struggling with involve both their inner emotional life and important others. For example, a client may see an aggressive manager as heartless, mean and sociopathic. After discussion, that client may come to see that this manager is overcompensating for insecurity and feelings of inadequacy. Taking the middle path may enable the client to not impulsively hand in their resignation letter but to talk to the boss about moving to another role with a different team because of this personality clash. The middle path may be a much better outcome for both the client and their organisation.

Healthy interdependency is the ability to balance the need to be a self-determined, free individual yet still rely on the kindness and concern of others. This can involve the client in accepting their unique individuality but also appreciating the impact others have on their well-being. For example, a client may want to leave their current position where they have felt overlooked and start their own company. They may feel torn because they want to strike out on their own and yet want to contract back to their company so that they have a financial buffer to bridge the gap between their former regular salary and the uncertain income of their own business. Using the idea of healthy interdependence, they may come to see that temporarily relying on their former company is a smart way to facilitate the start of their own business.

Compassion can be defined as the acceptance of and sensitivity towards the suffering of oneself and others (Szczygiel, 2014). It motivates clients to take action to help the physical, mental or emotional pain of others and themselves, while ensuring they do not become overwhelmed by such difficult emotions. This concept is explored in depth in the next chapter.

In coaching, these Buddhist concepts are used to help clients deal with frustration, anger, guilt, shame and pain and to move on from these difficult emotions and enrich their lives.

Using Buddhist Psychology to Deal with Difficult Emotions: A Case Study

Jasmin was a fluent Mandarin speaker who worked in the China Division of a major import–export company. She came to coaching to better manage her stress. In the first session it became clear that there were two main sources of stress for Jasmin. She worked for a very traditional boss who was uncaring and demanding. In addition, her husband was not very supportive of her work or understanding about the difficulties she was having. This combination generated lots of painful emotions and distress for her. Jasmin had been brought up in the Buddhist tradition and so it was an easy decision for the coach to suggest using the techniques of: sitting with, middle path, healthy interdependence and compassion. In the second session, Jasmin and the coach explored her challenges at work. Jasmin made it clear that, although her boss was very difficult, she really enjoyed working in the China Division and so did not want to look for another role. Also, her boss had stated directly to the team that he was going to retire at the end of the year, so Jasmin decided to stay in the job and wait things out.

She had practised Buddhist meditation for some years but had given up as she felt she had 'too much noise in her head'. The coach asked if she was willing to try to get back into regular meditation but this time with a greater willingness to sit with the noise in her head and quietly let it go rather than trying to fight it. Jasmin felt that this could be really useful and in the next session reported that she had gained a greater sense of acceptance which led to a better peace of mind. The coach went on to talk about the middle path and finding a balance between working hard but also not having work dumped on her by her boss. Jasmin found the idea of pushing back with her boss a challenge but during the next week was able to say to him that she was unable to take on more work at this stage and to her surprise he did not argue.

The idea of healthy interdependence was very easy for Jasmin to understand as she had an excellent relationship with her team members. With her husband it was more difficult, although Jasmin concluded that he would never be very supportive and that she should simply give up on expecting him to be so. In between sessions, she made a conscious effort to ask for more support and encouragement from her team members and subsequently this proved to be helpful.

The idea of compassion became very important to Jasmin as it motivated her to be more caring towards herself. She learned to not only accept her emotional pain but to be gentle and considerate towards herself when she was feeling bad.

Overall, the coaching was very successful as it tapped into Jasmin's understanding of Buddhist philosophy and provided a common language of change for her and the coach.

Reflective Practice Exercise: Using Buddhist Psychology to Deal with Difficult Emotions

Write a few sentences below about a difficulty you have in life.
Example: The death of my friend has resulted in me thinking more about my own eventual death.

Consider the four Buddhist coaching techniques: sitting with, middle path, healthy interdependency and compassion. How can you apply these to help you better deal with your difficult emotions?
Example: I can see that sitting with, middle path and compassion are all relevant to me. I will apply 'sitting with' and see how I feel.

What is your action plan?
Example: I will do a simple meditation on my own eventual death once a week on a Sunday evening after dinner. I will simply imagine myself in my nineties, feeling old, frail and preparing myself for the end. I will take the time to sit with and get used to the idea of death. I will reflect upon my life and what I have learned.

How will you hold yourself accountable for the change?
Example: I go to a meditation retreat every year in the autumn and will make a point of discussing my 'sitting with' experience with one of the retreat organisers.

The Importance of Meditation for the Coach

A common theme that runs through many Buddhist psychology and contemplative therapy books is the idea that if the therapist or coach wants to be effective and talk with conviction about openness, clarity and compassion to their clients they need to have an established, regular meditation practice themselves (Wegela, 2014).

> Here the psychotherapist meets her first client: herself. In the practice of sitting meditation, she has no compulsion to reduce, alter, or reject anything or anyone. All are welcome. All are simply thoughts. They manifest in varying intensity or appeal, and endless flavours, but their nature is always the same.
>
> (Trungpa, 2005, Kindle Location 166)

This does not mean, however, that the contemplative therapist or coach should become a Buddhist. As Trungpa (2005) asks, should an authentic psychologist become a Buddhist? Trungpa answers – of course not. The ideas of openness, clarity and compassion make perfect sense outside the Buddhist order.

Reflective Practice Exercise: The Importance of Meditation for the Coach

Do you use Buddhist psychology techniques in your coaching? Please describe what you do?
Example: I do use Buddhist psychology in my coaching. I find that getting my clients to sit with their pain is a very powerful way of reducing its intensity.

Do you have a meditation practice? Please describe what you do.
Example: My meditation practice is sporadic. Some months I do it every day and other months only a few times.

How do you want to improve your meditation practice? Please describe what you want to do.

Example: I want to use meditation for a few minutes everyday to prepare myself mentally for my coaching. I know that this will help me to be more present with my clients.

Are there areas for improvement or change in your use of Buddhist psychology techniques in your coaching? Detail these below.

Example: I want to read more about contemplative therapy and apply these ideas in my coaching.

Hall (2013) studied the impact of mindfulness meditation on coaching using an online international survey of over 150 coaches. The survey indicated that coaches practise mindfulness to help with the following:

- 74% said it was useful to be more present in the moment.
- 73% to be more self-aware.
- 67% to manage stress better.
- 65% to be more present with clients.

The reasons coaches explicitly used mindfulness with clients were as follows:

- 70% said it was to help clients be more self-aware.
- 59% to be calmer and less anxious.
- 55% to better manage stress and be more centred.
- 51% to better manage their reactions and responses.

Passmore and Marianetti (2007) suggest four specific uses of mindfulness for coaches:

- Preparing for the coaching session.
- Maintaining focus during the session.
- Remaining emotionally detached during coaching.
- Teaching mindfulness techniques to the client.

These uses from Passmore and Marianetti (2007) are explored more below.

Preparing for Coaching

Coaches are often very busy and can hurry from one session to another. This means coaches can be focused on ensuring they get to the right session, in the right place, at the right time rather than on being mentally and emotionally prepared for the session. One option is for the coach to spend four or five minutes before each session undertaking mindfulness meditation to help centre his or herself and prepare for the upcoming coaching. The brief meditation could involve breathing exercises and a body-scan to check the physical sensations being experienced. This can be followed by a review of the notes from the last meeting and planning for the coming session.

Maintaining Focus in the Session

Mindfulness can also be useful to help the coach to keep focused during the session as coaches sometimes suffer from distraction and a wandering mind during sessions. Mindfulness can be used during coaching sessions to maintain single-mindedness and watchfulness with an emphasis on continually bringing the mind back to the client. Intense listening to the client is only possible if the coach can minimise their internal dialogue.

Remaining Emotionally Detached

Mindfulness can be used to assist the coach to manage their own feelings, moods and emotions during coaching sessions and to remain suitably emotionally detached. Effective coaches can achieve a balance between subjectively experiencing the client's emotions and yet being objectively detached and looking for patterns of significance in the client's story. Being overwhelmed or flooded by the client's emotions and experiences is not helpful for assisting the client to find solutions and move forward with their challenges. On the other hand, being too detached can come across to the client as disinterest and even arrogance. To manage this balance, mindfulness techniques can help the coach to provide both empathy and constructive challenge.

Teaching Mindfulness to Clients

Appropriately trained coaches can teach mindfulness as a formal meditative practice or as an informal everyday awareness technique. If coaches are to teach or advocate mindfulness, they will need to have personal, direct, on-going experience with mindfulness practice. Segal et al. (2002) suggest that a swimming instructor is not someone who knows the physics of how bodies behave in water, but he or she does know how to swim. It is through personal practice and understanding that the coach can assist their clients.

Segal et al. (2002) provide a range of helpful suggestions on the skills needed in mindfulness teachings including:

- Concentration: this is critical to mindfulness and is the ability to focus one's full attention on one object or activity.
- Awareness: the conscious awareness and knowledge that life is 'as it is'.
- Acceptance: while awareness is important, however, one must accept the reality of life and let go of unhelpful struggles.
- De-centring: building the client's ability to see thoughts as just thoughts and not as reality, the truth or something that needs to be obeyed or even taken seriously.
- Being rather than doing: in this context *doing* means getting on with things while *being* means experiencing the moment-by-moment sensations as they ebb and flow. The coach can encourage the client to slow down, to rush around less, to enjoy the simple pleasures of life and when necessary, experience their painful moments going by.

Mindfulness Techniques in Meditation

In her book, *Mindful Coaching* (Hall, 2013), Liz Hall used the FEEL model to describe the mindful steps that coaches can undertake during their meditation practice:

F – Focus on what is going on – your thoughts, feelings and sensations.
E – Explore gently what is happening for you during the meditation being open and non-judgemental.

E – Embrace and accept what is going on without grasping or pushing – acknowledge what has arisen.

L – Let go of the thoughts, sensations and feelings, no matter whether they are good, bad or indifferent.

Reflective Practice Exercise: Using Mindfulness in Your Coaching Practice

Do you want to use the mindfulness approach more in your coaching?
Example: Yes, I want to be more mindful in my coaching sessions and spend less time thinking up clever advice for my clients.

How can you use mindfulness to better prepare for your coaching sessions?
Example: I will spend time each day reading my session notes and just sitting with the ideas that float into my mind.

How can you use mindfulness to better maintain focus during your coaching sessions?
Example: This is important for me to do as it quietens down my inner conversation.

How can you use mindfulness to better remain emotionally detached during your coaching sessions?
Example: I regularly coach a man who is very emotional, and I often feel myself getting drawn into a whirlpool of my own feelings. I will use mindfulness to be more compassionate but professionally detached in my sessions.

Do you want to improve the regularity of your own meditation practice as a way of improving your coaching skills? How?
Example: I will use the Health app on my phone to record my meditation every day.

Do you want to start to teach your clients formal or informal mindfulness practices?
Example: I feel I need to be a better meditation practitioner before I teach mindfulness to my clients.

Competencies for the Contemplative Coach

These five competences are based on the Tibetan Buddhist five wisdoms and energies (Trungpa, 2005). They are:

- Being present and letting be.
- Seeing clearly and not judging.

- Recognising and appreciating differences.
- Acting skilfully and letting go.

Wegela (2014, pp. 37–38)

1. Being present and letting go

As a contemplative coach our ability to be present with all our experiences is one of the most important things we offer our clients. If we are aware of whatever arises in us and sit with it, we are being fully present with our clients. As a coach we need to be aware of what we are thinking and feeling and not let these things distract us from being with the client. Coaches are often very well trained and have a strong need to be the 'expert'. However, in contemplative coaching it is a real advantage to not know and not feel the need to be the expert. Not knowing helps us to stay present, be curious and is a valuable skill. Less experienced coaches often feel that they need to be of help and solve problems. This can often get in the way of allowing the client to talk things through and get to the point where they develop their own unique solutions. Being present, letting go and sitting with uncertainty in coaching is important as often silence gives the client valuable time to think and make their own decisions (Wegela, 2014).

2. Seeing clearly and not judging

Seeing clearly and not judging is easy to say but difficult to do. During sessions coaches often want to analyse, categorise and even diagnose. This process can often stop the coach from listening clearly, seeing accurately and not judging. While coaching frameworks and models are very useful, they can easily be overdone and the inexperienced coach can find themselves thinking about where they are in the model rather than what the client is really saying. To see our clients clearly we need to understand our own preferences and prejudices. Knowledge of this is one of the things that can be obtained through the coach's own meditation practice. Wegela (2014) suggests that coaches practise 'being more stupid' and asking questions such as, 'What does anxiety mean for you?' or 'Are you saying you are really angry with your boss?' or 'Please tell me more about this, I really want to understand'.

3. Recognising and appreciating differences

Contemplative coaches recognise that they may see their world very differently from their clients. While many coaches have gone through personal difficulties themselves, these are often very different to the problems faced by the clients who come to see them. This is often the case in executive coaching, where clients are interacting with CEOs who are under great pressure from boards of directors, their staff and their other stakeholders. The coach may have never experienced such issues.

Inexperienced coaches often find that they are very keen to find points of similarity with their clients. This can often lead to coaches telling their own story and hoping to find a connection. This can be useful to build empathy but can easily be overdone. The clients who come to coaching typically want to be able to tell their own story and believe that they are unique in facing their own particular set of troublesome circumstances (Wegela, 2014).

4. Connecting with others and cultivating the relationship

According to Wegela (2014) Buddhist psychology suggests that connecting with our clients is not something that we need to do deliberately, rather it is something that we can allow to happen naturally over time, taking care not to create obstacles. A typical obstacle that interferes with being fully present in a session occurs when the coach does not want to have uncomfortable feelings, such as during an awkward silence, which the coach may fill with a comment or question, and so break the client's chain of thought. Or the coach may want to hold on to pleasant feelings such as believing their insights are critical and not listening carefully to the client's doubts about them.

For the contemplative coach the therapeutic relationship is the primary vehicle for healing and change. This idea fits well with O'Broin and Palmer's (2010) approach which indicates that the best predictor of coaching outcome is the quality of the working alliance or coaching relationship.

5. Acting skilfully and letting go

Wegela (2014) suggests that contemplative coaching does not have a set range of specific tips and techniques for acting skilfully. Rather the approach is for the coach to show up with an open and calm mind and to respond to what happens in a moment-by-moment way. It is important for the contemplative coach to tailor their actions to each therapeutic relationship. From a Buddhist psychology perspective, the aim of coaching is to reduce the clients' suffering and to better enable them to be fully aware of and experience the pains and pleasures of life. Acting skilfully in coaching means being responsive and creative. It is about being approachable, receptive and open to what the client brings to the session. It is also about listening for clues as to what might work to reduce the client's suffering. For example, a client may say, 'My cup is always empty' which may trigger the question from the coach, 'Is it equally empty all the time?' This may start a creative period of conversation where the coach and client look at the times when the 'cup is not quite empty' and find skilful ways to build on it.

Being creative and responsive can mean that sometimes we are wrong. It is important for coaches to be able to admit that they are wrong even if this makes them feel uncomfortable. Contemplative coaches can allow themselves to feel the physical discomfort of being wrong without the need to defend themselves or give in to other unhelpful impulses. During meditation the practitioner aims to let go every time they breathe out and in the same way coaches can let go when they are wrong or when holding on to a mistaken viewpoint (Wegela, 2014).

Reflective Practice Exercise: Assessing Your Mindfulness Competencies

How would you rate your own level of development in terms of being present and letting be?

Not well developed 1   2   3   4   5   6   7   8   9   10 Very well developed

How would you like to improve?
Example: I rate myself as 6 and will improve by using mindfulness more in my sessions to be more present.

How would you rate your own level of development in terms of seeing clearly and not judging?

Not well developed 1   2   3   4   5   6   7   8   9   10 Very well developed

How would you like to improve?
Example: I rate myself as 8 but will improve by using mindfulness to be less judgemental.

How would you rate your own level of development in terms of recognising and appreciating differences?

Not well developed 1   2   3   4   5   6   7   8   9   10 Very well developed

How would you like to improve?
Example: Same response as the last question.

How would you rate your own level of development in terms of acting skilfully and letting go?

Not well developed 1   2   3   4   5   6   7   8   9   10 Very well developed

How would you like to improve?
Example: I will use short periods of meditation before sessions to help me act more skilfully in my coaching.

When to Use Buddhist Psychology Techniques in Coaching

Buddhist psychology techniques are useful if the client is familiar with Buddhist concepts either because they grew up in that tradition or have become interested in it, for example through learning meditation. Building on the tradition that they learned as a child, or through meditation practice, can be a rapid way to connect empathetically with these clients.

The approach is also very useful if the client is suffering with an uncontrollable situation, for example a chronic disease or they have a spouse or partner with such a disease. The Four Noble Truths messages can help clients to accept the inevitable pain of life without making this worse by struggling with it and inducing additional suffering.

Using These Workbook Exercises in Professional Development

The reflective practice exercises in this chapter are designed to be used:

- In individual reflective practice sessions for students or coaches who want to develop their capability.
- With coaches who want to work in pairs to build their skills.
- For supervisors who want to use experiential learning in their work.
- With classroom instructors or academics teaching coaching skills.
- By senior practitioners who want to run professional development sessions for executive coaches.

Summary

This chapter presents a brief outline of Buddhist psychology based on the work of Trungpa, (2005), then it explores the use of this contemplative approach in therapy (Wegela, 2014). The chapter also focuses on how coaches can use Buddhist psychology to improve their practice. After reading the chapter any trained coach should be able to use a range of Buddhist psychology techniques in coaching and reflective practice sessions.

15
Using Compassion-focused Techniques

INTRODUCTION TO THE CHAPTER

This chapter aims to present a brief outline of two compassion-focused therapeutic approaches, firstly, Compassion-focused Therapy (CFT) developed by Gilbert (2005, 2009, 2010a, 2010b, 2014) and secondly, Mindful Self-Compassion (MSC) developed by Neff and Germer (2018) and Germer and Neff (2019). The chapter then focuses on a series of specific approaches and techniques from the two compassion approaches that can be used effectively in coaching and reflective practice sessions. The chapter does not aim to make the reader a CFT or MSC therapist but simply to give any competent coach a range of additional approaches they can use if needed. For a fuller explanation of CFT see Gilbert (2005, 2009, 2010a, 2010b, 2014) and for MSC see Neff (2003), Neff, Rude and Kirkpatrick (2007), Neff and Germer (2013, 2018), Neff and Pommier (2013).

Compassion-focused Therapy

Compassion-focused Therapy grew out of evolutionary biology and psychology and, according to Gilbert (2014), is based on the following understandings:

- The human brain is shaped by evolution, that is, the process that results in the survival and reproduction of individuals best adjusted to their environment. This has led to many mental well-being problems, for example the hypervigilant individuals who were more aware of threats survived and reproduced, so hypervigilance increased over evolutionary time. However, in modern society, with a relatively low level of threat, this hypervigilance becomes overdone and has led to many individuals suffering from anxiety and distress.

DOI: 10.4324/9781003285144-19

- The human brain has evolved for social processing and so is highly attuned to relationships, so our social interaction is critical to understanding mental well-being.
- Our relationships with ourselves can easily lack perspective and result in shame, and unhelpful self-criticism that can cause many mental well-being problems.
- Our recently evolved complex thinking abilities impact on our social motives and emotions, for example we can easily imagine a wide range of social slurs and insults and their 'disastrous' impact on our lives.
- Training people to be compassionate towards themselves and others has many physiological and psychological benefits (Desbordes et al., 2013), and well-being outcomes (Hoffmann et al., 2011).

Gilbert (2014) suggests that the group nature of our human evolution and survival has resulted in a range of important social interactions that include: wanting to be cared for, care giving, cooperation, competition and sexual relations. Each of these can be seen from the point of view of the self, the other and each has potential harmful aspects as illustrated in Table 15.1 which has been adapted from Gilbert (2014).

Table 15.1 Social interactions from the view point of the self, the other and their potentially harmful aspects

	Viewed from the point of view of the self.	Viewed from the point of view of the other.	Potential harmful aspects.
Being cared for	I need care, protection and guidance from others.	I can provide protection, reassurance and stimulation etc.	If others are not cared for, they withdraw, can be exploitative, threatening or harmful.
Care giving	I can provide others with care, protection and reassurance.	I can receive care, protection and reassurance.	If care is not given, the person can become overwhelmed, unable to provide care to others and can feel guilty about this.

	Viewed from the point of view of the self.	Viewed from the point of view of the other.	Potential harmful aspects.
Cooperation	I can be of value to others by sharing and helping.	I value others contribution and reciprocity.	If there is no cooperation the person can feel cheated, unappreciated and shamed for not cooperating.
Competition	I have either inferior or superior roles, am more or less powerful, harmful and benevolent.	I see others' inferior or superior roles, they are more or less powerful, harmful and benevolent.	If there is strong competition it can result in involuntary subordination, shaming and abuse.
Sexual	I am attractive and desirable.	I see others as attractive and desirable.	If there is no sexual attraction the other can feel undesirable and rejected.

This table illustrates that in nearly all aspects of our social interaction there are both positive and negative elements. CFT is designed to assist clients with the negative self-talk and emotions that are often generated in our social interaction. Gilbert (2014) outlines three emotional regulation systems that are often out of balance in clients who are distressed. These three systems are (1) drive, excitement and vitality, (2) contentment, safety and connection, (3) anger, anxiety and disgust. For example, a strong work drive can lead to positive outcomes such as excitement; however, it can also lead to frequent frustration with others and in turn little sense of contentment or safety. CFT helps clients address this imbalance.

A key to addressing this imbalance is compassion, which can be defined as:

- An intellectual and emotional awareness of suffering.
- A sympathetic concern for others who are suffering.
- A wish to see others relieved of this.
- A willingness to help do this (adapted from Gilbert, 2014, p. 19).

Recent Research on Compassion-focused Therapy

A sample of large-scale review research on CFT is presented below.

Wilson et al. (2019) undertook a systematic review and meta-analysis of whether self-compassion-related therapies, including CFT, are effective in improving self-compassion and decreasing psychopathology in clinical and subclinical populations. They found a total of 2,263 relevant studies of which 22 used randomised controlled trials. Their results indicated that self-compassion-related therapies produced improvements in all three outcomes of self-compassion, anxiety and depressive symptoms. Overall, this review provides evidence that these compassion-related therapies improve self-compassion and decrease psychopathology at a rate similar to other active psychological treatments.

Craig et al. (2020) reviewed research examining the effectiveness of CFT in clinical populations. They concluded that CFT showed promise in improving a wide range of mental health problems, especially when this therapy was used in a group approach with at least 12 hours duration. CFT was also well accepted by clients and clinicians. They suggested that there was a need for further randomised control trials that could reduce the existing research methodology limitations.

In a recent meta-analysis Thomason and Moghaddam (2021) assessed whether CFT was effective in improving self-esteem. They reviewed papers that had both 'compassion-based' and 'self-esteem' as a variable or outcome. They identified ten eligible papers and found that eight studies demonstrated a positive overall effect size which increased slightly when lowest quality studies were removed. They concluded that compassion-focused therapy or related compassion-based interventions can be effective in improving self-esteem.

In conclusion there is a range of research to indicate the value of CFT in building self-esteem and reducing clinical symptoms. CFT is therefore likely to be of value when used in coaching.

Using Compassion-focused Techniques in Coaching: Case Study

Julie was a social worker who originally came to coaching to talk about career options as she was feeling frustrated in her present role. However, within the first ten minutes of the initial session she was in tears talking about her physically abusive mother. Julie had been about ten years old when her mother had started to hit her. This abuse continued until Julie was about 14 years old and was physically stronger than her mother. Julie left home at 18 years and went to live in a nearby city with some friends. She was an academically talented woman and so was able to get a scholarship to study social work at university. She gained a job immediately after finishing her degree and married two years later. About ten years after this Julie made a great effort to reconcile her relationship with her mother. By now her mother was in her late sixties and not well. Julie and her mother spent a lot of time together and were able to talk about the pressure and strain when Julie was about ten years old and how this had led to the physical abuse. This was very helpful to Julie, although she felt hurt and deeply resentful because of the abuse she suffered. Julie explained that she liked her 60-year-old mother but hated the mother who had abused her. Julie and the coach talked about self-compassion and the need that Julie had to heal her psychological scars. The coach taught Julie the Developing Your Compassionate Self technique (see below) and this did reduce the pain somewhat. Julie practised this approach three times a week for a month. In the next session she reported feeling that the self-compassion was very helpful and that she was slowly letting go of the old pain. She reported being more comfortable when visiting her mother. Julie also said that she had used the approach when dealing with some of her very challenging social work clients. It seemed to be useful in this situation as well.

Compassion Building Exercises

There are several compassion-focused exercises produced by Gilbert (2010b) that are useful in CFC and a few of these have been adapted and are presented below.

Reflective Practice Exercise: Soothing Rhythmic Breathing

Find a time and place where you are not likely to be disturbed for 10 minutes or so. Sit comfortably in a chair with your feet flat on the floor and rest your hands on your lap. Gently close your eyes or look down at the floor a short distance in front of you.

Now gently focus on your breathing. Put one hand on your stomach just below your ribs and feel your diaphragm move as you breathe in and out. Quietly watch your breathing for a minute or two. Put your hand back on your lap.

You may find your breathing becomes slightly slower and deeper than normal. Let your in-breath last about 3 seconds . . . hold for a second . . . and then breath out for about 3 seconds. Make sure your breathing is smooth and even.

Spend some time just focusing on your breathing as the air comes in through your nose down into your lungs, then as your diaphragm lifts feel the air moving out through your nose.

Now turn your attention to your body and feel the weight of your body on the chair and your feet on the floor. Feel supported . . . at rest . . . in the moment.

Your mind will wander and that is okay, just gently guide yourself back to the awareness of your body and the flow of air coming in and out of your nose. There is no need to do anything but watch with curiosity and openness.

If you feel uncomfortable focusing on your breathing, just observe any object a few feet in front of you. Any object will do but a leaf or a small stone or candle is perfect. Just gaze at your object as best you can. When your mind wonders gently bring it back to the object.

Allow your breath and the view of the object to soothe you as much as you can.

After about 10 minutes slowly open your eyes, stretch if you want and bring your awareness back to the present moment. Quietly get on with the rest of your day.

What did you observe during the exercise?
Example: I felt restless at first but then calmness.

Are you able to observe what happens when you sit like this without evaluating the experience as good or bad?
Example: Not being evaluative is difficult and I will need to practise this.

Can you gently bring your mind back from wondering over and over again and accept that this is just how the process works?
Example: Initially I thought my wondering mind was a sign of failure, but now I see it differently.

What did you learn from this exercise?
Example: Soothing rhythmic breathing is important for slowing down.

How could you use this approach in your own coaching practice?
Example: After I have practised this a lot, I should feel comfortable using it with some of my clients.

Reflective Practice Exercise: Developing Your Compassionate Self

This exercise is designed to help you to build a view of yourself as a wise, strong, warm and responsible person.

Find a time and place where you are not likely to be disturbed for 20 minutes or so. Sit comfortably in a chair with your feet flat on the floor and rest your hands on your lap. Gently close your eyes or look down at the floor a short distance in front of you. When you feel rested and ready, start the exercise below.

Think about one or two compassionate people who you admire. These people will typically display wisdom, strength, warmth and responsibility. Spend two or three minutes sitting quietly thinking about them and their qualities.

Next, think about the ways in which they are wise. Do they have a good understanding of the human condition, how and why humans behave as they do? Then imagine yourself slowly developing these qualities. See yourself improving your ability to understand your own situation and that of others. See yourself developing the ability to understand your own mind and others' minds.

Then when you are ready and have a sense of your own wisdom, switch to imagining having strength, maturity and authority. Explore your body posture, your facial expressions, imagine ways in which you are getting stronger and more mature. Remember you are imagining yourself as a person that understands your own difficulties and those of others, in a non-judgemental way, and is sensitive and tolerant towards others' suffering.

When you are ready, focus on the qualities of warmth, building up a sense of your own gentle friendliness. Imagine yourself being warm, friendly and kind. See the sense of warmth in your posture, in your facial expression, in your voice, in your behaviour.

Then switch to imagining yourself building a sense of responsibility. See yourself as someone who has no interest in condemning or blaming themselves or others. Imagine you only want to do the best for yourself and others.

Lastly, imagine yourself being compassionate to yourself and to others. See this in your facial expression, in your words and in your actions. Help yourself and others out of difficult situations. Focus on committing yourself to becoming a more compassionate person.

It does not matter if you cannot see yourself as having all these qualities right now. Just imagine yourself slowly moving along the path of compassionate self-development. Notice how different you feel when you see yourself as wise, warm, responsible and compassionate.

During this exercise you will find that your mind wanders and you think of all sorts of other things. This is perfectly normal and typical. Just gently bring yourself back to the development path of compassion. Regular practice of this approach will help to build a stronger sense of your own compassion towards yourself and others.

What did you observe during the exercise?
Example: At first, I felt awkward and silly doing this, but after a few minutes it felt more natural.

What did you do that helped most to develop a sense of compassion?
Example: I can be very judgemental towards the junior team members at work and I will use this exercise to become more compassionate towards them.

How can you better develop compassion towards both yourself and others?
Example: I want to start by developing more compassion towards myself, to forgive myself for the mistakes I have made in life.

How and where would you like to practise this exercise?
Example: I can see I have a long way to go in developing self-compassion so I will practise this two or three times a week in the morning when I get up.

What did you learn from this exercise?
Example: I thought self-compassion was fixed and innate but now I can see that it can be learned.

How could you use this approach in your own coaching practice?
Example: So many of my clients are overly demanding of themselves and this could be very beneficial.

Mindful Self-Compassion

In a rather different approach to the topic, Mindful Self-Compassion (MSC) combines both mindfulness and compassion development into a single self-compassion programme. MSC is a mix of psychotherapy and personal training that is used to enhance self-compassion and was originally designed for use with the general public. It does not aim to explore past trauma as psychotherapy does but to teach a way of building kindness and understanding towards oneself and others (Germer & Neff 2019).

The concept of self-compassion in this context was developed from Buddhist psychology over a decade ago. It is designed to help individuals deal with their own inner dialogue and relationship with themselves in a compassionate rather than self-critical way. It is particularly useful when individuals face personal suffering. Self-compassion combines self-kindness, common humanity and mindfulness. Self-kindness means being gentle, supportive and understanding towards oneself. Common humanity means understanding that, like everyone else, we all make mistakes, fail and live imperfect lives. Mindfulness means building a balanced awareness of one's own present moment experience and not just focusing on the negative aspects of one's life (Germer & Neff, 2019).

The Effectiveness of Mindful Self-Compassion

Research on the effectiveness of self-compassion shows a positive relationship with psychological health (Barnard & Curry, 2011; Zessin et al., 2015). MacBeth and Gumley (2012) in a meta-analysis found a strong inverse relationship between self-compassion and depression, anxiety and stress in 20 studies. Self-compassion has been found to be associated with happiness, optimism and life satisfaction (Hollis-Walker & Colosimo, 2011; Neff et al., 2007), as well as to increased motivation, health behaviours, positive body image and resilience (Albertson et al., 2014; Allen et al., 2012; Breines & Chen, 2012; Sbarra et al., 2012). Self-compassionate individuals have been found to be more likely to understand others' perspectives, forgive them and be altruistic than those who are low in self-compassion (Neff & Pommier, 2013). People with high self-compassion are seen by their romantic partners as more supportive and emotionally connected and less controlling than those with low self-compassion (Neff & Beretvas 2013). In conclusion, there is a range of research to indicate the value of MSC in building psychological well-being and reducing distress. MSC is therefore likely to be of value when used in coaching.

Compassion-focused Coaching

Compassion-focused Coaching (CFC) uses the models and methods of CFT and MSC and applies these with the coaching population. Palmer (2013) has discussed the use of the compassion-focused approach with sports coaches. Passmore and Sinclair (2020) in their book, *Becoming a Coach: The Essential ICF Guide*, outline the 'Cultivating a compassionate mind' technique in which the client looks around at fellow passengers on public transport and offers a simple silent blessing, "May your day be blessed, and you carry with you joy and peace in your heart to the next people you meet" (p. 311). This work and the wealth of material from CFT and MSC are directly relevant to coaches. These fundamental ideas relevant to CFC are outlined below.

Compassion for clients is important in CFC and the key qualities are:

- Motivation – feeling the need to be concerned and caring towards ourselves and others – wanting to reduce suffering and misery.
- Sensitivity – learning to understand the feelings and needs of ourselves and others.
- Sympathy – being moved by the feelings of distress of others.
- Tolerance – accepting rather than avoiding difficult feelings, memories or situations.
- Insight – understanding how our mind works and why we feel and think how we do.
- Accepting – not dismissing, condemning or being submissive to ourselves and others (adapted from Gilbert, 2010b).

This author goes on to outline the skills of the compassionate helper, which are:

- Focused attention – paying close attention to the client and having a balanced compassionate perspective.
- Rational mind – helping the client to focus on reasoning and thinking about themselves, their relationships and situation in a compassionate and balanced way.
- Relieving distress – helping the client to plan and engage in ways that reduce pain and move themselves and others toward their life goals.

Critical elements for CFC can also be drawn from the eight-step MSC process for building self-compassion with clients which is set out below (Germer & Neff, 2019).

1. Discovering mindful self-compassion – which introduces this concept and process.
2. Practising mindfulness – which involves teaching both formal and informal mindfulness.
3. Practising loving-kindness – which introduces this concept and uses meditation to build feelings of love and kindness as key building blocks for compassion.
4. Discovering your compassionate voice – which broadens loving kindness meditation into a compassionate conversation that clients have with themselves.
5. Living deeply – which focuses on client's core values and the skill of compassionate listening.
6. Meeting difficult emotions – learning to apply the self-compassion skills to problematic emotions.
7. Exploring challenging relationships – where clients learn to understand and accept their own emotional needs and themselves with more compassion.
8. Embracing your life – which includes the practices of savouring, gratitude and self-appreciation.

In conclusion there are a wide range of important elements of both CFT and MSC that can be used in CFC.

Reflective Practice Exercise: How Would You Treat a Friend?

This exercise was adapted from the book by Neff & Germer (2018) called *The Mindful Self-Compassion Workbook: A Proven Way to Accept Yourself, Find Inner Strength, and Thrive.*

Take a piece of paper or a computer, phone etc. and write down the following:

1. Think about a time when you were with a close friend who was having a very hard time. Write down below the situation that you friend was in.
Example: My friend was feeling shame about a mistake they had made at work.

2. Think about how you would respond to your friend if you were being kind and caring. What would you say? What would you do?
Example: I would say that we all make mistakes and that my friend was being very hard on herself.

3. Now think about and write down a time when you were having a very hard time. What was the situation – write it below.
Example: I am now thinking about a time at work when I made an error in an important spreadsheet that went unnoticed for months.

4. Think about how you responded to your own difficult time. What did you say? What did you do?
Example: I was so angry at myself and would wake up at nights in a cold sweat.

5. Now carefully note the difference between how you treat yourself and how you have treated your friend. What were the main differences?
Example: Yes, I clearly see that I am much harder on myself than I am on my friend!

6. If there was a difference, write down how you would like to treat yourself when you are having a hard time. What would you change? What difference would this make? If you could treat yourself like a good friend how different would you feel.
Example: I would like to be gentler on myself and ask for others to double check important spreadsheet calculations.

Spend a few moments reflecting on what you have just done. What did you learn?
Example: This is a great exercise and I have learned that I am very hard on myself.

How could you use this approach in your own coaching practice?
Example: This is such a great exercise I will use it whenever it is relevant.

Reflective Practice Exercise: Self-Compassion Break

This exercise was adapted from Neff & Germer (2018).
Think about a time or situation in your life that is very problematic and stressful for you. Describe the situation below.
Example: I got very drunk a month ago and was unable to help a friend when he was in real need.

Now take a moment to feel your suffering. Write down exactly how it feels. (In MSC this is called the 'moment of suffering').
Example: I feel rotten to the core.

Now recognise that you are not alone in your suffering, but that suffering is an inevitable part of life. Reflect on the fact that we all suffer and you are not alone in feeling this way and write your thoughts below. (In MSC terms this is connecting with 'common humanity').
Example: I guess everyone makes mistake and does dumb things from time to time.

Now be kind to yourself by putting your hand over your heart and gently soothe yourself with a gentle touch. What do you feel as you do this? Write your thoughts and feelings below. (In MSC terms this is 'self-soothing'). It can be useful to say to yourself:
- May I be gentler on myself in future.
- May I learn to be more compassionate.
- May I forgive myself just as I would forgive a good friend.
- May I live my life with ease.

Spend a few moments reflecting on what you have just done. What did you learn?
Example: I do feel a lot better for being deliberately forgiving of myself – it does help.

How could you use this approach in your own coaching practice?
Example: This is a great exercise and I can immediately think of two clients who could benefit from it.

A great deal of helpful MSC material can be found on https://self-com passion.org.

Reflective Practice Exercise: The VOUCH Technique

LeJeune (2016) has a useful approach to dealing with self-criticism and self-shame called the VOUCH technique, which can be used in CFC. It is summarised below.

Reflective Practice Exercise: The VOUCH Technique

Find a quiet place where you will not be disturbed for 15 minutes. Sit upright and gently watch your breath for a few minutes.

Next think about a difficult or stressful situation that you want to work on. Allow yourself to get a clear picture in your mind of the situation and write down the details below. Then gently work through the following steps.

V – Vulnerability. Ask yourself, '*What is the vulnerability or difficulty that I am feeling?*'.

O – Open. Allow yourself to be *open to listening* and feeling the pain of the difficult situation.

U – Understanding. Allow yourself to be *understanding* about the difficult situation. Can you see how almost anyone would feel pain under these circumstances?

C – Compassion. Quietly feel *compassion* for yourself and your situation. What is the compassionate thing that you can tell yourself now? What can you do to take care of your hurt self?

H – Honour. How can you honour your deeply held values at this time? What is important for you to do so you can better live the life you want. How can you be more gentle and less self-critical in future?

Spend a few moments reflecting on what you have just done. What did you learn?
Example: I like the simple structured approach. I was able to feel the difference self-compassion made.

How could you use this approach in your own coaching practice?
Example: I can see lots of opportunities for using this in my practice.

When to Use Compassion-focused Techniques in Coaching

Compassion-focused techniques are extremely helpful when the client is facing a great deal of pain that they cannot do much about. For example, with a client who was neglected as a child by her depressed father but went on, many years later, to develop a genuine liking for him. After he died the client experienced very painful grief and a confusion of both love and hate. Using compassion meditation, she was able to sooth her archaic pain and so find a sense of peace.

Self-compassion techniques are also very helpful when working with clients who are deliberately self-punishing or who feel unworthy of love. For example, if the client has a chronic disease that makes them feel unworthy of care, then self-compassion can be helpful in slowly building a sense of self-worth despite the reality that their body is failing them.

Using These Workbook Exercises in Professional Development

The reflective practice exercises in this chapter are designed to be used:

- In individual reflective practice sessions for students or coaches who want to develop their capability.
- With coaches who want to work in pairs to build their skills.

- For supervisors who want to use experiential learning in their work.
- With classroom instructors or academics teaching coaching skills.
- By senior practitioners who want to run extended professional development sessions for coaches.

Summary

This chapter presented a brief outline of two compassion-focused therapeutic approaches, firstly Compassion-focused Therapy (CFT) developed by Gilbert (2005, 2009, 2010a, 2014) and secondly, Mindful Self-Compassion (MSC) developed by Germer and Neff (2019). The chapter then focuses on a series of specific approaches and techniques from the two compassion approaches that can be used effectively in coaching and reflective practice sessions.

16

Using Schema Therapy with Mindfulness Techniques

INTRODUCTION TO THE CHAPTER

This chapter introduces the key concepts of schema therapy and discusses the research on its effectiveness. The idea of mindfulness is then introduced and effectiveness research on mindfulness-based therapy is presented. The chapter moves on to a method used to combine the assessment phase of schema therapy with the therapeutic use of mindfulness. How the coach can combine schema therapy and mindfulness techniques in coaching and in reflective practice sessions is then presented. The chapter does not aim to make the reader a schema therapy or mindfulness therapist but simply to give any competent coach a range of additional approaches they can use if needed.

Schema Therapy

Schema therapy is an integrative approach that draws on methods and techniques from CBT, gestalt and psychodynamic therapy as well as attachment and object relations theories. It was developed by Jeffery Young and colleagues in the early 2000s (Young et al., 2003) and has been refined since then (Roediger et al., 2018).

Rafaeli, Bernstein and Young (2011) and Jacob and Arntz (2013) describe schema therapy as having the following distinguishing features.

- Schema therapy recognises a set of universal emotional human needs for safety, stability, nurturance, autonomy, competence, a sense of identity, freedom to express one's needs, spontaneity and play in a world with realistic limits that fosters self-control.
- It aims to help clients understand these needs and to find ways of meeting these in healthy ways.

DOI: 10.4324/9781003285144-20

- It places an emphasis on organised persistent patterns of dysfunctional childhood feelings, thinking and behaving, called early maladaptive schema.
- It is a highly experiential approach that includes the processing of aversive childhood memories to change maladaptive patterns.

Roediger et al. (2018) indicate that schema therapy has three levels of analysis:

1. The schemas themselves – that is, the painful patterns of dysfunctional feeling, thoughts and behaviours.
2. Coping mechanisms – that is, the methods clients use in their mistaken attempts to eliminate or reduce their schema pain.
3. Modes or the "moment-to-moment" emotional states seen in therapy sessions.

Schema can be thought of as more stable long-term traits while modes are like short-term feeling states. In the early stages of schema therapy, Young and colleagues (2003) primarily worked at the schema level; however, Roediger et al. (2018) suggested that, when treating disturbed clients, the schema level analysis became very complicated when clients jumped rapidly between different schema and coping styles. This led to the development and classification of these mood states as *schema modes* (Young et al., 2003).

Schema Types

Young and colleagues (2003) outline five broad categories of unmet needs and 18 early maladaptive schemas. Van Vreeswijk et al. (2014) added one more schema (social undesirability) to make 19, which are set out below.

- First Domain: Disconnection/rejection, which includes six schema: abandonment/instability, mistrust/abuse, emotional deprivation, defectiveness/shame, social undesirability and social isolation/alienation.
- Second Domain: Impaired autonomy and/or performance, which includes four schema: dependence/incompetence, vulnerability to harm or illness, enmeshment/undeveloped self and failure.
- Third Domain: Impaired limits includes two schemas: entitlement/grandiosity, insufficient self-control and/or self-discipline.
- Fourth Domain: Other directedness includes three schemas: subjugation, self-sacrifice, approval-seeking/recognition-seeking.
- Fifth Domain: Over-vigilance/Inhibition includes four schemas: negativity/pessimism, emotional inhibition, unrelenting standards/hyper-criticalness, punitiveness.

Young and colleagues (2003) suggest that there are three coping styles that clients use to try and minimise the impact of the pain caused by their schema.

- Schema surrender: The client capitulates and acts out the schema without trying to change it. For example, the client with the approval-seeking schema will regularly please others at their own long-term expense and then feel deeply resentful.
- Schema avoidance: The client tries to run away and escape the schema. For example, a client with defensiveness/shame schema may work extremely hard and gain a highly influential role but, despite the prestige of the job, feel deeply inadequate.
- Schema compensation: The client reacts in precisely the opposite way that is indicated by the schema. For example, a client with a negativity/pessimism schema may develop a 'polly-anna' type positivity and take great risks, believing that everything will work out well.

The Effectiveness of Schema Therapy

This section aims to provide a brief overview of more recent meta-analyses and systematic reviews on the effectiveness of schema therapy and does not attempt to provide a comprehensive coverage.

Bakos et al. (2015) produced an extensive systematic review of the effectiveness of schema therapy. They identified 3,200 published research abstracts but after applying their selection criteria for sound methodological research they were left with only nine studies that were used in their review. They concluded that there was preliminary but growing evidence about the effectiveness of schema therapy in the treatment of personality disordered patients. They suggested that there was a need for more randomised controlled trials to increase the utility of the research findings.

Avramchuk and Hlyvanska (2018) reviewed studies using dialectical behaviour therapy, mentalisation-based therapy and schema therapy to treat borderline personality disorders. They found 309 articles in total but after applying their selection criteria for sound methodological research they were left with 33 studies. They concluded that all three therapeutic approaches were useful for patients diagnosed with borderline personality disorder. They found that schema therapy produced the longest periods without recurrence of co-morbid states and the lowest dropout rates. They also concluded that schema therapy produced greater quality of life improvements compared to other psychotherapies.

Körük & Özabacı (2018) completed a meta-analysis of 35 studies of schema therapy used to treat depression. They concluded that schema therapy had a high level of efficacy in the treatment of depressive disorders and this effect was not significantly impacted by the type of depressive disorder, the number of participants, the number of sessions, the type of session (individual or group), the duration of the session (minutes), the number of sessions per week or the country or culture the work was undertaken in.

McCormick (2022b) concluded there is a wide range of research to demonstrate the effectiveness of schema therapy. However, more large-scale random controlled trails are needed in future to build further empirical support.

Mindfulness

The term *mindfulness* is associated with Buddhist psychology and is derived from the Sanskrit word 'Smr̥ti', which means 'that which is remembered' (Naik et al., 2013). Jon Kabat-Zinn, a founder of the field, defined mindfulness as, 'paying attention in a particular way: on purpose, in the present moment, and nonjudgmentally' (Kabat-Zinn, 1994). To better understand the term mindfulness, it can be contrasted with experiences of mindlessness. The latter occurs 'when attention and awareness capacities are scattered due to preoccupation with past memories or future plans and worries; this, in turn, leading to a limited awareness and attention to experiences in the present moment' (Black, 2011, p. 1).

The Use of Mindfulness in Therapy

Mindfulness-based therapeutic interventions are widely accepted in the helping professions (Shapiro & Carlson, 2009). There are four broadly recognised therapy models that use mindfulness techniques.

- Mindfulness-Based Stress Reduction developed by Jon Kabat-Zinn (Kabat-Zinn, 1994) which is an eight-week training programme originally created for chronically ill patients but is now used for a wide variety of symptoms and conditions including anxiety, cancer pain, coronary heart disease and depression (Nehra et al., 2013).
- Dialectical Behaviour Therapy (Linehan, 1993) which is a comprehensive multicomponent therapy that includes mindfulness and has been used extensively in the treatment of borderline personality disorder.

- Acceptance and Commitment Therapy (ACT), which was developed in the late 1980s by Steven Hayes and colleagues (Hayes, Strosahl & Wilson, 1999), used to treat a wide variety of conditions including workplace stress, test anxiety, social anxiety disorder, depression, obsessive-compulsive disorder and psychosis.
- Mindfulness-Based Cognitive Therapy for depression, which was developed by Segal, Williams and Teasdale (2002) and consists of an eight-session programme that has been demonstrated to improve the recovery from depression and reduce relapse.

The Effectiveness of Mindfulness-Based Therapy

Below is a summary of a wide-ranging study on the effectiveness of mindfulness-based therapy which is designed to give the trained coach some confidence in the evidence base behind this approach.

Khoury et al. (2013) undertook a comprehensive meta-analysis of the effectiveness of mindfulness-based therapy (MBT). They reviewed studies published in journals and dissertations up until May 2013. This resulted in a total of 209 studies involving 12,145 subjects. They found that, based on effect-size estimates, MBT is moderately effective in pre-post evaluations, in comparisons with waitlist controls and when contrasted with other psychological treatments. They concluded that 'MBT is an effective treatment for a variety of psychological problems, and is especially effective for reducing anxiety, depression, and stress' (Khoury et al., 2013, p. 763).

Mindfulness in Schema Therapy

According to Van Vreeswijk et al. (2014), schema therapy has two phases: the assessment phase where schemas are identified and secondly, the transformation phase where schemas and modes are treated. This second phase typically draws on psychodynamic theory and uses visual exercises to confront past difficulties and traumas. Schema therapy also uses gestalt therapy chair work and inner dialogue experiments to challenge persistent punitive ruminations and build the Healthy Adult voice.

Van Vreeswijk et al. (2014) introduces a new third stage using mindfulness to challenge schema. This stage uses non-judgemental mindful attention focused on the client's schema experience to quietly let go of inner conflict, unhelpful thoughts and feelings.

Indications and Contra Indications for Using Mindfulness in Schema Therapy

Van Vreeswijk et al. (2014) suggest that indications for the use of mindfulness techniques in schema therapy include:

- A willingness to become aware of long-standing troublesome life patterns.
- A desire to address persistent rumination and negative thoughts.
- An aspiration to deal with ongoing difficulties managing emotion.
- A desire to change impulsiveness.
- A wish to address persistent difficulties with social interchange.
- An openness to undertaking schema therapy.

Contra indications include:

- Severe disorders resulting in clients being unable to concentrate on exercises.
- Severe learning challenges.
- An unwillingness to invest time into the process.
- Socio-economic circumstances that mean the person is unable to attend sessions, e.g., financial crisis or personal health problems.

Mindfulness in the Schema Therapy Process

Van Vreeswijk et al. (2014) outline a mindfulness group training programme which consists of eight treatment sessions and then two follow-up sessions.

- Prior to the first session there is an initial assessment using the Brief Symptom Inventory, the Young Schema Questionnaire and the Schema Mode Inventory.
- Session 1 includes an introduction to schema, modes and mindfulness training. Homework exercises are then undertaken between sessions.
- Session 2 includes a review of the homework, learning body scan meditation and learning how to build everyday mindful awareness.
- Session 3 includes mindfulness breathing, an exercise to use present moment focus to reduce the impact of painful memories, mindfulness walking and, at the conclusion of the session, a three-minute breathing space exercise.
- Session 4 includes a review of homework, a three-minute breathing exercise, how to use mindfulness to better cope with schema and a discussion of homework for the upcoming week.

- Session 5 includes a review of homework, a three-minute breathing space exercise, mindfulness acceptance of self and others and then, at the conclusion, assignment of further mindfulness homework.
- Session 6 includes a three-minute breathing space meditation, an exercise to reinforce the idea that schema thoughts are simply just thoughts and not facts, a method for letting go of schema impacts and setting homework for the next session.
- Session 7 focuses on clients caring for themselves through fostering the Healthy Adult and Happy Child. The session includes reviewing the level of schema mindfulness over the last week, the three-minute breathing space exercise, an approach to develop the Healthy Adult and Happy Child and to start to better prepare for the future.
- Session 8 focuses on the future and the maintenance of progress. It includes a review of schema intensity levels in the past week, a three-minute breathing exercise, a discussion of the utility of the Healthy Adult and Happy Child exercise and an evaluation of the programme.

Van Vreeswijk et al. (2014) also outline the two follow-up sessions. The first takes place one month after the end of the eighth session and the second two months later. The focus of these sessions is to refresh past learnings and to reinforce the positive changes that clients have already made.

Comparing Schema Therapy and Schema Coaching

McCormick (2022b) argues that schema therapy and schema coaching both use the same approach and techniques and aim to help clients meet their core needs by challenging their maladaptive schemas and learning new functional ways of coping. However, schema therapy is a widely practised approach with research demonstrating its effectiveness, while schema coaching is new with no research demonstrating its effectiveness yet. Schema therapy is typically used with clinical and forensic clients, while schema coaching is used with business leaders. Schema therapy utilises a broad range of schema, while executives typically only report a limited number which often include *unrelenting standards*, *self-sacrifice* and *approval-seeking/recognition-seeking*. Schema therapy clients typically employ the full range of coping mechanisms to deal with the pain of their schema, while schema coaching clients typically only use surrender coping. Schema therapy frequently uses mode analysis and treatment, while this is less common in schema coaching.

McCormick (2016, 2022b) describes using the full range of schema therapy treatment techniques in schema coaching, which includes imagery work to deal with past pain and trauma, transformational chairwork, emotional reg-ulation techniques and schema homework. While all these approaches are useful, they need considerable training and experience to employ with con-fidence. For the coach wanting to start using schema techniques it is recom-mended they employ the approach advocated by Van Vreeswijk et al. (2014) which includes schema assessment and mindfulness methods. This approach can usefully be supplemented with CBT-based schema challenge techniques (Young et al., 2003). The three mindfulness techniques are set out below in more detail.

Mindfulness and Schema Techniques in Coaching

Van Vreeswijk et al. (2014) provide a useful Participant Workbook for us-ing schema therapy with mindfulness. The exercises below are adaptions of methods from Van Vreeswijk et al. (2014) which have proven to be useful in coaching.

Body Scan to Build Non-Judgemental Observation: Instructions

- Sit in a comfortable chair with your back upright and with your feet flat on the floor. Close your eyes or keep them half opened but focused a short distance in front of you.
- Focus on the sensation of your breathing. For two or three minutes, experi-ence the rhythmical way the air moves through your nose down into your lungs then back again.
- Now become aware of your head, focus on the sensations in your forehead and scalp. Breathe gently and notice any feelings in this area. Now focus on your eyes, lips, tongue and jaw. Breathe gently and notice any sensations in this area.
- Now slowly focus on other parts of your body and notice the sensations – your neck, shoulders, left arm, hand and fingers, right arm, hand and fin-gers, your chest, stomach, upper back, lower back, your hips, thighs, calves, shins, feet and toes. Spend five or six minutes doing this.
- Notice what you feel – the sensations. Quietly try not to label them as good or bad, helpful or unhelpful. Just notice them in a non-judgemental way.
- Now notice the sensations in your body as a whole. Take a few breaths and gently scan from head to toe noticing any sensations. Again, just

notice them in a non-judgemental way. Spend two or three minutes doing this.
- When you are ready slowly open your eyes and return to your day.
- Regularly practise this exercise to build your awareness of bodily sensations.

Mindfulness and Schema Techniques: Case Study

Carmen was a partner in an accounting firm who was highly intelligent and capable. She came to coaching to discuss her career options. Carmen had been a partner for ten years and was now well off financially. She came to coaching to deal with a sense of what she called 'ennui'. This involved regular feelings of listlessness, dissatisfaction and lack of interest in her work. She said that these emotions had started when she was quite young and had tormented her for a long time. She felt that she was intellectually able to undertake her role but emotionally disinterested. In the case conceptualisation it was agreed that Carmen suffered from a *lack of spontaneity* schema. She felt that she needed suppress her spontaneous feelings, actions and communications to avoid disapproval by others, particularly her fellow partners. As a result, she stopped herself from doing things that are enjoyable and worthwhile. In particular she felt that that the commercial focus of the firm was stifling and that the seemingly endless discussions around new cars, boats and holiday homes at partner lunches was nauseating. Carmen's goal in coaching was to let go of her feelings of dissatisfaction, to explore her deeply held values and decide what she wanted for the next part of her career.

The coach taught Carmen body-scan meditation and she immediately felt that having a regular time to let go of painful emotions was very helpful. Together Carmen and the coach drew up a list of her top ten frustrations at work and these included attending partner meetings, joining partner lunches and other firm social occasions. As she practised her meditation on a regular basis and focused on letting go the frustrations, Carmen found she gained a greater interest at work. In particular, she became much more interested in developing the capability of the large staff group in her department. After about a year, Carmen made the decision that she wanted to stay in the firm and to build a legacy as a dedicated, caring partner, passionate about building skills and collaboration in the team. Carmen felt she was much more able to let go of her feelings of dissatisfaction, to explore her deeply held values and decide what she wanted for the next part of her career. She described her personal growth and change as a result of coaching as 'a major!'

Reflective Practice Exercise: Body Scan to Body Scan to Build Non-Judgemental Observation

Try the body scan using the instructions above and write a sentence or two to describe your experience.
Example: I had persistent distressing tension in my shoulders that remained throughout the body scan.

Review the words you used in your description above. Were these words simple descriptions, e.g., tightness in my chest, air moving into my lungs, or were your words judgements or evaluations, e.g., painful tightness in my legs, welcome warmth in my hands. Remember, mindfulness involves being non-judgemental toward whatever arises in the moment. This means that sensations, thoughts and emotions are not judged as good or bad, pleasant or unpleasant; they are simply noticed until they eventually pass. Write down your observations.
Example: OK so my description 'distressing' is very judgemental!

Think about a range of non-judgemental words you can use to describe your body scan. Write these below.
Example: Tension in my shoulders that was present for much of the body scan.

What did you learn from this self-reflection?
Example: I see how labelling the tension 'distressing' magnifies the problem.

What do you want to apply to your own coaching practice?
Example: I have a long way to go before I apply this in my coaching.

Combining Schema and Mindfulness Techniques in Coaching

The ten-session group training approach of Van Vreeswijk et al. (2014) is not appropriate for individual coaching with time-poor executives. It is recommended that coaches consider the following brief approach.

- Start with solution-focused or another recognised coaching method and assess the degree to which the client's problems can be addressed using this approach. If the nature of the problem is more prolonged or deep-seated the coach may move on to use schema and mindfulness techniques.
- Undertake a psychoeducation phase by asking the client to read material on schema therapy such as *Reinventing Your Life: The Breakthrough Program to End Negative Behaviour and Feel Great Again* (Young & Klosko, 1994). Identify the client's relevant schema and hold a discussion on the nature of schema and schema coping. The session would also include a conversation about how schemas are not facts but are painful mental traps.
- The next step would involve teaching the client a mindfulness meditation approach, such as the body scan, the use of mindfulness to lessen distressing schema-based memories and exercises on the acceptance of self and others (see below).

- The final step could include a review of schema intensity levels since the last session, a three-minute breathing space meditation, exercises on developing the Healthy Adult and Happy Child (see below) and an evaluation of the programme.

Mindfulness to Lessen Schema-Based Memories: Instructions

- Sit in a comfortable chair with your back upright and with your feet flat on the floor. Close your eyes or keep them half opened but focusing a short distance in front of you.
- Direct your attention to the sensation of your breathing. For two or three minutes, experience the rhythmical way the air moves through your nose down into your lungs then back again.
- Now undertake a body scan, gently observing your body from head to toe.
- Let yourself become aware of past situations, memories, sounds, smells that bother you or that cause pain. Allow the memory to unfold in your mind. What do you see? What do you smell? What do you feel? What are your thoughts? What is going on in your body? How intense are the feelings?
- Now direct your attention to the sensation of your breathing. For two or three minutes, experience the rhythmical way the air moves through your nose down into your lungs then back again.
- Focus on a painful schema-based memory and allow yourself to feel the full intensity of the memory without trying to change it. Perhaps say to yourself 'I accept my pain. I will allow it to exist and not try to escape or avoid it'. 'Accepting and not fighting the memory will ease my pain over time'. 'My courage will conquer the pain'.
- When you are ready, slowly open your eyes and return to your day.
- Regularly practise this exercise to gradually accept and lessen the impact of your painful memories.

Reflective Practice Exercise: Mindfulness to Lessen Memories

What did you learn from this exercise?
Example: I imagined being bullied at school and it was a very raw memory. I learned that these memories are very powerful and concrete.

How do you personally want to use this approach in the future?
Example: I can see how these memories have held me back in life and I want to let go of them.

What do you want to apply to your own coaching practice?
Example: Yes, I can see the value of this for my coaching practice. I will use it with a range of clients.

Three-minute Breathing Space Meditation: Instructions

- Sit in a comfortable chair with your back upright and with your feet flat on the floor. Close your eyes or keep them half opened but focused a short distance in front of you.
- Direct your attention to the sensation of your breathing. For two or three minutes, experience the rhythmical way the air moves through your nose down into your lungs then back again.
- Now become aware of your body. What do you feel as you sit here, the weight of your body on the chair, the feeling of your feet on the floor?
- Notice the thoughts in your head as they arrive and fade away. Observe them as if they were clouds in the sky passing by – no need to hang on to them, no need to push them away.
- Notice your emotions – what do you feel, what is arriving, what is passing away? Again, observe them as if they were clouds in the sky passing by – no need to hang on to them, no need to push them away.
- Direct your attention back to the sensation of your breathing. For two or three minutes, experience the rhythmical way the air moves through your nose down into your lungs then back again.
- Direct your awareness to your whole body. If you have any pain or discomfort allow yourself to accept this with a sense of compassion. Be gentle and kind with yourself and your pain and discomfort.

- When you are ready, slowly open your eyes and return to your day.
- Regularly practise this exercise to gradually accept your bodily sensations, thoughts and emotions.

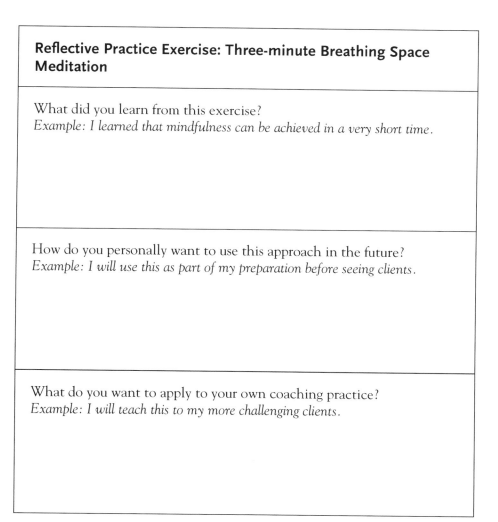

Reflective Practice Exercise: Three-minute Breathing Space Meditation

What did you learn from this exercise?
Example: I learned that mindfulness can be achieved in a very short time.

How do you personally want to use this approach in the future?
Example: I will use this as part of my preparation before seeing clients.

What do you want to apply to your own coaching practice?
Example: I will teach this to my more challenging clients.

Developing the Healthy Adult and Happy Child: Instructions

- Sit in a comfortable chair with your back upright and with your feet flat on the floor. Close your eyes or keep them half opened but focused a short distance in front of you.

- Direct your attention to the sensation of your breathing. For two or three minutes, experience the rhythmical way the air moves through your nose down into your lungs then back again.
- Now become aware of that part of yourself that is your Healthy Adult. This is the part of you that offers protection, kindness, compassion and composure. This part of you sets healthy boundaries in a calm and caring way.
- Alternatively become aware of your Happy Child. This is the part of you that is spontaneous, joyful and loves to have fun. This is the part of you that can bring you joy and happiness.
- Develop a few positive, constructive accepting thoughts from either your Healthy Adult or Happy Child and repeat these to yourself.
- For example – the Healthy Adult: 'I do my best and that is good enough'. 'I will not beat myself up for not doing better'. 'I do not need to constantly please others'. 'If others are annoyed at me, I can accept this but treat it lightly, even with indifference'.
- For example – the Happy Child: 'I can be open to new fun ideas'. 'I can enjoy myself without feeling guilty'. 'I deserve to be happy'. 'I can allow myself to be spontaneous and enjoy my life'.
- Now direct your attention to the sensation of your breathing. For two or three minutes, experience the rhythmical way the air moves through your nose down into your lungs then back again.
- When you are ready slowly open your eyes and return to your day.
- Regularly practise this exercise to gradually strengthen your Healthy Adult or Happy Child.

Reflective Practice Exercise: Developing the Healthy Adult and Happy Child

What did you learn from this exercise?
Example: I learned that my Healthy Adult needs to develop a bit and my Happy Child needs to develop a great deal!

How do you personally want to use this approach in the future?
Example: I will practise this Happy Child exercise three times a week in the morning.

What do you want to apply to your own coaching practice?
Example: I am not sure how this will work with many of my senior leader clients.

Using these Workbook Exercises in Professional Development

The reflective practice exercises in this chapter are designed to be used:

- In individual reflective practice sessions for students or coaches who want to develop their capability.
- With coaches who want to work in pairs to build their skills.
- For supervisors who want to use experiential learning in their work.
- With classroom instructors or academics teaching coaching skills.
- By senior practitioners who want to run professional development sessions for coaches.

Summary

This chapter introduced the key concepts of schema therapy and discussed the research on its effectiveness. The idea of mindfulness was also introduced and effectiveness research on mindfulness-based therapy was presented. There was an explanation of how these two methods can be combined by using the assessment phase of schema therapy with the therapeutic use of mindfulness. Practical steps to using this approach in coaching and with reflective practice professional development sessions have been set out.

17
Using Cognitive Analytic Therapy Techniques

INTRODUCTION TO THE CHAPTER

The aim of this chapter is to introduce the concepts, stages and techniques of Cognitive Analytic Therapy, to discuss its effectiveness and how and when it can be used in Cognitive Analytic Coaching. The chapter includes a case study and a range of reflective practice exercises.

Introduction to Cognitive Analytic Therapy

Cognitive Analytic Therapy (CAT) was developed by a British psychodynamic therapist, Anthony Ryle, in the late 1970s. Ryle worked originally as a General Practitioner and then as a Consultant Psychotherapist. He was troubled by the large numbers of clients with readily treatable dysfunctions who received very little psychotherapy. He observed that there were a small number who received long-term psychoanalytic psychotherapy; however, the majority were only given psychotropic medication due to staff shortages (Llewelyn, 2003).

Ryle produced CAT with the aim of creating a brief, highly focused, effective psychotherapy that could be delivered to large numbers of clients in the public system by front-line clinic staff. He also aimed to clarify and simplify the complex language of psychoanalysis and replace it with clear concepts that could be easily explained to clients and bring about change. Ryle wrote a great deal with the aim of de-mystifying psychoanalysis (see Ryle, 1991, 1992, 1993, 1994a, 1994b, 1994c, 1995a, 1995b, 1996, 1997). He was influenced by the research that demonstrated that clients can be helped equally by a variety of forms of therapy. Ryle and Kerr (2002) used this insight to develop an integrative approach that drew on a range of different schools of psychotherapy, including the psychoanalytic, personal construct theory, and cognitive therapy.

DOI: 10.4324/9781003285144-21

Ryle and Kerr (2002) suggest that CAT differs from other models of therapy in several ways:

- Therapists work collaboratively with the client in activities such as mapping out the behavioural sequences that generate unhappiness, sharing their understandings and inviting their ideas, comments and modifications.
- They demonstrate how problems have been formed and maintained, therapists also use a 'narrative reconstruction' by writing several letters to the client setting out the links between past experience and current behaviour.
- By using written and diagrammatic tools, the therapist generates a common agenda for the therapy.

Core Concepts of Cognitive Analytic Therapy

CAT has several core concepts. The client is seen in dynamic and wholistic terms (e.g., a struggling volatile executive) not as a static diagnostic entity (e.g., a borderline personality case) but as someone whose actions and relationships all need to be understood to appreciate the person. For example, a client is seen as struggling with their volatile behaviour, which has multiple external triggers (e.g., bullying by work colleagues) that interact with their own inability to gain perspective on the situation (e.g., the belief that 'Everything would be alright if they just left me alone').

Another key concept in CAT is the value and power of the collaborative relationship between therapist and client (Llewelyn, 2003). This is used to generate a common understanding of the problem, the sequence of events that generate it and joint agreement on the actions the client will take to improve their well-being.

In CAT, the idea of a 'symptom' is replaced by a 'procedure' which is seen as a 'linked chain of mental processes and actions' used to achieve a goal (Ryle, 1985). Procedures are used all the time and an everyday example would be the driving of a car where the procedure might be, insert the car key, put your foot on the break, turn the key, etc. However, not all procedures are helpful. For example, a person is unsure of what they want so they end up doing what their friend wants to do. After a while they feel resentful as they do not get to do what they want. Consequently, they get angry and make hurtful comments to their friend which damages their relationship and causes both parties to feel bad. This becomes a circular and dysfunctional snare. The client may come to therapy with a specific problem such as anxiety, loneliness, depression; however, the role of the CAT therapist is to work collaboratively with the client to discover the linked chain of thinking patterns and events that led to the presenting problem. The CAT therapist looks for the trigger, what the linked chain is, what the consequences are and how the pattern is maintained. Once the procedure is understood, the client and therapist can develop a range of ways of addressing the problem (Llewelyn, 2003).

Ryle provided a simple way to describe the three main types of dysfunctional procedures: the snag, the trap and the dilemma (Llewelyn, 2003).

- Snags are procedures where the client believes that expressing or meeting their own needs will have a bad outcome. For example, a person wants to do well at university but fears that any success will be resented by their family, so they repeatedly procrastinate, which leads to academic failure. This results in the person and their family both feeling frustrated and disappointed.
- Traps are circular patterns of behaviour where the client's attempt to solve a problem makes it worse. For example, a client drinks alcohol to reduce stress but wakes the next day with a hangover and feels even more stressed.
- Dilemmas are false but untested beliefs that result in maladaptive rigid patterns. For example, the client believes they must do their work perfectly, so they take a long time to finish it which results in their boss criticising them for not doing enough. Or they rush their work and feel bad about their own poor quality. This repeats itself until the person is fired or resigns from their job.

CAT was originally developed to last for 16 sessions, plus one or two follow-up sessions. Ryle and Kerr (2002) note the importance of naming the number of sessions, especially as the end of therapy approaches. They argue this clear number of sessions leads to an intensification of the therapy and more rapidly addresses critical problems. It also reduces any chance of the client becoming overly dependent on the therapist. CAT places a special emphasis on 'ending well' and includes the use of a 'goodbye letter' in the penultimate session. The aim of this letter is to enable the therapist to provide the client with a positive but accurate reflection on the course of therapy and what has been achieved.

However, the number of sessions does vary depending on the needs of the client. For example, Sheard et al. (2000) used one to three CAT sessions for clients presenting with repeated deliberate self-harm. By contrast Ryle (1997) suggests that up to 26 sessions may be needed for clients with borderline personality disorder.

Ryle and Kerr (2002) suggest that the aim of CAT is modest as it simply seeks to remove the 'roadblocks' that maintain distress for the client and prevent personal growth. This takes place in a supportive therapeutic relationship that provides a 'new beginning' for the client. It places an emphasis on the discovering of the repeated patterns of snags, traps and dilemmas that trick the client into unhappiness. Once the patterns are clear, the therapist and client can identify a range of ways of breaking the 'roadblocks' and freeing themselves from the painful cycles.

The Stages of Cognitive Analytic Therapy

The first stage of CAT is to build a supportive therapeutic relationship and to accurately identify the client's procedures or destructive cyclical behaviour patterns. This is done by the therapist listening very attentively to the client's story and using the history of relationship patterns to identify the cycles of problem generation. The therapist makes use of transference and countertransference during the therapy sessions. Transference is the subconscious association of one person in the present with a past relationship. For example, the therapist meeting a new client that reminds him or her of a former lover, a parent or a school friend. Countertransference involves the therapist responding to the client with the feelings and thoughts associated with that past relationship. The therapist uses their own experience of transference to help the client understand how humans subconsciously associate one person in the present with a past experience. This distortion often helps to generate the unhelpful behavioural cycle. For example, the CAT therapist may ask the client 'Who does your critical boss remind you of?' The client may reply 'He reminds me of a sadistic school teacher who used to punish me for not being able to catch a ball!' Identifying this may help the client to understand why he or she has such intense automatic feelings of hatred and disgust whenever their boss is critical of them. The therapist aims to provide an independent observation of the client's experience and help them to make sense of it (Llewelyn, 2003).

After the first four sessions, the therapist gives the client a written summary, often in the form of a letter, which cautiously sets out in a sympathetic way the origins and consequences of the client's behaviour patterns. The letter also points out the client's strengths in dealing with their problems and suggests how these patterns may have developed in a vain attempt to resolve earlier challenges. The client is asked to comment on the letter and together the pair jointly produce a document that spells out the areas they will work on. This stage of the therapy helps the client to become aware of his or her own procedures and to start to change them (Llewelyn, 2003).

Ryle and Kerr (2002) set out some general principles to use in the writing of reformulation letters:

- The therapist makes it clear that the letter is a draft and so 'open to revision by the client' (Ryle & Kerr, 2002, p. 102).
- The letter provides a general account of what the client wanted to work on in therapy and a summary of the important milestones in their life history.

- It shows the client the behaviour patterns that have developed because of their past experience and how these have become repeated and unhelpful.
- The letter provides a summary of the client's current challenges and a list of the unhelpful snags, traps and dilemmas.
- It provides a realistic but positive opinion on what can be achieved in therapy.

In the next stage, the client and therapist aim to deepen their understanding of the unhelpful procedures using the Sequential Diagrammatic Reformulation (SDR). The SDR is a rough sketch or map of the client's relationships and behaviour patterns, which summarise the steps that give rise to the client feeling bad and why. The client will be encouraged to bring the SDR to sessions and use it to better understand things that happen between sessions. Simplified examples of SDRs for snags, traps and dilemmas are given in Figures 17.1, 17.2 and 17.3.

A snag where the client believes that expressing or meeting their own needs will and does have a bad outcome.

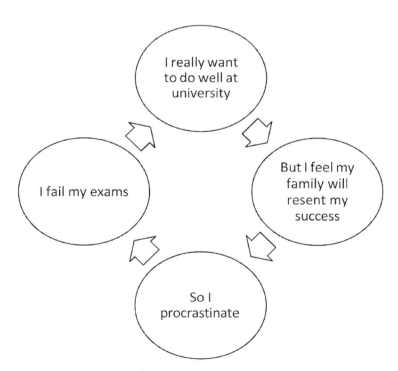

Figure 17.1 An example of a snag

Figure 17.2 An example of a trap

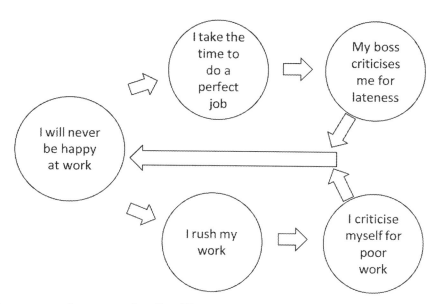

Figure 17.3 An example of a dilemma

A trap is a circular procedure where the attempt to solve a problem makes it worse.

A dilemma is a false but untested belief that results in maladaptive rigid patterns.

The SDR diagrams of traps, dilemmas and snags can roughly be sketched out during sessions as a collaborative way of working with the client to develop a mutual understanding of the problem. Developing these diagrams helps to spell out and explain the entrapment that the client so often feels. It builds the working alliance and deepens the client–therapist relationship. The rough sketch developed in the session can be corrected and refined over time either during or between sessions by the client.

These diagrams naturally lead to the development of options for change. For example, the diagram above can be broken down into its individual steps and options of change constructed at each point:

- 'I will never be happy at work' – the client can learn to become aware of these unhappy feelings at an early stage and take corrective action before they build up, e.g., going for a walk, talking to a friend, doing some relaxation.
- 'I take the time to do a perfect job' – the client can practise challenging the idea that the work must be 'perfect' and can learn to aim for a good but not perfect job.
- 'My boss criticises me for lateness' – the client can learn to see the boss's perspective and clarify the precise time frame for job completion.
- 'I rush my work' – the client can learn to talk to their boss early about the quality level the customer is expecting and draw up a simple project plan to ensure the work is done to an agreed quality standard and deadline.
- 'I criticise myself for poor work' – the client can learn to challenge their inner critic and be more compassionate with themselves.

When the range of change steps are presented to the client, they are typically surprised at the number of options they have for change. The client can work with the therapist to select the easiest and most effective step to take first. The client typically sees that the chain of events can be broken at multiple points which can be very reassuring for someone who has felt trapped and powerless in the face of the problem.

CAT involves homework like that undertaken in CBT. The important point is for the therapist and client to work collaboratively to develop a set of actions to be undertaken between sessions that support the progress made in therapy. Common examples of CAT homework (Ryle and Kerr, 2002) involve agreeing with the client to:

- Write a brief autobiography to clarify the development of the problem.
- Draw up a life chart to show how the problem has changed over time by drawing a graph with the intensity of the problem on the vertical axis and the months of the year on the horizontal axis. The life chart can also include notes about when important events occurred, e.g., when the client started therapy.
- Complete a brief family tree and show the important challenges each generation of your family faced, e.g., my grandparents went through the great 1930s depression and my grandmother became depressed. This family tree can help to show how each generation has faced major challenges and that the client is not alone in having problems.
- Write a never to be sent letter to an important person who may be dead or alive. This can help the client 'vent' their emotions and so feel a sense of emotional relief.
- Carry out an important ritual for someone who has died, e.g., visiting the grave of a friend and talking to them about how much you miss them.
- Undertake a series of steps to overcome a fear or build up a routine. For example, driving on the motorway at a quiet time of the day to overcome a fear of fast-moving traffic.
- Practise a range of ways to deal with troublesome emotions. For example, practising doing work to an adequate and not perfect state and tolerating the bad feelings associated with not doing things perfectly.
- Rehearse constructive self-talk, for example, 'I am feeling uncomfortable driving in the busy city centre, but I am just going to focus on what the other cars are doing and not focus on how I am feeling'.
- Regularly undertaking Tai Chi or other types of active meditation to help reduce stress and anxiety.

CAT places a lot of emphasis on ending well. This may involve the therapist writing a 'goodbye letter'. This letter can include the therapist describing what the client wanted to work on in therapy, the degree of openness and courage the client brought to therapy, the approaches or techniques that were helpful, the degree of progress made so far, the steps the client can take to maintain the current level of achievement – and the therapist can also provide encouragement for the future.

The Effectiveness of Cognitive Analytic Therapy

Below is a recent meta-analysis of CAT effectiveness that will give any coach confidence about the efficacy of using these techniques in coaching.

Hallam et al. (2021) conducted a meta-analysis into the effectiveness of CAT, the durability of the therapeutic outcomes and the level of client dropouts. They identified 846 relevant studies and after applying their research quality criteria they reviewed 25 studies with pre–post CAT treatment outcomes. These studies examined CAT effectiveness in improving global functioning, depression and interpersonal problems. Improvements in global functioning were assessed using measures such as the Symptom Checklist-Revised-90 and the Clinical Outcomes in Routine Evaluation Outcome Measure. Hallam et al. (2021) reported large pre–post improvements in global functioning, moderate-to-large improvements in interpersonal problems and large reductions in depression symptoms. At follow-up, all the therapeutic effects were maintained or improved. The effectiveness of CAT treatment was not impacted by client age, gender, study type, e.g., random controlled trials versus practice-based evidence, level of therapist qualification, individual versus group treatment format or diagnosis, e.g., personality disorder versus other types. CAT showed small to moderate, but significant post-treatment benefits compared to a range of other therapies in nine clinical trials. The average dropout rate for CAT was 16% with a range from 0 to 33%. The authors concluded that CAT produced durable improvements in clients with a range of presenting problems. A coordinated research strategy to further develop the CAT evidence base in a targeted and productive manner is recommended.

Cognitive Analytic Coaching

Cognitive Analytic Coaching (CAC) uses the approach and techniques of CAT with executives. To summarise how this approach can be used, the coach can:

- Develop a supportive relationship with the client.
- Identify the range of behaviours that are causing the problems.
- Write a reformulation letter to the client to set out the problems the client brought to coaching and the range of behaviours causing the problems, offer a positive but realistic view of what can be achieved and provide support.
- Jointly draw a diagram to illustrate the sequence of the snags, traps or dilemmas – the Sequential Diagrammatic Reformulation (SDR).
- Develop a range of possible changes that can be made to break the snag, trap or dilemma.
- Identify the most practical and easily achieved steps that the client can undertake to change.
- Agree the homework, which may be practising these agreed steps.

CAC is best offered to clients who have a repetitive problematic behaviour that they are unable to easily change. For example: giving in to pressure at work to take on an unsustainable workload, being unassertive with other colleagues, eating, drinking or other related challenges.

Cognitive Analytic Coaching Case Study

Robert was a highly successful account manager in a large advertising agency. He came to coaching to improve his stress management. Robert was responsible for several large advertising campaigns and a sizable team. In the first session Robert and the coach were easily able to establish rapport and a very effective working relationship. The coach noted Robert's very positive approach to life and his willingness to openly explore the issues.

As a homework exercise after this first session the coach asked Robert to write a brief two-page autobiography to clarify the development of the problem.

In reviewing the autobiography and further exploring the stress issues in the second session it became clear that Robert had two areas of challenge. The clients he worked for had very high expectations of the agency's ability to drive sales as several were long-standing clients who had previously been able to generate large revenue increases because of very successful past campaigns. After considerable discussion, it appeared that Robert had built his career on being able to say 'Yes' to almost any client demand and then actually delivering, even if it was a major challenge. He was very successful because clients felt that he could achieve almost anything.

The second issue Robert had was dealing with his team. He felt he had a very talented, hardworking team but his ability to take on almost impossible client demands and succeed generated a major issue with ownership of work by several team members. He had two staff whose attitude Robert described as 'When the going gets tough, they just get going'. Meaning that for most of the time these team members were great but when the pressure was really on, they left Robert to solve the problems. In discussing the issue with the coach, Robert could see that his willingness to pick up and solve problems had in part generated the staff reaction. His staff felt that Robert could solve the big problems, so they did not need to worry. The coach wrote Robert the following email.

Dear Robert

You have come to coaching to better manage your stress and you already have some great insights into the causes of the troubles you find yourself in. You can clearly see the impact of the combination of your willingness to say 'Yes' to almost any client demand, combined with an extraordinary ability to solve problems and get results. This challenge you have is exacerbated by the attitude of some of your team who feel that they can relax when there is a major problem because you can always solve it. I understand that you feel like you are stuck between a rock and a very hard place.

Despite your difficulties I am deeply impressed with your openness and willing-ness to explore these very serious issues. These qualities are very important in coaching and are a key contributor to your long-term success. I understand that you love the agency and want to stay but you need to be able to face and deal with these problems. Your ability to solve problems has 'saved your skin' many times in the past but it will not work forever.

I greatly enjoy working with you and feel that with determination and time we can together make a big improvement in your stress levels.

I welcome the opportunity to talk this email through with you in our next session and I will be very interested to see how well I have summarised your challenges.

Kind regards,

In the next session, Robert reported that the coach had understood his issues well and the email was very useful because it was an objective and independ-ent view of his situation. The coach and client then went on to map out the sequence of events in an SDR. The circular traps that Robert had built for himself are illustrated in Figure 17.4 and Figure 17.5.

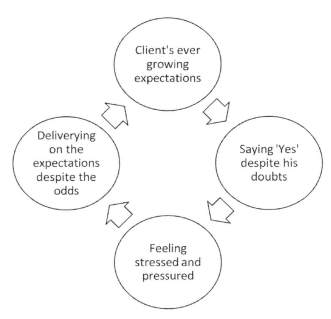

Figure 17.4 Robert's client trap

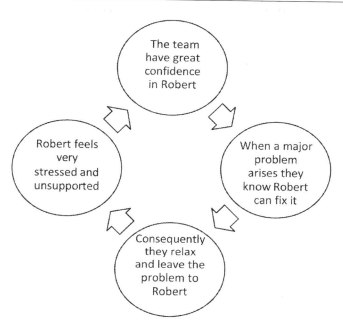

Figure 17.5 Robert's team trap

Robert said that he found the mapping of the sequence of his problems very helpful as it provided a clear and concrete way of understanding the issues. Together the coach and Robert used the SDR to draw up a potential list of ways of addressing each problem.

The client expectation problem could be addressed by Robert:

- Holding a discussion with each client early on in any assignment about the realistic outcomes from an advertising campaign and so starting to manage the client's expectations early on.
- Systematically challenging his automatic tendency to say 'Yes' to clients. Robert could spend time before each important client meeting thinking about the range of requests the client may make and how he could say things like 'I would be keen to do that, but I just need a little time to think through the implications and I will get back to you'.
- Learning yoga or meditation as a means of better dealing with work stress whenever it arose.
- Holding post-campaign debriefs with clients and openly discussing the successful results but being careful to separate the impact of luck and timing with the impact that Robert made on the result.

The team confidence problem could be addressed by Robert:

- Showing more vulnerability and talking to his team about the level of stress he experienced to provide them with a more realistic account of his ability.
- Asking for help from the team as soon as a problem arose.
- Assertively requesting help from the team if they started to relax and leave the problem to him.
- Holding one-on-one sessions with members of his team and reinforcing the point that he got stressed and needed their ongoing support.

With this list of possible actions drawn up Robert felt greatly relieved. What had started as a confusing problem that resulted in uncontrolled stressed was now distilled down to a clear set of diagrams and list of specific actions.

Robert's homework after the session was to write up a summary of the session and to send a clear and realistic action plan back to the coach.

In the penultimate session Robert reported back on the progress he had made. What had gone well was his discussions with the client to manage their expectations and the requests to staff for assistance. What needed more work was Robert's automatic tendency to say 'Yes' to clients without thinking about the consequences.

Robert's homework after the session was to practise saying 'No' clearly and firmly. He started with simple situations like saying 'No' to his local café owner who often wanted to sell him a muffin with his coffee. He went on to say 'No' to his staff members who wanted him to undertake tasks they were not interested in. He even went on to say 'No' to a social invite when he was tired and wanted to rest.

The coach wrote the following email to Robert to ensure that their coaching would end well.

> *Dear Robert*
>
> *You have come to coaching wanting to better manage your stress and you have already made excellent progress. I believe that you have a deep understanding of how both client expectations and staff confidence in you generate the stress. You have tackled both these issues with gusto.*
>
> *You have enthusiastically embarked upon practising your assertiveness and clearly saying 'No' when this is important. Based on my experience, you will need to keep practising this for some months as your tendency to say 'Yes'*

is deeply ingrained. I have great confidence that you can keep saying 'No' when needed.

The aim of our work is to start you on the road to comprehensive change and as you have said you now have a wide range of ways to tackle your challenges. It will take determination and courage to keep pushing ahead but I am sure you will do it.

I welcome the opportunity to talk this email through with you in our next session and I will be very interested to see how well I have summarised progress to date.

Kind regards,

In the final session Robert and the coach reflected on the past sessions and identified the learnings for Robert. They reviewed the SDRs and the range of possible actions that Robert could take to address the problems. The coach thanked Robert for his openness and willingness to learn. Robert said the coaching had changed his life.

When to Use Cognitive Analytic Techniques in Coaching

CAT techniques are particularly useful in coaching when the client has a complex and entangled set of problems. The CAC approach is very helpful because it deeply engages the client, it provides a clear framework for breaking problems down into manageable pieces, it helps clients understand the sequence of events that lead to painful outcomes, it provides a clear way to generate a whole range of possible solutions and reinforces understanding and change using emails sent by the coach.

Cognitive Analytic Techniques: Reflective Practice Exercise

Think about a problem you have that you have not yet found a good solution to. Identify a problem that could be a snag, trap or dilemma. Write a brief autobiography and describe how the problem arose.

Example: I did really well at university, gaining a master's degree in Marketing with First Class Honours. I have had a range of jobs over the last ten years, but I only last in any role for about two years.

Now map out the sequence of your problem using a Sequential Diagrammatic Reformulation. Draw this below. See for example Figure 17.4.

Now carefully review your Sequential Diagrammatic Reformulation and draw up a whole range of possible actions that could break the chain of events.
Example: Now I see the SDR I can see there are many things I can do. I need to be more realistic when I start a job – it will not be perfect. I will learn to tolerate the inevitable disappointments and frustrations as the job goes on. I want to be less disappointed when reality hits and tolerate this. I want to resist the magic thinking that changing jobs will change my life.

Write up the long list of possible helpful actions and identify a small number that you can realistically achieve over the next month.
Example: I will print out the SDR and put it on my bedroom wall at home. I will work with my coach on ways to build my tolerance for disappointment.

Write an email to yourself setting out the nature of the problem, your understanding of how it arises, the actions you will take. Be sure to offer yourself encouragement as you start to deal with the problem.
Example: I am a bright and able person who has fallen into the trap of believing that the next job will be perfect. I now understand much more about what is going on and will work hard with my coach to build resilience and realism. I know I can do it.

Identify a friend, colleague or supervisor who you can share your story with and gain encouragement to continue to address it.

Example: I am going out to lunch next week with my friend from university days and will talk to her about my story and I am sure she will be very encouraging.

Using These Workbook Exercises in Professional Development

The reflective practice exercises in this chapter are designed to be used:

- In individual reflective practice sessions for students or coaches who want to develop their capability.
- With coaches who want to work in pairs to build their skills.
- For supervisors who want to use experiential learning in their work.
- With classroom instructors or academics teaching coaching skills.
- By senior practitioners who want to run professional development sessions for coaches.

Summary

This chapter introduced the concepts and techniques of Cognitive Analytic Therapy; these included developing a supporting relationship with the client, identifying the range of behaviours that are causing the problems, writing a reformulation letter to the client to set out the problems and what can be done. Following this, the client and coach can jointly draw a diagram to illustrate the sequence of the snag, trap or dilemma – the Sequential Diagrammatic Reformulation (SDR). They can develop a range of possible changes that can be made to break the problematic sequence. Finally, they can identify the most practical and easily achieved steps that the client can undertake to change. During the therapy they can agree on the homework to be undertaken between sessions. The chapter shows how these CAT techniques can be used in coaching and reflective practice sessions.

18

Using Stress Inoculation Therapy Techniques

INTRODUCTION TO THE CHAPTER

The aim of this chapter is to introduce the concepts and techniques of Stress Inoculation Therapy (SIT) and to show how these can be used in coaching and reflective practice sessions. The chapter covers the four phases of SIT, awareness and knowledge building, skill development, application and review. It also includes the research that evaluates the effectiveness of SIT. The chapter includes a SIT case study and a reflective practice exercise.

Stress Inoculation Therapy

SIT is an effective strategy for mitigating the adverse effects of stress (Robson & Manacapilli, 2014). It builds resistance to stress by combining cognitive and behavioural skill development with carefully managed exposure to stressful stimuli. SIT is analogous to medical inoculation against disease because it aims to expose individuals to just enough stress to engage defences, such as coping skills. However, the level of exposure must be small and manageable and never overwhelm the individual (Meichenbaum, 1985). Through this combination of training and exposure the individual learns ways to deal with stress and to build their confidence in their ability to handle it in the future.

Meichenbaum (1985) sets out the following characteristics of SIT:

- SIT helps clients understand that stress and coping arise out of a sequence of circumstances and beliefs about what is happening, that is, they are transactional in nature.
- It teaches clients to self-monitor unhelpful thoughts, beliefs, images, feelings and behaviours and so to better cope with stress.

DOI: 10.4324/9781003285144-22

- It trains clients to problem solve, that is, to define the problem, to anticipate the consequence, to make choices and to evaluate what happens.
- It provides models and the opportunity to rehearse concrete actions, emotional regulation and self-control mechanisms.
- SIT helps clients to use their unhelpful stress responses as cues to apply their coping skills.
- It provides practice both in imagination and in vivo with graded exposure that intensifies over time.
- SIT helps clients gain the knowledge, self-understanding and coping skills to enable them to handle unexpected stressful circumstances.

Types of Stress

Meichenbaum (2007) outlines a range of different types of stress that can be aided by SIT.

- Acute time-limited stressors that include preparing for challenging medical procedures such as surgery, invasive examinations such as colonoscopies, or having to confront specific evaluations such as PhD oral examinations.
- Acute stressors with subsequent extended episodes such as the series of stressful events that follow traumatic occasions such as a terrorist attack or a natural disaster that results in a major loss.
- Chronic intermittent stressors that involve recurring exposures to stressors such as musical or athletic competitions, repeated medical tests or treatments, or episodic physical disorders such as repeated headaches or the stress that comes with certain occupational roles, such as police dealing with domestic violence.
- Chronic continual stressors where individuals need to cope with incapacitating medical or physical conditions resulting from burns, traumatic brain injuries etc., or prolonged distress from marital or family discord, violence, poverty, racism, as well as from ongoing occupational dangers such as police work or certain highly challenging types of nursing or teaching.

The Phases of Stress Inoculation Therapy

SIT originally had three phases – awareness and knowledge building, skill development and application (Meichenbaum, 1985). However, Robson and

Manacapilli, (2014) added a fourth phase – the review and evaluation of the effectiveness of SIT.

The Awareness and Knowledge Building Phase

This first phase aims to build awareness of frequently occurring stressors, the individual's psychological and physical responses to these, and the impact of the stress on performance. For example, in a military setting trainers might discuss one type of equipment failure and how this may impact on anxiety, heart rate and breathing.

Driskell and Johnston (1998) recommend that this phase include teaching clients about the importance of stress management by using case studies of performance failures or accidents that resulted from high stress levels. This phase can also include 'stress experiments' where clients are asked to perform a well-known task, e.g., long division, under varying levels of stress such as time pressure, loud noise or flashing lights.

After clients have a full understanding of the adverse impacts of stress, the programme can focus on a discussion of the specific stressors relevant to the client. For example, a meeting with a hostile customer, an email containing a formal complaint or a report of a serious injury of a team member. Simply knowing that specific stressors are likely to occur can help the client to mentally prepare for their arrival. A fundamental idea of SIT is that pre-exposure to the stress reduces the impact and novelty of stressful situation and increases a sense of control (Robson & Manacapilli, 2014).

The Skill Development Phase

The second phase of SIT aims to build the cognitive and behavioural skills necessary to sustain or even enhance performance under the stressful conditions. Driskell and Johnston (1998) suggest a range of skills training in this phase: cognitive control skills, physiological control strategies, overlearning, mental practice, decision making/prioritisation skills and team skills. These are summarised below (Robson & Manacapilli, 2014).

- Cognitive control approaches are designed to increase focus and concentration by diminishing distractions such as negative thinking. The core idea is that worry and negative thoughts consume working memory and therefore reduce performance, so reducing the focus on these can improve functioning.

- Physiological control strategies include slow breathing or deep muscle relaxation to reduce tension and unhelpful thinking. The use of biofeedback equipment to measure and provide information on heart rate, blood pressure etc. can be useful.
- Overlearning involves the repetition of tasks to a point beyond proficiency to generate very high levels of knowledge, skills and abilities. This strategy enables tasks to be performed automatically or on autopilot even under stressful conditions.
- Mental practice is a strategy used by elite athletes to prepare for competition by mentally rehearsing outstanding performance. Also known as imagery rehearsal, the technique improves performance, particularly in tasks that require considerable mental effort.
- Decision making and prioritisation skills can be used to overcome problems such as information overload, multiple high-priority tasks and increased time pressures. Decision making skills may include systematic assessment of information and its sources as well as maintaining vigilance during this process.
- Team skills are critical in roles where key tasks require communication, cooperation and interdependence. Team performance can easily be eroded by stress as individuals narrow their attention and become less sensitive to important social cues. Team skill development includes building awareness between team members of their knowledge and expertise so they can easily identify who is best to contribute to success.

The Application Phase

After receiving the knowledge and skills to perform under stress, individuals can begin to apply it. The knowledge and skills can be applied in imagination and in vivo with general stressors such as information overload, time pressure and ambiguity. It is also helpful for clients to practise with more specific stressors such as difficult customers or suppliers, problematic bureaucrats, troublesome team members and so on.

In the application phase it is best to ensure that the inoculation approach is applied and that the client is only exposed to a small amount of toxic stimulus. For example, if the SIT is being used to reduce the stress response to information overload, a hierarchy of relevant items should be developed, ranging from overload that is a minor nuisance to overload that is nearly overwhelming. The client can then systematically work up the items and gradually get used to the pressure and learn to maintain their focus and performance under increasingly difficult conditions.

The Review and Evaluation Phase

After the client has worked to apply the SIT techniques it is important for them to set aside a specific time to review and evaluate the awareness, skill development and application phases. Important questions include:

- Does the client understand the sequential and transactional nature of stress and coping?
- Can the client self-monitor unhelpful thoughts, beliefs, images, feelings and behaviours to cope with stress?
- Has the client learned to effectively problem solve by clearly defining the problem, anticipating the consequences, making sound choices and evaluating what happens?
- Has the client been able to rehearse emotional regulation, self-control mechanisms and concrete actions? How effective were these techniques? What needs to be improved?
- Is the client able to use their unhelpful stress responses as cues to apply their coping skills?
- Have they been able to practise the SIT techniques both in imagination and in vivo with graded exposure that intensifies over time?
- Is the client better able to handle unexpected stressful circumstances because of the training?

The Effectiveness of Stress Inoculation Training

A range of meta-analyses have been conducted into SIT and several of these are summarised below.

In an early review of SIT effectiveness studies in applied work settings, Saunders et al. (1996) identified 37 control group type studies and found that SIT has a moderate to strong impact on diminishing both state and performance anxiety. They also found that SIT had a moderate effect on improving performance, with effect sizes in the range .31 to .56. SIT was effective for clients with either normal or high anxiety. They found that more SIT sessions generally resulted in greater effectiveness when compared to smaller numbers of sessions, with four to seven sessions needed to produce average-level declines in state and performance anxiety. Interestingly, clients involved with less experienced trainers, that is those without a doctoral degree, did slightly better than those with more experienced trainers.

Chemtob et al. (1997) used a randomised group design to evaluate a 12-session anger and PTSD treatment programme for Vietnam War veterans. They found that adding SIT routine VA clinical care was effective in decreasing state-anger (angry moods), improving anger control and coping skills and reducing general anxiety and PTSD symptoms.

DiGuiseppe and Tafrate (2001) conducted a meta-analytic review of SIT and related cognitive-behavioural interventions for adults and adolescents with anger and aggression problems. They concluded that these interventions: 'work equally well for all age groups and all types of populations and are equally effective for men and women. The average effect sizes across all outcome measures ranged from .67 to .99 with a mean of .70' (p. 263). The meta-analyses suggested that SIT was moderately successful with clients who were 76% better off than control group untreated clients. Post-treatment stress scores improved by 83% on pre-test levels. Improvement was sustained at follow-up which ranged from 2 to 64 weeks.

Similar results were found in the meta-analysis of Beck and Fernandez (1998) with anger management clients involving 50 SIT and cognitive-behavioural interventions and 1,640 subjects across a wide age range. In both these meta-analytic studies they found that standardised manuals and treatment fidelity checks contributed to effectiveness.

In academic settings, using first-year law students, SIT has been found to be effective in reducing stress and anxiety as well as improving performance (Sheehy & Horan, 2004).

Military personnel with no prior flying experience who received SIT performed better in a flight task compared to those who had not (McClernon et al., 2011). In this case, SIT did not significantly improve subjective stress ratings compared to the control group; however, flight performance assessed from aircraft telemetry data and flight instructor ratings was better for the group that undertook the SIT training. Barwood et al. (2006) found that SIT improved the ability of subjects to hold their breath when immersed in cold water compared to a control group matched on initial breath-hold times. Robson and Manacapilli (2014) concluded that the majority of well conducted research in the military suggested that SIT enhanced performance under stress.

Based on the above range of studies, it appears that SIT has the potential to decrease stress symptoms and improve performance under pressure.

Stress Inoculation Coaching

Stress Inoculation Coaching (SIC) uses the same four phase approach as SIT:

1.   Awareness and knowledge building.
2.   Skill development.

3.   Application.
4.   Review and improvement.

However, in this context the clients are senior managers and leaders in organisations rather than the clinical population (McCormick, 2021a).

Awareness and Knowledge Building Phase

In the awareness and knowledge building phase the client is taught about the nature and four types of stress as summarised below:

1.   One-time not often repeating events – e.g., dental procedure.
2.   One event that triggers a cascade – e.g., job loss, divorce.
3.   Chronic but intermittent – e.g., musical performance, athletic competition, combat.
4.   Chronic and continual – e.g., illness, marital conflict, abuse, nursing, teaching, police work.

Next the client is taught about the rationale for SIC, which is to help clients understand stress and better manage their feelings. The stages in stress reduction are presented, which are:

• Preparing for stressful situations.
• Emotional preparation.
• Cognitive preparation.
• Behavioural preparation.
• Social preparation.
• Confronting the situation.
• Coping with critical moments.
• Recognising achievements.

The client is provided with information about stress such as 'experiencing stress is normal for everyone and it is not a sign that you are going crazy', 'Distressing reactions are a very common reaction to difficult and challenging stressful situations', 'The body's way of dealing with threat is to increase heart rate, blood pressure, cortisol, etc. The mind's way of dealing with threat is to have intrusive thoughts, which is a method used to try to make sense of the situation', 'At a behavioural level we typically deal with stress by flight (running away), fight (standing up to the threat) or freeze (remaining completely still). Stressful situations are often not predictable so the surprise element often makes it much worse.'

The Yerkes Dobson Law is then presented as an upside-down U-shaped curve in which the left side of the curve represents low arousal, or stress and the right side represents high arousal. At the centre is a medium level of arousal which is the optimal state for high performance. Too much stress or too little stress is suboptimal for performance.

In an awareness building exercise the client is asked to think about a recent stressful situation and to describe how their body reacted, what they thought and what they did.

Skill Building Phase

This starts with teaching the client emotional preparation and inoculation skills. The client is taught that avoidance of unpleasant emotions intensifies them and that quietly sitting with them typically allows emotions to subside. They are then asked to:

- Review their calendar and write a list of upcoming stressful events, e.g. stuck in traffic, difficult client discussion, disagreement over child custody.
- Then to experience the detail of the situation with eyes closed for three to five minutes.
- During this time they allow the emotion to arise and wait it out. They imagine a clock slowly rotating:
  - o 12 o'clock represents the start of the time when they imagine the scene.
  - o 3 o'clock represents the intensity of emotion building.
  - o 6 o'clock represents maximum intensity.
  - o 9 o'clock represents the emotion subsiding.
  - o 12 o'clock represents feeling back to normal.

The skill building phase then moves to cognitive preparation and inoculation. The client is asked to think about an upcoming stressful situation and assess whether they can control it or not. If they cannot control all or most of the situation they are asked to try to accept it and give up the hopeless task of fighting when they have little control. If they have some control they are asked to think about what they can say to themselves to assist with stress management. Useful phrases might be, 'I can manage myself in this situation', 'I know I can regulate my emotion by slowing down my breathing', 'If I find I am getting upset, I will just wait for the emotion to subside', 'I am not going to get into an argument', 'This is a difficult situation but I have the skills to handle it' or 'I do not like this but it will soon pass'.

The behavioural preparation and inoculation is the next skill building task. The client is asked to spend a minute or two anticipating the stressful situation and thinking through how they can behave. They develop a plan of action and think through the steps.

Social preparation is the next step. The client is asked to think about who they could call upon to assist during or after the stressful situation. They think about a trusted individual who they can talk to and how they can generate social support for themselves.

The final step in skill building is reflective practice and the recognition of their achievements. The client is asked to spend a minute or two reflecting on their stress inoculation skill development, what they learned and how they can apply it. They might then say to themselves, 'Preparation is the key to my handling stress better', 'I did well by not struggling with the stressful thoughts – I just let them go' or 'I can see I will get better every time I use these procedures'.

Application Phase

The client then decides how they will use the stress inoculation steps to proactively deal with difficult situations. They are encouraged to undertake regular practice to build up their capability. For many clients picking a regular occasion to practise dealing with upcoming challenges can be useful. A typical example is for the client to book a private meeting room when they arrive at work, then to take five minutes to think through the upcoming potentially stressful events of the day and practise the emotional, cognitive, behavioural, social and self-reflective techniques.

Stress Inoculation Coaching: Case Study

Paul was a senior architect designing a major new shopping mall. He had many years of successful experience but came to coaching because he wanted 'to do his job and leave the stress behind at the end of the day'. In the first session Paul talked over the stresses of the job, which included: a shortage of qualified design staff, a demanding client, the rapid rise in construction costs and the pressure from Head Office to ensure the project was profitable. Paul said he found the most difficult part of his job was the seemingly random and unexpected arrival of very demanding challenges. He talked through his day yesterday which had included a difficult client meeting, followed by a senior member of his team resigning because he had just received a cancer diagnosis and the day finished with the firm's CFO ringing him to discuss the deteriorating profitability of the job. Paul felt that if he had time to prepare for any of these situations, he would be OK, but they were all unexpected and left him feeling 'shell shocked'. The coach discussed the stress inoculation process to Paul who was immediately impressed by the idea of being better prepared for his daily challenges. He did express the concern that he did not want the daily preparation to turn into a depressing ritual and the coach was able to reassure him that this was the opposite of what would happen.

In the next session the coach went over the SIC phases: awareness and education, skill building, the development of an action plan to implement the approach and review of achievements.

A month later Paul came back for another coaching session. He reported that initially he had struggled to make the time to implement the stress inoculation. However, he decided that the best time was sitting in his car before driving to work. This was quiet and sitting in his garage at home he was not going to be disturbed. When he started to practise regularly, he came to the frightening realisation that the number of stressful events each day at work was large. Initially he felt daunted by this but then decided that this was the very reason he needed to be practising stress inoculation. After these initial hurdles, he settled into a regular pattern of five to ten minutes of stress inoculation preparation for his day and it started to make a big difference to his life. He felt more in control and that he understood the importance of not struggling with painful emotions but simply waiting them out. Overall, he felt that stress inoculation was a powerful approach for proactively dealing with challenges.

Reflective Practice Exercise: Stress Inoculation

Think about an upcoming potentially stressful event in your life and write about it below.

Example: I am often hugely disappointed at the performance of my team members, particularly Jake. He will either refuse to take on work, telling me he is too busy, or he will take on work but not deliver on time.

Decide what type of stress it is.

- One time not often repeating – e.g., dental procedure.
- One event that triggers a cascade – e.g., job loss, divorce.
- Chronic but intermittent – e.g., musical performance, athletic competition, combat.
- Chronic and continual – e.g., illness, marital conflict, abuse, nursing, teaching, police work.

Write a summary of the type of stressful situation.
Example: This is a chronic but intermittent problem.

Write down your typical emotional response to this type of stress.
Example: I feel resentful, bitter and frustrated.

Write down your typical thoughts in this type of situation.
Example: Jake is just bone lazy and why does our boss not do anything about this situation?

Write down your typical behaviour pattern in this situation.
Example: I go quiet and do the work myself, often working very long hours and feeling stressed.

Write down your typical use of social support in this situation.
Example: I withdraw and do not get any support from others.

Now develop a stress inoculation plan, which should include:

- How you will rehearse the stressful event and experience the reality of your emotions. How you will be able to wait for these emptions to pass.
- What constructive thoughts you can say to yourself in the middle of the stressful event.
- What actions you can take to better deal with the situation.
- Who can you call upon to provide you with social support under these circumstances?
- How you can reflect on your stress inoculation skill building and recognise your achievements.

Example: I will imagine Jake at his worst, feel the burning resentment and stay with it until it goes. I will practise thinking, 'Jake does this because no one tells him about his impact on other team members'. I will rehearse, saying, 'Jake I know you are busy but this is urgent client work that needs to be done this week, can you please just do this small part of it'. I will recognise my small steps moving froward, not expecting Jake to change immediately but celebrate my speaking up.

Now develop an action plan to implement stress inoculation. When will you practise it? For how long? How will you assess whether it is working? If you have difficulties in the process, who can you get help from?
Example: Book a meeting room each day and spend ten minutes practising my stress inoculation. I will talk to my coach about my achievements and challenges.

When to Use Stress Inoculation

There are three conditions where stress inoculation is useful:

- A simple stressful event that triggers a cascade of distress.
- A chronic but intermittent series of stresses.
- A chronic and continual stress.

It is not generally useful for a single stressful event that is not often repeating – e.g., a dental procedure.

Using This Workbook Exercise in Professional Development

The reflective practice exercise in this chapter is designed to be used:

- In individual reflective practice sessions for students or coaches who want to develop their capability.
- With coaches who want to work in pairs to build their skills.
- For supervisors who want to use experiential learning in their work.
- With classroom instructors or academics teaching coaching skills.
- By senior practitioners who want to run professional development sessions for coaches.

Summary

This chapter introduced the concepts and techniques of Stress Inoculation Therapy and showed how these can be used in coaching and reflective practice sessions. The chapter covered the four phases of SIT, awareness and knowledge building, skill development and application and the review and evaluation of the effectiveness of SIT. The research into the effectiveness of SIT was summarised. The chapter includes a SIT case study and a reflective practice exercise.

19
When to Use Which Therapeutic Technique or Approach

INTRODUCTION TO THE CHAPTER

This chapter argues for employing a planned integrated approach to using the range of therapeutic techniques in coaching, then sets out a simple model for better understanding client problems and then suggests readings for the coach to undertake to better assist with a range of client challenges.

The Importance of Using an Integrative Approach

In Chapter 11 the case for using an integrated rather than an eclectic approach to coaching was advanced. Integrative means to form, coordinate, or blend into a functioning or unified whole (Merriam-Webster, 2021). Cooper and McLeod (2007) suggest that the underlying principle of an integrative approach is that client problems have multiple causes and so using only one therapeutic method is unlikely to be successful. Nothing is appropriate in all situations as different clients are helped by different processes at different times. In practice, integrative coaching means in any one session the coach will primarily adhere to one coaching model but supplement this with the use of other therapeutic techniques as needed. This approach aims to produce a coherent, clear and unified method to coaching which can be easily explained to the client, if needed.

For example, in an integrative approach the coach may use the solution-focused model (Szabo & Meier, 2008) and work systematically through this until they reach a point where the client is stuck and unable to generate their own solutions. At this point the coach can ask if the client would like to try a therapeutic approach and explain the background and logic behind the change. If

DOI: 10.4324/9781003285144-23

the client agrees, the coach will use the technique, then after this move back to the solution-focused approach by asking, for example, 'If you use this therapeutic approach regularly how much of the problem will that solve on a scale of 1, *not at all*, to 10, *the problem is totally solved?*' If the client provides a rating of 7 or 8 the coach can move on to action planning. If the client provides a low rating the coach can explore why this approach is not very successful and what needs to be done to improve its impact. Towards the end of the session the coach can encourage the client to draw up an action plan and set goals to be achieved before the next coaching session.

This is in sharp contrast to the eclectic model where the coach may move between coaching models and therapeutic approaches in a spontaneous and unplanned manner. For example, the coach could use parts of different coaching models (solution focused, GROW or CLEAR) and then move between therapeutic techniques (ACT, CAT or SIT). The moves between models and approaches are often determined in a spur-of-the-moment manner, depending on the issues raised by the client and without a systematic or thoughtful approach.

In conclusion, it is strongly recommended that coaches employ a planned integrated approach to using the range of therapeutic techniques in coaching.

Understanding Client Problems

To know which therapeutic technique or approach to use in coaching it is critical that the client's problems and the reasons for coming to coaching are understood. This is then the key to designing and implementing an effective coaching programme. Greenberger and Padesky (2016) suggest a useful framework for understanding problems which includes:

- Environment, life situation and changes – 'What changes have been going on in your life recently?' 'What long-term problems or challenges do you experience?'
- Physical reactions – 'What unwanted physical reactions do you have – poor appetite, pain levels, sleep etc.?'
- Moods or emotions – 'What single words most accurately define your difficult mood or emotions – anger, sadness, anxiety, guilt etc.?'
- Behaviours – 'How do you react when you are feeling like this – what is your behaviour?'
- Thoughts – 'When you have powerful unwanted feelings, what are your thoughts – about yourself, others near you, the prospects etc.?'

Once the coach has a sound understanding of the client, they can go on to identify what approach may be useful.

Suggested Readings

Table 19.1 gives a range of problems and a range of suggested readings in this book. However, many of these problems below such as sleep problems, irritability and fatigue many have underlying medical causes which much be addressed before coaching is undertaken.

Table 19.1 Client problem and reading suggestions

Client problem	Reading suggestions
Anxiety and fear	Chapter 12: Unified Protocol Cognitive Behavioural Therapy Techniques
	Chapter 13: Internet Supplemented Acceptance and Commitment Therapy Techniques
Emotional upset, lability, rapid shifts in emotions	Chapter 14: Using Buddhist Psychology Techniques
	Chapter 15: Using Compassion-Focused Techniques
	Chapter 18: Using Stress Inoculation Techniques
	Chapter 12: Unified Protocol Cognitive Behavioural Therapy Techniques
	Chapter 16: Using Schema Therapy with Mindfulness Techniques
Enduring painful situations	Chapter 14: Using Buddhist Psychology Techniques
	Chapter 15: Using Compassion-Focused Techniques
Extreme and chronic fatigue	Chapter 12: Unified Protocol Cognitive Behavioural Therapy Techniques
	Chapter 13: Internet Supplemented Acceptance and Commitment Therapy Techniques
Stress and inability to respond effectively to it	Chapter 18: Using Stress Inoculation Techniques
	Chapter 12: Unified Protocol Cognitive Behavioural Therapy Techniques

(Continued)

Table 19.1 (Continued)

Client problem	Reading suggestions
Troublesome thoughts	Chapter 12: Unified Protocol Cognitive Behavioural Therapy Techniques
	Chapter 13: Internet Supplemented Acceptance and Commitment Therapy Techniques
	Chapter 14: Using Buddhist Psychology Techniques
	Chapter 15: Using Compassion-Focused Techniques
Other troublesome emotions	Chapter 12: Unified Protocol Cognitive Behavioural Therapy Techniques
	Chapter 13: Internet Supplemented Acceptance and Commitment Therapy Techniques
	Chapter 14: Using Buddhist Psychology Techniques
	Chapter 15: Using Compassion-Focused Techniques
	Chapter 18: Using Stress Inoculation Techniques
Troublesome behaviours	Chapter 13: Internet Supplemented Acceptance and Commitment Therapy Techniques
	Chapter 16: Using Schema Therapy with Mindfulness Techniques
Persistent problem behaviour patterns	Chapter 16: Using Schema Therapy with Mindfulness Techniques
	Chapter 17: Using Cognitive Analytic Therapy Techniques
Unclear or conflicting values	Chapter 13: Internet Supplemented Acceptance and Commitment Therapy Techniques

Summary

This chapter argues for using a planned integrated approach to using therapeutic techniques in coaching, then it sets out a simple model to better understand client problems and provides suggested readings for the coach to undertake to better assist with a range of client challenges.

Part V
Conclusion

This final part of the book draws together the range of material that has been presented so far and sets out how, at a practical level, the coach can start a regular reflective practice.

DOI: 10.4324/9781003285144-24

20
Final Reflections

INTRODUCTION TO THE CHAPTER

This chapter challenges the reader to look back and reflect on what is of value to them in this book and to implement reflective practice on a regular basis. The reader is encouraged to develop a regular systematic process of reflection and to have this as a core element of their ongoing professional development as a coach.

Reflective Practice Exercise: Main Learnings and Applications

Having read this book, use the following questions to reflect on what you learned and how you want to become a better coach.

Reflective Practice Exercise: Main Learnings and Applications

What are your main learnings from this book? How will you apply these in your coaching practice? What do you want to do to continue your professional practice as a coach?
Example: I learned that there are a wealth of newly developed approaches that can keep my coaching both current and evidence based.

DOI: 10.4324/9781003285144-25

What did you learn about the importance of reflective practice for coaches? Why do many international professional coaching bodies stress the importance of self-reflection?
Example: I learned that reflective practice is recognised by many international professional coaching bodies as critical to effective coaching practice.

What practical steps did you learn about to set up a reflective practice? What approach to reflective practice is most relevant to you?
Example: I learned that there are a whole range of ways to develop reflective practice and I will do more of it.

What did you learn about how to build psychological connection, safety and confidentiality? How will you apply this?
Example: I want to run group reflective practice programmes and I now understand how critical safety is for these groups.

What did you learn about how to establish an assessment of outcome in reflective practice sessions? How will you apply this?
Example: Evaluating reflective practice group sessions is both easy and useful.

What did you learn about coaching generally, the range of conceptual coaching models and the nature of coaching? How will you apply your new learnings?
Example: I really understand much more about the power of the coaching alliance and will work on this next month.

What did you learn about coaching effectiveness? How will you reinforce the evidence-based approach to coaching to your clients?
Example: I learned how much recent well-conducted research there is in the coaching area. I will explain this where relevant to my clients.

What did you learn about solution-focused coaching? What do you want to apply in your own coaching practice?
Example: I now see how this model is very effective at generating powerful coaching questions. I want to start to use it in my next coaching session.

What did you learn about coaching skills? What are your coaching skill strengths? What skills do you want to improve? How will you do this?
Example: I want to improve my deep listening and intuition skills by reflecting more after each coaching session.

Do you use an eclectic or integrated approach in your coaching? Why? What do you want to change?
Example: I tend to be eclectic but now understand how being planned and systematic is critical in coaching.

What did you learn about using a unified protocol approach to cognitive behavioural techniques in coaching? Which techniques will you apply in your own practice?
Example: This opened my eyes to a whole new approach to coaching. I will use the Unified Protocol approach when relevant.

What did you learn about using internet supplemented acceptance and commitment therapy techniques in coaching? Which techniques will you apply in your own practice?
Example: I will look further into the ACT Coach app which I will start to use to supplement my work.

What did you learn about using Buddhist psychology techniques in coaching? Which techniques will you apply in your own practice?
Example: Understanding how important it is for coaches to have a regular meditative practice, if they want to suggest mindfulness to their clients, will be a great source of motivation for me.

What did you learn about using compassion-focused techniques in coaching? Which techniques will you apply in your own practice?
Example: I have a small number of clients where the self-compassion meditation techniques will be extremely useful.

What did you learn about using schema therapy and mindfulness techniques in coaching? Which techniques will you apply in your own practice?
Example: I want to work on one of my own schema before I find some additional training in this area.

What did you learn about using cognitive analytical techniques in coaching? Which techniques will you apply in your own practice?
Example: I like the idea of drawing a chart of the sequence of troublesome behaviours to help my clients better understand their problems and I will use this when relevant in my coaching.

What did you learn about using stress inoculation techniques in coaching? Which techniques will you apply in your own practice?
Example: I am very keen to apply this proactive approach to managing my own stress. Later I will use it with relevant clients.

The Reflective Coach

The focus of this book has been to build up an understanding and practice of reflective practice for coaches. At an operational level this can be implemented by adopting a regular self-reflective practice on a daily, monthly and annual basis.

Try using these Reflective Practice exercises.

Daily Reflective Practice Exercise

Looking back over my coaching today – what went well?
Example: I felt that I listened really deeply to my first client of the day and this added a great deal to the session's effectiveness.

Looking back over my coaching today – what did not go well?
Example: I had my second session of the day postponed at the last minute and I found this very frustrating.

What did I learn from my coaching today?
Example: Once again I learned the power of taking the time to listen deeply to the client and to understand their world view before moving forward.

What do I want to improve?
Example: Keep listening deeply and actively to my clients.

Monthly Reflective Practice Exercise

Looking back over the last month – what are the most important lessons I learned?
Example: I have been a coach for many years but this month I learned, once again, that I can still learn a great deal more.

How will I apply these lessons?
Example: I will undertake more systematic written reflective practice.

How will I hold myself accountable?
Example: I will add a discussion about my reflective practice to my supervision sessions.

What do I want to improve?
Example: I want to improve the quality of my reflection.

Annual Reflective Practice Exercise

Looking back over the last year – what are the most important lessons I learned?
Example: I went to a schema coaching course and worked on my own schema. I now feel ready to apply this with clients.

What new innovative approaches or techniques did I learn about this year?
Example: The use of stress inoculation in coaching. It will prove to be extremely helpful for a wide range of clients.

Did I live by my deeply held personal values this year? Am I living my life in a way that brings me satisfaction and adds something useful to my community?
Example: I greatly enjoy my coaching work and feel that I am helping my clients a lot. I am sure this is adding something to my community.

Am I keeping up to date with the evidence base of coaching?
Example: This is always a challenge and I want to do more reading in this area next year.

What do I want to achieve in 12 months' time?
Example: To be a more powerful, effective and self-reflective coach.

Summary

This chapter challenges the reader to look back and reflect on what is of value to them in this book and to set up a regular self-reflective practice. The reader is encouraged to develop a regular systematic process of reflective practice and to have this as a core element of their ongoing professional development as a coach.

References

AC, Association for Coaching (2019). https://cdn.ymaws.com/www.association forcoaching.com/resource/resmgr/accreditation/coach_accreditation/supporting_documentation/ca_supervision_guide.pdf

AC, Association for Coaching. (2021a). *Coaching Competency Framework*. https://cdn.ymaws.com/www.associationforcoaching.com/resource/resmgr/Accreditation/Accred_General/Coaching_Competency_Framewor.pdf

AC, Association for Coaching. (2021b). *About Us*. www.associationforcoaching.com/page/AboutUs

Adcroft A. (2011). The mythology of feedback. *Higher Education Research & Development*, 30(4), 405–419.

Albertson, E.R., Neff, K.D., & Dill-Shackleford, K.E. (2014). Self-compassion and body dissatisfaction in women: A randomized controlled trial of a brief meditation intervention. *Mindfulness*, 25 January, 1–11.

Allen, A.B., Goldwasser, E.R., & Leary, M.R. (2012). Self-compassion and wellbeing among older adults. *Self and Identity*, 11(4), 428–453.

Allport, G. (1960). *Personality and social encounter*. Beacon Press.

Ambady, N., & Rosenthal, R. (1992). Thin slices of expressive behavior as predictors of interpersonal consequences: A meta-analysis. *Psychological Bulletin*, 111(2), 256–274.

Animas (2021). *9 Powerful Types of Life Coaching Questions*. www.animascoaching.com/blog/9-powerful-types-of-coaching-questions/

Ashworth, M., Shepherd, M., Christey, J., Matthews, V., Wright, K., Parmentier, H., Robinson, S., & Godfrey, E. (2004). A client-generated psychometric instrument: The development of 'PSYCHLOPS'. *Counselling and Psychotherapy Research*, 4(2), 27–31.

Atkins, S., & Murphy, K. (1993). Reflection: A review of the literature. *Journal of Advanced Nursing*, 18, 1188–1192.

Avramchuk, O., & Hlyvanska, O. (2018). Comparative analysis of modern methods of psychotherapy for patients with borderline personality disorder. *European Journal of Interdisciplinary Studies, 10*(1), 50–61.

Bachkirova, T., Jackson, P., Hennig, C., & Moral, M. (2020). Supervision in coaching: systematic literature review. *International Coaching Psychology Review.* https://radar.brookes.ac.uk/radar/file/b6abc742-08ba-41b9-b4f5-4c058a1e0536/1/Supervision%20in%20coaching%20systematic%20literature%20review%20-%202020%20-%20Bachkirova%20Jackson%20Hennig%20Moral.pdf

Bakos, D.S., Gallo, A.E., & Wainer, R. (2015). Systematic review of the clinical effectiveness of schema therapy. *Contemporary Behavioral Health Care, 1*(1), 11–15.

Barbagallo, M.S., (2021). Nursing students' perceptions and experiences of reflective practice: A qualitative meta-synthesis. *Teaching and Learning in Nursing, 16*(1), 24–31.

Barlow, D.H, Farchione, T.J., Fairholme, C.P., Ellard, K.K., Boisseau, C.L., Allen, L.B., Ehrenreich-May, J. (2011). *The unified protocol for transdiagnostic treatment of emotional disorders: Therapist guide.* Oxford University Press.

Barnard, L.K., & Curry, J.F. (2011). Self-compassion: Conceptualizations, correlates, & interventions. *Review of General Psychology, 15*(4), 289–303.

Barnes, C., Bullard, M., & Kohler-Evans, P. (2017). Essential Coaching Skills for Affective Development. *Journal of Education and Culture Studies, 1*(2), 176.

Baron, L., & Morin, L. (2009). The coach–client relationship in executive coaching: A field study. *Human Resource Development Review, 20*(1), 85–106.

Baron, L., & Morin, L. (2012). The working alliance in executive coaching: Its impact on outcomes and how coaches can influence it. In E. de Haan & C. Sills (Eds.), *Coaching relationships* (pp. 213–226). Libri.

Barwood, M.J., Dalzell, J., Datta, A.K., Thelwell, R.C., & Tipton, M.J. (2006). Breath-hold performance during cold water immersion: Effects of psychological skills training. *Aviation Space and Environmental Medicine, 77*(11), 1136–1142.

Beck, J.S. (1995). *Cognitive therapy: Basics and beyond.* Guilford Press.

Beck, R., & Fernandez, E. (1998). Cognitive-behavioral self-regulation of the frequency, duration and intensity of anger. *Journal of Psychopathology and Behavioral Assessment, 20,* 217–229.

Benito, M.J. (2018). The fine line between integration or eclecticism and syncretism in new therapists: Dual diagnosis. *Open Access, 3*(3), 8.

Bennett-Levy, J., & Lee, N.K. (2012). Self-practice and self-reflection in cognitive behaviour therapy training: What factors influence trainees' engagement and experience of benefit? *Behavioral and Cognitive Psychotherapy, 42*(1), 48–64.

Bennett-Levy, J., Turner, F., Beaty, T., Smith, M., Paterson, B., & Farmer, S. (2001). The value of self-practice of cognitive therapy techniques and self-reflection in the training of cognitive therapists. *Behavioural and Cognitive Psychotherapy, 29,* 203–220.

Bennett-Levy, J., Thwaites, R., Haarhoff, B., & Perry, H. (2015). *Experiencing CBT from the inside out: A self-practice/ self-reflection workbook for therapists.* Guilford Press.

Bisson, M. (2017). *Coach yourself first: A coach's guide to self-reflection.* Matador.

Black, D.S. (2011). A brief definition of mindfulness. *Mindfulness Research Guide.* https://classroommindfulnessdotcom.files.wordpress.com/2012/10/a-brief-definition-of-mindfulness.pdf

Blackman, A., Moscardo, G., & Gray, D.E. (2016). Challenges for the theory and practice of business coaching: A systematic review of empirical evidence. *Human Resource Development Review, 15*(4), 459–486.

Blakey, J., & Day, I. (2012). *Challenging coaching: Going beyond traditional coaching to face the FACTS.* John Murray Press.

Bolton, G., & Delderfield, R. (2018). *Reflective practice: Writing and professional development.* SAGE.

Bond, F. W. & Bunce, D. (2000). Mediators of change in emotion-focused and problem- focused worksite stress management interventions. *Journal of Occupational Health Psychology, 5,* 156–163.

Bono, J.E., Purvanova, R.K., Towler, A.J., & Peterson, D.B. (2009). A survey of executive coaching practices. *Personnel Psychology, 62*(2), 361–404.

Bordin, E.S. (1979). The generalizability of the psychoanalytic concept of the working alliance. *Psychotherapy: Theory, Research & Practice, 16,* 252–260.

Bordin, E.S. (1994). Theory and research on the therapeutic working alliance: New directions. In A.O. Horvath and L.S. Greenberg (Eds.), *The working alliance: Theory, research and practice.* Wiley.

Boyce, L.A., Jackson, R.J., & Neal, L.J. (2010). Building successful leadership coaching relationships: Examining impact of matching criteria in a leadership coaching program. *Journal of Management Development, 29,* 914–931.

Bozer, G., & Jones, R.J. (2018). Understanding the factors that determine workplace coaching effectiveness: A systematic literature review. *European Journal of Work and Organizational Psychology, 27*(3), 342–361.

Brazier, C. (2003). *Buddhist Psychology.* Robinson.

Brazier, D. (1995). *Zen therapy: Transcending the sorrows of the human mind.* Wiley.

Breines, J.G., & Chen, S. (2012). Self-compassion increases self-improvement motivation. *Personality and Social Psychology Bulletin, 38*(9), 1133–1143.

Brown, R.P., Varghese, L., Sullivan, S, & Parsons, S. (2021). The impact of professional coaching on emerging leaders. *International Journal of Evidence-Based Coaching and Mentoring, 19*(2), 24–37.

Burt, D., & Talati, Z. (2017). The unsolved value of executive coaching: A meta-analysis of outcomes using randomised control trail studies. *International Journal of Evidence-Based Coaching and Mentoring, 15*(2), 17–24.

Carlucci, L., Saggino, A., & Balsamo, M. (2021). On the efficacy of the unified protocol for transdiagnostic treatment of emotional disorders: A systematic review and meta-analysis. *Clinical Psychology Review, 87*, 101999.

Castonguay, L., & Beutler, L.E. (2006). Principles of therapeutic change: a Task Force on participants, relationships, and techniques factors. *Journal of Clinical Psychology, 62*, 631–638.

Cavanagh, M.J., & Grant, A.M. (2010). The solution-focused approach to coaching. In E. Cox, T. Bachkirova, & D. Clutterbuck (Eds.), *Complete handbook of coaching* (pp. 54–67). SAGE.

Cercone, K. (2008). Characteristics of adult learners with implications for online learning design. *AACE Journal, 16*(2), 137–159.

Chemtob, C.M., Novaco, R.W., Hamada, R.S., & Gross, D.M. (1997). Cognitive-behavioral treatment for severe anger in posttraumatic stress disorder. *Journal of Consulting and Clinical Psychology, 65*(1), 184–189.

Cheng, F.K., & Tse, S. (2014). The use of Chinese Buddhist theories in counselling, psychotherapy, psychology, and mental health research: An integrative review. *International Journal for the Advancement of Counselling, 36*, 229–242.

CIPD, The Chartered Institute of Personnel and Development. (2021). *Reflective practice*. https://beta.cipduat.co.uk/Images/reflective-practice-guide_tcm18-12524.pdf

Clark, T.R., (2020). *The 4 stages of psychological safety: Defining the path to inclusion and innovation*. Berrett-Koehler.

Cooper, M. (2008). *Essential research findings in counselling and psychotherapy*. SAGE.

Cooper M., & McLeod, J. (2007). A pluralistic framework for counselling and psychotherapy: Implications for research. *Journal of Counselling Psychology Research, 7*, 135–143.

Costa, A.L., & Garmston, R.J. (2002). *Cognitive coaching: A foundation for renaissance schools* (2nd ed.). Christopher-Gordon.

Craig, C., Hiskey, S., and Spector, A. (2020). Compassion focused therapy: A systematic review of its effectiveness and acceptability in clinical populations. *Expert Review of Neurotherapeutics, 20*, 385–400.

Dahl, J., Wilson, K.G., & Nilsson, A. (2004). Acceptance and commitment therapy and the treatment of persons at risk for long-term disability resulting from stress and pain symptoms: A preliminary randomized trial. *Behavior Therapy, 35*, 785–802.

Dalgleish, T., Black, M., Johnston, D., & Bevan, A. (2020). Transdiagnostic approaches to mental health problems: Current status and future directions. *Journal of Consulting and Clinical Psychology*, 88(3), 179–195.

de Haan, E.D. (Ed.). (2019). *Critical moments in executive coaching: Understanding the coaching process through research and evidence-based theory* (1st ed.). Routledge.

de Haan, E., Culpin, V., & Curd, J. (2011). Executive coaching in practice: What determines helpfulness for clients of coaching? *Personnel Review*, 40, 24–44.

de Haan, E., & Duckworth, A. (2013). Signalling a new trend in coaching outcome research. *International Coaching Psychology Review*, 8(1), 6–20.

de Haan, E., Molyn, J., and Nilsson, V. O. (2020). New findings on the effectiveness of the coaching relationship: Time to think differently about active ingredients. *Consulting Psychology Journal: Practice and Research*, 72, 155–167.

de Shazer, S., Berg, I.K., Lipchik, E., Nunnally, E., Molnar, A., Gingerich, W., Weiner-Davis, M. (1986). Brief therapy: Focused solution development. *Family Process*, 25(2), 207–221.

Dembkowski, S., & Eldridge, F. (2003). Beyond GROW: A new coaching model. *The International Journal of Mentoring and Coaching*, 1(1), 21.

Desbordes, G., Negi, L.T., Pace, T.W., Wallace, A.B., Raison, C.L., & Schwartz, E.L. (2013). Effects of mindful-attention and compassion meditation training on amygdala response to emotional stimuli in an ordinary, non-meditative state. *Frontiers in Human Neuroscience*. Advance, 292. doi:10.3389/fnhum.2012.00292

Dewey, J. (1933). *How we think: A restatement of the relation of reflective thinking to the educative process*. DC Heath.

DiGuiseppe, R., & Tafrate, R. C. (2001). Anger treatment for adults: A meta-analytic review. Unpublished manuscript. St. John's University, Jamaica, New York. Cited in Meichenbaum, D. (2007). Stress inoculation training: A preventative and treatment approach. In R. L. Woolfolk and W. S. Sime (eds.), *Principles and practice of stress management* (3rd ed., pp. 497–518). Guilford Press.

Dilts, R. 6-Step reframing. http://www.scrutz.net/~rdilts/pattern2.htm. 1996.

Di Stefano, G., Gino, F., Pisano, G., & Staats, B. (2016). Making experience count: The role of reflection in individual learning (June 14, 2016). Harvard Business School NOM Unit Working Paper No. 14-093, Harvard Business School Technology & Operations Mgt. Unit Working Paper No. 14-093, HEC Paris Research Paper No. SPE-2016-1181, Available at SSRN: https://ssrn.com/abstract=2414478 or http://dx.doi.org/10.2139/ssrn.2414478

Driskell, J.E., & Johnston, J.H. (1998). Stress exposure training. In J.A. Cannon-Bowers & E. Salas (eds.), *Making decisions under stress: Implications for individual and team training*. American Psychological Association.

Duncan, B.L., Miller, S.D., Sparks, J.A., Claud, D.A., Reynolds, L.R., Brown, J., & Johnson, L.D. (2003). The session rating scale: Preliminary psychometric properties of a 'working' alliance measure. *Journal of Brief Therapy*, 3, 3–12.

ECF, Executive Coaching Forum (2015). *The executive coaching handbook: Principles and guidelines for a successful coaching partnership.* http://theexecutivecoachingforum. com/docs/default-document-library/tecf-6th-ed.pdf

Edgerton, N., & Palmer, S. (2005). SPACE: A psychological model for use within cognitive behavioural coaching, therapy and stress management. *The Coaching Psychologist, 2*(2), 25–31.

Edmondson, A.C., & Lei, Z. (2014). Psychological safety: The history, renaissance, and future of an interpersonal construct. *Annual Review of Organizational Psychology and Organizational Behavior, 1,* 23–43.

Efstation, J.F., Patton, M.J., & Kardash, C.M. (1990). Measuring the working alliance in counselor supervision. *Journal of Counseling Psychology, 37*(3), 322–329.

Elliott, R., Wagner, J., Sales, C., Rodgers, B., Alves, P., & Café, M.J. (2016). Psychometrics of the personal questionnaire: A client-generated outcome measure. *Psychological Assessment, 28*(3), 263.

Ellis, A. (1994). *Reason and emotion in psychotherapy* (Rev. ed.). Carol Publishing Group. www.theexecutivecoachingforum.com

EMCC, European Mentoring and Coaching Council (2015). *Global competence framework V2.* https://emccdrive.emccglobal.org/api/file/download/0gzGExIyhoRp VFnq5DB7ucXeu1FpQ6pJZk35YbTh

EMCC, European Mentoring and Coaching Council (2021). *Our purpose.* www.emc cglobal.org

Ennis, S., Goodman, R., Hodgetts, W., Hunt, J., Mansfield, R., Otto, J., & Stern, L. (2015). *The executive coaching handbook: Principles and guidelines for successful coaching partnerships.* The Executive Coaching Forum. http://theexecutivecoach ingforum.com/docs/default-document-library/tecf-6th-ed.pdf

Erskine, R.G., & Moursund, J.P. (1988). *Integrative psychotherapy in action.* SAGE.

Erskine, R., & Trautmann, R. (1996). Methods of an integrative psychotherapy. *Transactional Analysis Journal, 26,* 316–328.

Farrell, J.M., & Shaw, I.A. (2018). *Experiencing schema therapy from the inside out: a self-practice/self-reflection workbook for therapists.* Guilford.

Finlay, L. (2015). *Relational integrative psychotherapy: Process and theory in practice,* Wiley.

Freeston, M.H., Thwaites, R., & Bennett-Levy, J. (2019). 'Courses for horses': Designing, adapting and implementing self-practice/self-reflection programmes. *The Cognitive Behaviour Therapist, 12*(28), 1–19.

Friedlander, M.L., & Snyder, J. (1983). Trainees' expectations for the supervisory process: Testing a developmental model. *Counselor Education and Supervision, 22*(4), 342–348.

Friedlander, M., & Ward, L. (1984). Development and validation of the Supervisory Styles Inventory. *Journal of Counseling Psychology*, 31, 541–557.

Froggatt, W. (2006). *A brief introduction to cognitive-behaviour therapy*. https://rational.org.nz/prof-docs/Intro-CBT.pdf

Gale, C., & Schröder, T. (2014). Experiences of self-practice/self-reflection in cognitive behavioural therapy: A meta-synthesis of qualitative studies. *Psychology and Psychotherapy Theory Research and Practice*, 87, 373–392.

Germer, C. & Neff, K. D. (2019). Mindful self-compassion (MSC). In I. Itvzan (Ed.), *The handbook of mindfulness-based programs: Every established intervention, from medicine to education* (pp. 357–367). Routledge.

Gibbs, G. (1988). *Learning by doing: A guide to teaching and learning methods*. Oxford Further Education Unit.

Gibbs, G. (2001). *Learning in doing*. London: Oxford Centre for Staff and Learning Development, Oxford Brooks University. https://thoughtsmostlyaboutlearning.files.wordpress.com/2015/12/learning-by-doing-graham-gibbs.pdf

Gilbert, P. (2005). *Compassion: Conceptualisations, research and use in psychotherapy*. Routledge.

Gilbert, P. (2009). *The compassionate mind*. Constable Robinson and New Harbinger.

Gilbert, P. (2010a). *Compassion focused therapy*. Routledge

Gilbert, P. (2010b). *Training our minds in, with and for compassion: An introduction to concepts and compassion-focused exercises*. www.getselfhelp.co.uk/docs/GILBERT-COMPASSION-HANDOUT.pdf

Gilbert, P. (2014). The origins and nature of compassion focused therapy. *British Journal of Clinical Psychology*, 53, 6–41.

Gladwell, M. (2005). *Blink: The power of thinking without thinking*. Back Bay Books.

Gloster, A.T., Walder, N., Levin, M.E., Twohig, M.P., & Karekla, M. (2020). The empirical status of acceptance and commitment therapy: A review of meta-analyses. *Journal of Contextual Behavioral Science*, 18, 181–192.

Gore, J., & Zeichner, K. (1991). Action research and reflective teaching in preservice teacher education: A case study from the United States. *Teaching and Teacher Education*, 7(2), 119–136.

Graßmann, C., Schölmerich, F., & Schermuly, C. C. (2020). The relationship between working alliance and client outcomes in coaching: A meta-analysis. *Human relations*, 73(1), 35–58.

Graf, E., & Dionne, F. (2021). Coaching research in 2020: About destinations, journeys and travelers (Part 1). *International Coaching Psychology Review*, 16(1), 38–53.

Grant, A.M. (2011). Is it time to REGROW the GROW model? Issues related to teaching coaching session structures. *The Coaching Psychologist, 7*(2), 118–126.

Grant, A.M. (2019). Solution-focused coaching: The basics for advanced practitioners. *Coaching Psychologists, 15*(2), 444–453.

Grant, A.M. (2012). Making a positive change: A randomized study comparing solution-focused vs. problem-focused coaching questions. *Journal of Systemic Therapies, 31*(2), 21–35.

Grant, A.M., & Cavanagh, M.J. (2007). Evidence-based coaching: Flourishing or languishing? *Australian Psychologist, 42*, 239–254.

Grant, A.M., Franklin, J., & Langford, P. (2002). The self-reflection and insight scale: A new measure of private self-consciousness. *Social Behavior and Personality: An International Journal, 30*(8), 821–835.

Grant, A.M., & Gerrard, B. (2020). Comparing problem-focused, solution-focused and combined problem-focused/solution-focused coaching approach: Solution-focused coaching questions mitigate the negative impact of dysfunctional attitudes. *Coaching: An International Journal of Theory, Research and Practice, 13*(1), 61–77.

Grant, A.M., Passmore, J., Cavanagh, M.J., & Parker, H. (2010). The state of play in coaching today: A comprehensive review of the field. *International Review of Industrial and Organizational Psychology, 25*, 125–167.

Gray, D.E. (2006). Executive coaching: Towards a dynamic alliance of psychotherapy and transformative learning processes. *Management Learning, 37*(4), 475–497.

Green, D. (2006). CPD: Why bother? In L. Golding & I. Gray (Eds.), *Continuing professional development for clinical psychologists: A practical handbook*. BPS Blackwell.

Greenberger, D., & Padesky, C.A. (2016). *Mind over mood: A cognitive therapy treatment manual for clients*. Guilford.

Grover, S., & Furnham, A. (2016). Coaching as a developmental intervention in organisations: A systematic review of its effectiveness and the mechanisms underlying it. *PloS One, 11*(7), e0159137.

Haarhoff, B.A. (2006). The importance of identifying and understanding therapist schema in cognitive therapy training and supervision. *New Zealand Journal of Psychology, 35*, 126–131.

Haarhoff, B., & Thwaites, R. (2016). *Reflection in CBT*. Sage.

Haley, J. (1973). *Uncommon therapy: The psychiatric techniques of Milton H. Erickson, M.D.* Norton.

Hall, L. (2013). *Mindful coaching: How mindfulness can transform coaching practice*. Kogan Page.

Hallam, C., Simmonds-Buckley, M., Kellett, S., Greenhill, B., & Jones, A. (2021). The acceptability, effectiveness, and durability of cognitive analytic therapy: Systematic review and meta-analysis. *Psychology and Psychotherapy: Theory, Research and Practice, 94*, 8–35.

Hamid, B.A., & Azman, H. (1992). Making supervisory intentions clear: Adapting the six category intervention analysis to promote facilitative type supervisory feedback in teaching practice. In E. Sadtono (Ed.), *Language teacher education in a fast-changing world (anthology series)*. Singapore: SEAMEO RELC.

Harris, M. (1999). Look, it's an I-O psychologist . . . no, it's a trainer . . . no, it's an executive coach. *The Industrial-Organizational Psychologist, 36*(3), 1–5.

Harris, R. (2006). Embracing your demons: An overview of Acceptance and Commitment Therapy. *Psychotherapy in Australia, 12*, 2–8.

Harris, R. (2007). *The happiness trap: Stop struggling and start living*. Exisle.

Harris, R. (2009). *ACT made simple*. New Harbinger.

Hawkins, P., & Smith, N. (2013). *Coaching, mentoring and organizational consultancy: Supervision and development* (2nd ed.). Open University Press/McGraw-Hill.

Hayes, A.M., & Harris, M.S. (2000). The development of an integrative treatment for depression. In S. Johnson, A.M. Hayes, T. Field, N. Schneiderman, & P. McCabe (Eds.), *Stress, coping, and depression* (pp. 291–306). Lawrence Erlbaum.

Hayes, S.C., Strosahl, K., & Wilson, K.G. (1999). *Acceptance and commitment therapy: An experiential approach to behavior change*. Guilford.

Hayes, S.C. (2021). *My ACT tool kit*. https://stevenchayes.com/my-act-toolkit/

Heron, J. (1976). A six-category intervention analysis. *British Journal of Guidance & Counselling, 4*(2), 143–155.

Hicks, M.D., & Peterson, D.B. (1999). The development pipeline: How people really learn. *Knowledge Management Review, 9*, 30–33.

Hodgetts, W.H. (2002). Using executive coaching in organizations: What can go wrong (and how to prevent it). In C. Fitzgerald & J. Garvey Berger (Eds.), *Executive coaching: Practices and perspectives*. Davies-Black.

Hofmann, S.G., Asnaani, A., Vonk, I.J., Sawyer, A.T., & Fang, A. (2012). The efficacy of Cognitive Behavioral Therapy: A review of meta-analyses. *Cognitive Therapy and Research, 36*(5), 427–440.

Hoffmann, S.G., Grossman, P., & Hinton, D.E. (2011). Loving-kindness and compassion meditation: Potential for psychological intervention. *Clinical Psychology Review, 13*, 1126–1132.

Hollis-Walker, L., & Colosimo, K. (2011). Mindfulness, self-compassion, and happiness in non-meditators: A theoretical and empirical examination. *Personality and Individual Differences, 50*, 222–227.

Horvath, A.O., & Greenberg, L. (1986). The development of the Working Alliance Inventory. In L. Greenberg & W. Pinsoff (Eds.), *Psychotherapeutic processes: A research handbook* (pp. 529–556). Guilford.

Horvath, A.O., & Greenberg, L.S. (1989). Development and validation of the Working Alliance Inventory. *Journal of Counseling Psychology*, 36(2), 223.

Hullinger, A.M., DiGirolamo, J.A., & Tkach, J.T. (2019). Reflective practice for coaches and clients: An integrated model for learning. *Philosophy of Coaching: An International Journal*, 4(2), 5–34.

ICF, International Coaching Federation (2019). *Updated ICF Core Competency Model*. https://coachfederation.org/app/uploads/2019/11/ICFCompetencyModel_Oct2019.pdf

ICF, International Coaching Federation (2020). *Membership and credentialing fact sheet July 2020*. https://coachfederation.org/app/uploads/2020/07/July2020_FactSheet.pdf

ICF, International Coaching Federation (2021). *About*. https://coachfederation.org/about

Jacob, G.A., & Arntz, A. (2013). Schema therapy for personality disorders: A review. *International Journal of Cognitive Therapy*, 6(2), 171–185.

Jelly, B., & McCormick, I. A. (2022). Transformational learning and continuous professional development in coaching psychology. *Psychology Aotearoa*, 14(1), 23–30.

Johns, C. (1995). The value of reflective practice for nursing. *Journal of Clinical Nursing*, 4, 23–30.

Jones, R.J., Woods, S.A., & Guillaume, Y.R.F. (2016). The effectiveness of workplace coaching: A meta-analysis of learning and performance outcomes from coaching. *Journal of Occupational and Organizational Psychology*, 89(2), 249–277.

Joo, B-K. (2005). Executive coaching: A conceptual framework from an integrative review of practice and research. *Human Resource Development Review*, 4(4), 462–488.

Jug, R., Jiang, X.S., & Bean, S.M. (2019). Giving and receiving effective feedback: A review article and how-to guide. *Archives of Pathology & Laboratory Medicine*, 143(2), 244–250.

Kabat-Zinn, J. (1994). *Wherever you go, there you are: Mindfulness meditation in everyday life*. Hyperion Books.

Kampa-Kokesch, S., & Anderson, M.Z. (2001). Executive coaching: A comprehensive review of the literature. *Consulting Psychology Journal: Practice & Research*, 53(4), 205–228.

Kampa, S., & White, R. P. (2002). The effectiveness of executive coaching: What we know and what we still need to know. In R.L. Lowman (Ed.), *Handbook of organizational consulting psychology* (pp. 139–158). Jossey-Bass.

Katz, J. and Hemmings, B. (2009). *The professional relationship*. In J. Katz & B. Hemmings (Eds.). *Counselling skills handbook for the sport psychologist*. The British Psychological Society.

Katzenbach, J.R., & Smith, D.K. (1993). The discipline of teams. *Harvard Business Review, 71*(2), 111–120.

Kelley, F.A., Gelso, C.J., Fuertes, J.N., Marmarosh, C., & Lanier, S.H. (2010). The real relationship inventory: Development and psychometric investigation of the client form. *Psychotherapy: Theory, Research, Practice, Training, 47*(4), 540–553.

Kelson, J., Rollin, A., Ridout, B., & Campbell, A. (2019). Internet-delivered acceptance and commitment therapy for anxiety treatment: Systematic review. *Journal of Medical Internet Research, 21*(1), e12530.

Kennedy, B. (2021). *Professional development: Beyond the shiny goldfish*. Paper presented at the 11th International Congress of Coaching Psychology, 8 October 2021.

Khakpoor, S., & Omid S. (2018). Transdiagnostic cognitive behavioral therapy based on unified protocol: New approach to emotional disorders. *Asia Pacific Journal of Clinical Trials: Nervous System Diseases, 3*(4), 151. Gale Academic OneFile. https://go.gale.com/ps/i.do?p=AONE&u=auclib&id=GALE%7CA580721906&v=2.1&it=r&sid=bookmark-AONE&asid=f800e386

Khoury, B., Lecomte, T., Fortin, G., Masse, M., Therien, P., Bouchard, V., Chapleau, M.A., Paquin, K., & Hofman, S.G. (2013). Mindfulness-based therapy: A comprehensive meta-analysis. *Clinical Psychology Review, 33*(6), 763–771.

Kilburg, R.R. (2000). *Executive coaching: Developing managerial wisdom in a world of chaos*. American Psychological Association.

Kilburg, R.R., & Lowman, R.L. (2002). Individual interventions in consulting psychology. *The California School of Organizational Studies: Handbook of organizational consulting psychology: A comprehensive guide to theory, skills, and techniques*, 109–138.

Kishita, N., Gould, R.L., Farquhar, M., Contreras, M., Van Hout, E., Losada, A., Cabrera, I., Hornberger, M., Richmond E., & McCracken L.M. (2021). Internet-delivered guided self-help acceptance and commitment therapy for family carers of people with dementia (iACT4CARERS): A feasibility study, *Aging & Mental Health, 26*(10), 1933–1941.

Knowles, M.S. (1980). *The modern practice of adult education: From pedagogy to androgogy* (2nd ed.). Cambridge Books.

Knowles, M.S. (1984). *Andragogy in action*. Jossey-Bass.

Kolb, D.A. (1984). *Experiential learning: Experience as a source of learning and development*. Prentice Hall.

Körük, S., & Özabacı, N. (2018). Effectiveness of schema therapy on the treatment of depressive disorders: A meta-analysis. *Current Approaches in Psychiatry/Psikiyatride Guncel Yaklasimlar, 10*(4), 460–470.

Kowalski, K., & Casper, C. (2007). The coaching process: An effective tool for professional development. *Nurses Administrative Quarterly*, 31(2), 171–179.

Laborde, G.Z. (1983). *Influencing with integrity: Management skills for communication and negotiation.* Syntony.

Lai, Y.L., & McDowall, A. (2014). A systematic review (SR) of coaching psychology: Focusing on the attributes of effective coaching psychologists. *International Coaching Psychology Review*, 9(2), 120–136.

LeJeune J. (2016). *Teaching clients to 'VOUCH' for themselves: Using perspective taking to facilitate learning in those who are highly self-critical and shame prone.* www.actwith compassion.com/teaching_clients_to_vouch_for_themselves

Levinson, H. (1996). Executive coaching. *Consulting Psychology Journal: Practice and Research*, 48(2), 115–123.

Libri, V. (2004). Beyond GROW: In search of acronyms and coaching models. *The International Journal of Mentoring and Coaching*, 2(1), 1–8.

Lines, R.L.J., Pietsch, S., Crane, M., Ntoumanis, N., Temby, P., Graham, S., & Gucciardi, D. F. (2021). The effectiveness of team reflexivity interventions: A systematic review and meta-analysis of randomized controlled trials. *Sport, Exercise, and Performance Psychology*, 10(3), 438–473.

Linehan, M.M. (1993). *Cognitive-behavioral treatment of borderline personality disorder.* Guilford.

Llewelyn, S. (2003). Cognitive Analytic Therapy: time and process. *Psychodynamic Practice*, 9(4), 501–520.

Lynham, S.A. (2000). Theory building in the human resource development profession. *Human Resource Development Quarterly*, 11(2), 159–178.

MacBeth, A., & Gumley, A. (2012). Exploring compassion: A meta-analysis of the association between self-compassion and psychopathology. *Clinical Psychology Review*, 32, 545–552.

Machin, S. (2010). The nature of the internal coaching relationship. *International Journal of Evidence Based Coaching and Mentoring, Special Issue*, 4, 37–52.

Mattila, A. (2001). 'Seeing things in a new light': Reframing in therapeutic conversation. In *Rehabilitation foundation research report.* Helsinki University Press. https://helda.helsinki.fi/bitstream/handle/10138/22824/seeingth.pdf

McCauley, C.D., & Hezlett, S.A. (2001). Individual development in the workplace. In N. Anderson, D. Ones, H.K. Sinangil, & C. Viswesvaran (Eds.), *Handbook of industrial, work, and organizational psychology* (Vol.2, pp. 313–335). SAGE.

McClernon, C.K., McCauley, M.E., O'Connor, P.E., & Warm, J.S. (2011). Stress training improves performance during a stressful flight. *Human Factors*, 53(3), 207–218.

McCormick, I.A. (2016). *Using schema therapy in executive coaching*. Paper presented to the Industrial and Organisational Special Interest Group of the New Zealand Psychological Society. www.organisationalpsychology.nz/_content/Schema_therapy_in_ executive_coaching.pdf

McCormick, I.A. (2020). *Self-practice/self-reflection: A new world of professional development for coaches*. Presentation made to a Coaching Psychology Special Interest Group of the New Zealand Psychological Society by Dr Iain McCormick of the Executive Coaching Centre on Tuesday, 9 June 2020. www.eccltd.co.nz/post/self-practice-self-reflection-a-new-world-of-professional-development-for-coaches

McCormick, I.A. (2021a). *Stress inoculation coaching*. www.eccltd.co.nz/post/stress-inoculation-coaching

McCormick, I.A. (2021b). *Next level professional development: Self-practice self-reflection*. Paper presented at the 11th International Congress of Coaching Psychology, 8 October 2021. www.eccltd.co.nz/post/11th-international-congress-of-coaching-psychology-2021

McCormick, I.A. (2021c). Next level professional development for coaches: Self-practice self-reflection. *Coaching Psychology International*, 14(1), 16–26. www.isfcp.info/journals/coaching-psychology-international/cpi-volume-14/cpi-volume-14-article-3/

McCormick, I.A. (2022a). *NZPSS Connect 22 Series: Reflective practice for coaching psychologists*. Paper presented to the New Zealand Psychological Society, 5 July 2022.

McCormick, I.A. (2022b). Schema coaching: Theory, research and practice. In J. Passmore & S. Leach (Eds.), *Third wave cognitive behavioural coaching: Contextual, behavioural and neuroscience approaches for evidence-based coaches*. Pavilion Publishing and Media.

McCormick, I.A., & Forsyth, S. (2019). *Using Buddhist psychology in executive coaching*. From a paper presented at the NZPsS Conference Rotorua, August 2019. www.eccltd.co.nz/post/using-buddhist-psychology-in-executive-coaching

McGinn, L.K. (2015). Enhancing Cognitive-Behavioural Therapy (CBT) skill acquisition through experiential and reflective learning: A commentary on studies examining the impact of self-practice and self-reflection in CBT. *Australian Psychologist*, 50, 340–343.

McInerney, E., Giga, S., & Morris, A.S. (2021). Does it last? A systematic review of the enduring effects on manager from executive coaching. *International Coaching Psychology Review*, 16(2), 22–50.

Meichenbaum, D. (1985). *Stress inoculation training*. Pergamon Press.

Meichenbaum, D. (2007). Stress inoculation training: A preventative and treatment approach. In R.L. Woolfolk & W.S. Sime (Eds.), *Principles and practice of stress management* (3rd ed., pp. 497–518). Guilford.

Merriam, S.B. (2001). Andragogy and self-directed learning: Pillars of adult learning theory. *New Directions for Adult and Continuing Education*, 89, 3–13.

Merriam-Webster, (2021). *The on-line dictionary.* www.merriam-webster.com/dictionary. Accessed 19 July 2021.

Mezirow, J. (1991). *Transformative dimensions of adult learning.* Jossey Bass.

Morley, S. (2013). *EasyPQ: Yet another version of Shapiro's Personal Questionnaire.* Unpublished manuscript. www.researchgate.net/publication/235463593_EasyPQ_-Yet_another_version_of_Shapiro%27s_Personal_Questionnaire

Mudd, K. (2021). The observing self. http://eightfoldcounseling.com/wordpress/wp-content/uploads/The-Observer-Self-Handout.pdf

Murphy, M.G., Rakes, S., & Harris R.M. (2020). The psychometric properties of the session rating scale: A narrative review. *Journal of Evidence-Based Social Work*, *17*(3), 279–299.

Murray, E. (2004). Intuitive coaching: Summary. *Industrial and Commercial Training*, 36(5), 203–206.

Naik, P., Harris, V.W., & Forthun, L.F. (2013). *Mindfulness: An introduction.* www.researchgate.net/publication/261528260_Mindfulness_An_Introduction

Neff, K.D. (2003). Self-compassion: An alternative conceptualization of a healthy attitude toward oneself. *Self and Identity*, 2, 85–102.

Neff, K.D., & Beretvas, S.N. (2013). The role of self-compassion in romantic relationships. *Self and Identity*, *12*(1), 78–98.

Neff, K.D., & Germer, C.K. (2013). A pilot study and randomized controlled trial of the mindful self-compassion program. *Journal of Clinical Psychology*, 69(1), 28–44.

Neff, K.D., & Germer, C.K. (2018). *The mindful self-compassion workbook: A proven way to accept yourself, find inner strength, and thrive.* Guilford.

Neff, K.D., & Pommier, E. (2013). The relationship between self-compassion and other- focused concern among college undergraduates, community adults, and practicing meditators. *Self and Identity*, *12*(2), 160–176.

Neff, K.D., Rude, S.S., & Kirkpatrick, K. (2007). An examination of self-compassion in relation to positive psychological functioning and personality traits. *Journal of Research in Personality*, *41*, 908–916.

Nehra, D.K., Sharma, N.R., Kumar, P., & Nehra, S. (2013). Mindfulness based stress reduction: An overview. In D. Hooda & N.R. Sharma (Eds.), *Mental health risk and resources* (pp. 197–231). Global Vision.

Nikolic, N. (2021). *Sky metaphor.* https://neshnikolic.com/sky-metaphor

O'Broin, A., & Palmer, S. (2007). Reappraising the coach–client relationship. In S. Palmer and A. Whybrow (Eds.), *Handbook of coaching psychology: A guide for practitioners*. Routledge.

O'Broin, A., & Palmer, S. (2010). The coaching alliance as a universal concept spanning conceptual approaches. *Coaching Psychology International*, 3(1), 3–6.

Page, N., & de Haan, E. (2014). Does executive coaching work?. *The Psychologist*, 27(8), 582–586.

Paget, T. (2001). Reflective practice and clinical outcomes: Practitioners' views on how reflective practice has influenced their clinical practice. *Journal of Clinical Nursing*, 10, 204–214.

Palmer, S. (2009). Rational coaching: A cognitive behavioural approach. *The Coaching Psychologist*, 5(1), 12–18.

Palmer, S. (2013). Compassion-focused imagery for use within compassion-focused coaching: Stephen Palmer [Internet]. Version 8. *Journal of the International Academy for Professional Development*. 22 February. https://stephenpalmer.wordpress.com/article/article-compassion-focused-imagery-for-use-within-compassion-focused-coaching/.

Palmer, S., & McDowall, A. (Eds.). (2010). *The coaching relationship*. Routledge.

Pascal, G.R., & Zax, M. (1956). Psychotherapeutics: Success or failure. *Journal of Consulting Psychology*, 20, 325–331.

Passmore, J., & Marianetti, O. (2007). The role of mindfulness in coaching. *The Coaching Psychologist*, 3(3), 131–137.

Passmore, J., & Sinclair, T. (2020). *Becoming a coach: The essential ICF guide*. Springer.

Paterson, C. (1996). Measuring outcome in primary care: A patient-generated measure, MYMOP, compared to the SF-36 health survey. *British Medical Journal*, 312, 1016–1020.

Peltier, B. (2001). *The psychology of executive coaching: Theory and application*. Brunner-Routledge, Taylor & Francis Group.

Peltier, B. (2010). The psychology of executive coaching: Theory and application. *NHRD Network Journal*, 3(2), 84–87.

Peterson, D.B. (1996). Executive coaching at work: The art of one-on-one change. *Consulting Psychology Journal: Practice and Research*, 48(2), 78–86.

Peterson, D.B. (2010). Executive coaching: A critical review and recommendations for advancing the practice. In S. Zedeck (Ed.), *APA handbook of industrial and organizational psychology, Vol. 1. Building and developing the organization*. American Psychological Association.

Perls, F. (1969). *In and out the garbage pail*. Real People Press.

Perls, F., Hefferline, R., & Goodman, P. (1951). *Gestalt therapy: Excitement and growth in the human personality*. Julian.

Phillips, R. A., Bain, J., McNaught, C., Rice, M., & Tripp, D. (2000). *Handbook for learning-centred evaluation of computer-facilitated learning projects in higher education*. https://researchrepository.murdoch.edu.au/id/eprint/12141/1/handbook.pdf

Pomerantz, S. (2020). Global coaching survey from ICF. https://libraryofprofessional coaching.com/research/coaching-surveys/global-coaching-survey-from-icf/

Porter, J. (2017). Why you should make time for self-reflection (even if you hate doing it). *Harvard Business Review*, *21*. https://hbr.org/2017/03/why-you-should-make-time-for-self-reflection-even-if-you-hate-doing-it

Rafaeli, E., Bernstein, D.P., & Young, J. (2011). *Schema therapy: Distinctive features.* Routledge.

Ragins, B.R., & Kram, K.E. (2007). *The handbook of mentoring at work: Theory, research, and practice.* SAGE.

Reinholt, N., & Krogh, J. (2014). Efficacy of transdiagnostic cognitive behaviour therapy for anxiety disorders: A systematic review and meta-analysis of published outcome studies. *Cognitive Behaviour Therapy*, *43*(3), 171–184.

Reynolds, M. (2020). *Person not the problem: A guide to using reflective inquiry.* Berrett-Koehler Publishers.

Robson, S., & Manacapilli, T. (2014). *Enhancing performance under stress: Stress inoculation training for battlefield airmen.* www.rand.org/content/dam/rand/pubs/research_reports/RR700/RR750/RAND_RR750.pdf

Roediger, E., Stevens, B.A., & Brockman, R. (2018). *Contextual schema therapy: An integrative approach to personality disorders, emotional dysregulation, and interpersonal functioning.* New Harbinger Publications.

Rothberg, D. (2006). *The engaged spiritual life: A Buddhist approach to transforming ourselves and the world.* Beacon Press.

Ruth-Sahd, L.A. (2003). Reflective practice: a critical analysis of data-based studies and implications for nursing education. *Journal of Nursing Education*, *42*(11), 488–497.

Ryle, A. (1985). Cognitive theory, object relations and the self. *British Journal of Medical Psychology*, 58, 1–7.

Ryle, A. (1991). Object relations theory and activity theory: A proposed link by way of the procedural sequence model. *British Journal of Medical Psychology*, 64, 307–316.

Ryle, A. (1992). Critique of a Kleinian case presentation, *British Journal of Medical Psychology*, 65, 309–317.

Ryle, A. (1993). Addiction to the death instinct? A critical review of Joseph's paper 'Addiction to near death'. *British Journal of Psychotherapy*, 10, 88–92.

Ryle, A. (1994a). Response: Psychoanalysis and cognitive analytic therapy. *British Journal of Psychotherapy*, 10, 402–404.

Ryle, A. (1994b). Projective identification: A particular form of reciprocal role procedure, *British Journal of Medical Psychology*, 67, 107–114.

Ryle, A. (1994c). Consciousness and psychotherapy. *British Journal of Medical Psychology*, *167*, 115–123.

Ryle, A. (1995a). Transference and counter-transference variations in the course of the cognitive-analytic therapy of two borderline patients: The relation to the diagrammatic reformulation of self-states. *British Journal of Medical Psychology*, 68, 109–124.

Ryle, A. (1995b). *Cognitive analytic therapy: Developments in theory and practice.* Wiley.

Ryle, A. (1996). Ogden's autistic-contiguous position and the role of interpretation in psychoanalytic theory building. *British Journal of Medical Psychology*, 69, 129–138.

Ryle, A. (1997). *Cognitive analytic therapy and borderline personality disorder: The model and the method.* Wiley.

Ryle, A., & Kerr, I. (2002). *Introducing cognitive analytic therapy: Principles and practice.* Wiley.

Sasaki, N., Imamura, K., Nishi, D., Watanabe, K., Sekiya, Y., Tsuno, K., Kobayashi, Y., & Kawakami, N. (2021). Internet-based acceptance and commitment therapy programme 'Happiness Mom' for well-being: a protocol for a randomised controlled trial. *British Medical Journal Open*, 11, e042167.

Saunders, T., Driskell, J.E., Johnston, J.H., & Salas, E. (1996). The effect of stress inoculation training on anxiety and performance. *Journal of Occupational Health Psychology*, *1*(2), 170–186.

Sbarra, D.A., Smith, H.L., & Mehl, M.R. (2012). When leaving your Ex, love yourself: Observational ratings of self-compassion predict the course of emotional recovery following marital separation. *Psychological Science*, *23*(3), 261–269.

Scanlan, J.M., Care, W.D., & Udod, S. (2002). Unraveling the unknowns of reflection in classroom teaching. *Journal of Advanced Nursing*, *38*, 136–143.

Schon, D.A. (1979). *The reflective practitioner.* Taylor & Francis.

Scoular, A., & Linley, P.A. (2006). Coaching, goal setting and personality type. What matters? *The Coaching Psychologist*, *2*, 9–11.

Segal, Z.V., Williams, J.M.G., & Teasdale, J.D. (2002). *Mindfulness-based cognitive therapy for depression: A new approach to preventing relapse.* Guilford Press.

Sellars, M. (2017). *Reflective practice for teachers.* SAGE.

Shapiro, M.B. (1961). A method of measuring changes specific to the individual psychiatric patient. *British Journal of Medical Psychology*, *34*, 151–155.

Shapiro, S.L., & Carlson, L.E. (2009). *The art and science of mindfulness: Integrating mindfulness into psychology and the helping professions.* American Psychological Association.

Sheehy, R., & J.J. Horan (2004). Effects of stress inoculation training for 1st-year law students. *International Journal of Stress Management*, *11*(1), 41.

Sheard, T., Evans, J., Cash, D., Hicks, J., King, A., Morgan, N., Nereli, B., Porter, I., Rees, H., Sandford, J., Slinn, R., Sunder, K., & Ryle, A. (2000). A CAT-derived one to three session intervention for repeated deliberate self-harm: A description of the model and initial experience of trainee psychiatrists in using it. *British Journal of Medical Psychology*, 73, 179–196.

Siegel, D.J. (2010). *The mindful therapist: A clinician's guide to mindsight and neural integration*. W.W. Norton.

Siegel, D.J. (2012). *The developing mind: How relationships and the brain interact to shape who we are* (2nd ed.). Guilford.

Segal, Z.V., Williams, J.M.G, & Teasdale, J.D. (2002). *Mindfulness-based cognitive therapy for depression*. Guildford.

Smither, J.W. (2011). Can psychotherapy research serve as a guide for research about executive coaching? An agenda for the next decade. *Journal of Business and Psychology*, *26*(2), 135–145.

Sonesh, S.C., Coultas, C.W., Lacerenza, C.N., Marlow, S.L., Benishek, L.E., & Salas, E. (2015). The power of coaching: A meta-analytic investigation. *Coaching: An International Journal of Theory, Research and Practice*, 8(2), 73–95.

Sperry, L. (1993). Working with executives: Consulting, counseling, and coaching. *Individual Psychology*, *49*(2), 257–266.

Starr, J. (2016). *The Coaching Manual: The definitive guide to the process, principles and skills of personal coaching*. Pearson Education.

Stewart, L.J., Palmer, S., Wilkin, H., & Kerrin, M. (2008). The influence of character: Does personality impact coaching success? *International Journal of Evidence-Based Coaching and Mentoring*, 6(1), 32–43.

Strong, S.D. (2021). Contemplative psychotherapy: Clinician mindfulness, Buddhist psychology, and the therapeutic common factors. *Journal of Psychotherapy Integration*, *31*(2), 146–162.

Szabo, P., & Meier, D. (2008). *Coaching plain & simple: Solution-focused brief coaching essentials*. W.W. Norton.

Szczygiel, P. (2014). A Buddhist-informed conceptual framework for approaching difficult emotions in psychotherapy (Dissertation). University of Pennsylvania, Philadelphia, PA. https://repository.upenn.edu/cgi/viewcontent.cgi?article=1059&context=edissertations_sp2

Taylor, B. (2001). Identifying and transforming dysfunctional nurse–nurse relationships through reflective practice and action research. *International Journal of Nursing Practice*, 7, 406–413.

Telio, S., Ajjawi, R., & Regehr, G. (2015). The 'educational alliance' as a framework for reconceptualizing feedback in medical education. *Academy of Medicine, 90*(5), 609–614.

Thomason, S., & Moghaddam, N. (2021). Compassion-focused therapies for self-esteem: A systematic review and meta-analysis. *Psychology and Psychotherapy: Theory, Research and Practice, 94*(3), 737–759.

Theeboom, T., Beersma, B., & van Vianen, A.E.M. (2014). Does coaching work? A meta-analysis on the effects of coaching on individual level outcomes in an organizational context. *The Journal of Positive Psychology, 9*, 1–18.

Ting, S., & Hart, E.W. (2004). Formal coaching. In C.D. McCauley & E. Van Velsor (Eds.), *The Center for Creative Leadership handbook of leadership development* (pp. 116–150). Jossey-Bass.

Tobias, L.L. (1996). Coaching executives. *Consulting Psychology Journal: Practice & Research, 48*(2), 87–95.

Trungpa, C. (2005). *The sanity we are born with.* Shambhala (Kindle edition).

Twohig, M.P., Hayes, S.C., & Masuda, A. (2006). Increasing willingness to experience obsessions: Acceptance and Commitment Therapy as a treatment for obsessive compulsive disorder. *Behavior Therapy, 37*(1), 3–13.

Van Manen, M. (1977). Linking ways of knowing with ways of being practical. *Curriculum Inquiry, 6*(3), 205–228.

van Goethem, A., van Hoof, A., Orobio de Castro, B., Van Aken, M., & Hart, D. (2014). The role of reflection in the effects of community service on adolescent development: A meta-analysis. *Child Development, 85*(6), 2114–2130.

Van Vreeswijk, M., Broersen, J., & Schurink, G. (2014). *Mindfulness and schema therapy.* Wiley.

Wang, Q., Lai, Y.L., Xu, X., & McDowall, A. (2022). The effectiveness of workplace coaching: A meta-analysis of contemporary psychologically in-formed coaching approaches. *Journal of Work-Applied Management, 14*(1), 77–101.

Watzlawick, P., Weakland, J., & Fisch, R. (1974). *Change: Principles of problem formation and problem resolution.* W.W. Norton.

Wegela, K.K. (2014). *Contemplative psychotherapy essentials: Enriching your practice with Buddhist psychology.* W.W. Norton.

Whitmore, J. (1996). *Coaching for performance* (2nd ed.). Nicholas Brealey.

Whybrow, A., & Palmer, S. (2006). Taking stock: A survey of coaching psychologists' practices and perspectives. *International Coaching Psychology Review, 1*(1), 56–75.

Williams, H., Edgerton, N., & Palmer, S. (2010). Cognitive behavioural coaching. In E. Cox, T. Bachkirova & D. Clutterbuck (Eds.), *The complete handbook of coaching* (pp. 37–53). SAGE.

Wilson, A.C., Mackintosh, K., Power, K., & Chan, S.W. (2019). Effectiveness of self-compassion related therapies: A systematic review and meta-analysis. *Mindfulness*, 10, 979–995.

Winter, B., & Katrivesis, M. (2016). *Reflective practice: Why different points of view matter*. National Disability Service. www.nds.org.au/images/resources/person-centred/Reflective-Practice.pdf

Witherspoon, R., & White, R.P. (1996). Executive coaching: A continuum of roles. *Consulting Psychology Journal: Practice & Research*, 48(2), 124–133.

Young, J.E., & Klosko, J.S. (1994). *Reinventing your life: The breakthrough program to end negative behaviour and feel great again*. Plume.

Young, J.E., Klosko, J.S., Weishaar, M.E. (2003). *Schema therapy: A practitioner's guide*. Guilford.

Yürekli, A. (2013). The six-category intervention analysis: A classroom observation reference. *ELT Journal*, 67(3), 302–312.

Zessin, U., Dickh[symbol]user, O., & Garbade, S. (2015). The relationship between self-compassion and well-being: A meta-analysis. *Applied Psychology: Health and Well-Being*, 7(3), 340–364.

Zettle, R.D., & Raines, J.C. (1989). Group cognitive and contextual therapies in treatment of depression. *Journal of Clinical Psychology*, 45, 438–445.

Index

Printed in the United States
by Baker & Taylor Publisher Services